The Family Reunion Sourcebook

The Family Reunion Sourcebook

by EDITH WAGNER

LOWELL HOUSE

LOS ANGELES

NTC/Contemporary Publishing Group

Library of Congress Cataloging-in-Publication Data

Wagner, Edith, 1938–
     The family reunion sourcebook / by Edith Wagner.
        p. cm.
     Includes bibliographical references and index.
     ISBN 0-7373-0100-7 (pbk.)
     1. Family reunions—United States—Planning. 2. United States—Social life and
customs. I. Title.
     GT2424.U6W34   1999
     394.2—dc21   99-21483
                                                            CIP

Published by Lowell House, a division of NTC/Contemporary Publishing Group, Inc., 4255
West Touhy Avenue, Lincolnwood, Illinois 60646-1975 U.S.A.

Copyright © 1999 by Edith Wagner.
Text design by Nancy Freeborn/Freeborn Design

Printed and bound in the United States of America
International Standard Book Number: 0-7373-0100-7
10 9 8 7 6 5 4 3 2 1

*For Magda Wagner and Wenzel Zierold, who established
the most special family I've ever known.*

Contents

Preface

A family reunion is a gift of love a family gives to itself. Reunions are holidays families create for themselves to celebrate and enjoy the importance of closest kin. Reunions continually strengthen bonds and build traditions.

The Family Reunion Sourcebook offers information you'll need to organize a family reunion: ideas and experiences, suggestions and leads, sites, vendors, services, books, magazines, newsletters, and activities.

I was contacted to write a book for family reunion organizers and turned, as I always have, to the people who inspire me and keep my curiosity about family reunions alive and exciting. They are among the thousands of family reunion organizers about whom I have had the pleasure to report as editor of *Reunions magazine.*

Reunions, you'll soon discover, are no longer backyard picnics, though picnics are still an important feature of larger and longer events. Many reunions now include everything from workshops, tournaments, talent shows, and adventure experiences to just plain sittin' around and gossipin' with cousins who don't live as close as they once did.

Reunion organizers are very special people who are willing to give of themselves for the pleasure and often preservation of their families. Organizing a reunion is a very special gift of time, creativity, and effort by its organizer and the committees who help. Organizers may sometimes complain of frustration, of promises not met, of no response to requests for registration or reservation. But in the end, most reunions are enormously successful and enjoyed by everyone from the centenarians to the toddlers.

The Family Reunion Sourcebook uses a two-part approach. First are the reports, anecdotes, vignettes, and tips from other reunions to inform and inspire you. Draw from the experiences, incorporate the ideas, but your reunion will uniquely suit and enchant *your* family. Second is a compilation of resources that can assist you in achieving your family's dreams. It should be emphasized, though, that this selection of resources is just that—it's by no means exhaustive.

When we started *Reunions magazine* almost ten years ago, there existed one book about class reunions and little else to help reunion organizers. Now there is a whole reunion marketplace. *The Family Reunion Sourcebook* introduces and orients you to that marketplace, so you can use it to your advantage and make yours the best reunion ever.

Acknowledgments

This book would not have happened without the people you meet throughout its pages. You will meet them because they have very important things to offer your reunion: help, inspiration, and encouragement.

There are also many others who must be acknowledged because they helped me over and under obstacles to meet deadlines in record time.

Thanks to my friend, Margaret Henningson, whose energy never ceases to amaze, for enviable appendices. To Conor Liston and Jean Salzer for notable machine editing, and to gentle readers Jeff Perso and Susan Welsh.

I also thank Ione Vargus, Ph.D., founder of the Family Reunion Institute, for her constant and special support and inspiration. The Js, who always wondered how a project of this magnitude could take any time. My favorite cousin, Heike Lotterschmid, who has known before I that I can do anything I set out to do. Tammy Stark, whose support is stalwart. Margaret A. Persia, without whom the East Stroudsburg University study of reunions would never have happened. And Krishna Campbell, who was there as I struggled to find the voice for this book.

A very special thanks to Bill and Beth Webb, whose generosity knows no bounds and who were extraordinary in giving me the undistracted time and place to work on this book.

To *Reunions magazine* staff writers and editors over the years whose collaboration has made their articles stand out: Mary Thiele Fobian, Carol Burns, Andi McKenna, and Susan Welsh. To all the reunion reporters you'll meet throughout this book, without whom there would not be the breadth of material that exists today, and especially to Sharon DeBartolo Carmack, Debbie and Gary Dill, Jacalyn Eis, Beth Gay, Richard Johnson, Robin Longman, Bill Masciangelo, Tom Ninkovich, Karen Robertson, Marilou Robinson, Paula Sheagley, Ron Slaughter, Jean Timpel, and Cindi Wood. To those anonymous E-mailers from whom we've gotten excellent ideas if not their names. To the Beckley, Linquist, Paque, and Seideman families, for use of their reunion photos.

I recognize specially the creators and editors of Successful Meetings, Meetings & Conventions, and Meeting News, who provide lessons and inspiration regularly.

And last but not least, to the people who have the last word, after all, my Lowell House editors Maria Magallanes, Claudia McCowan, and Bud Sperry; designers Nancy Freeborn and Laurie Young; copyeditor Amy Spitalnik; and proofreaders Janet Brown and Nancy McKinley.

Introduction

The Family Reunion Sourcebook is a resource for anyone contemplating or already in the throes of organizing a reunion. Its extensive resources show evidence of a very friendly marketplace—a strong ally in facing the challenge of a reunion.

Along with resources, The Family Reunion Sourcebook offers anecdotes from hundreds of reunions by seasoned organizers who've known both the exhaustion and joy of producing a successful event. Start to finish, this book includes myriad details to help someone just starting to think about organizing a family reunion as well as someone wanting to add sparkle to a well-established family event.

Organizing a reunion takes the juggling skills of a four-star general, the patience of Job, and the stamina of Superman. It also takes imagination and, sometimes, the courage to try something different. After all, reunions don't have to be the same year after year. Plus, reunions may be taking up someone's vacation time. So make them very special.

Let's be candid. Some relatives come to family reunions under protest. They are sure there will be nothing for them to do. *Surprise them.*

How do you entice your teenage nephew to join the fun? Convince your career-minded daughter to steal time away from her busy life? Lure the reluctant homebody? By planning exciting, once-in-a-lifetime reunions that family members want to pen in on their calendar.

Because family reunions are more a creative undertaking than a methodology, more an art than a science, this book is essentially written by the families who've shared their reunion stories with me as editor of *Reunions magazine*. I've spent close to ten years intrigued and delighted by reports from thousands who generously shared their invaluable experiences. *Reunions* is a reader-driven publication making the most of suggestions, ideas, and material from people who organize these events. I myself do not organize a reunion year after year. I'm from a tiny family—two whole generations can sit at my dining table with the addition of only one extension leaf!

How does a reunion get started? Sometimes one person wants to get to know the rest of the family. Other times, relatives determine it's important to have a family gathering other than at funerals.

In her book *The Value of Family*, Dr. Ruth Westheimer cites family reunions as "a growing and wonderful trend in American society." American mobility, Dr. Ruth points out, separates families who miss much by living far apart. "Reunions link generations and are the perfect place to transmit values and tradition from one generation to the next. They play an important role in connecting families." The Westheimer Family Reunion draws about eighty people eager to maintain contact with relatives who have moved to other countries. For the Westheimers, reunions are occasions for making friends with newly found family.

Family reunions have seen a revival in recent years, in part because of renewed interest in family history and genealogy.

Patty Fisher, editorial writer for the *San Jose Mercury News* in California, pondered her first family reunion in a generation in Lake Geneva, Wisconsin. "Family is serious stuff to Fishers, who trace ancestors back to a guy who arrived in New York in 1742. Like all families, we've endured disease, divorce, childhood deaths, substance abuse, and bankruptcy. We've also faced interracial marriage, homosexuality, and single parenthood. Yet family is family. Our family values are our connections, not our differences. And we accept—sometimes grudgingly—each family member's right to choose a lifestyle, a mate, a career."

Constructing a reunion from scratch requires answers to the questions: Why? Who? Where? When? How and how much? It takes a commitment to the family and the reunion and a willingness to work at making a special gathering for a group of special people.

A reunion is a gift to your family. If you're the spearhead, be prepared to confront sometimes thankless tasks, last-minute registrations, and, invariably, complaints. Still, all in all, your efforts will be much appreciated.

Never do a reunion alone. Assess interests, skills, and specialties of family members. Don't overlook any age group. For example, kids have access to the Internet. Consider how a relative can contribute time, talent, or money. Then ask.

Start now to use the suggestions in this book, and you can expect success (short of predicting or controlling the weather!). An example of such success is the Rahm Family Reunion.

Myron R. Halpin writes that when Sarah Rahm's eleven grandchildren were growing up in New Haven, Connecticut, they were always together at their grandmother's house. They attended school together and shared friends. Then they scattered throughout the United States, Israel, and England. By the mid-1980s, when only aunts from the older generation survived, the idea for a family reunion caught on.

Aunts Martha and Eva arrived by stretch limousine. Aunt Martha, who died a month later, met two great-grandsons for the first time. Relatives shared remembrances and listened to a reading of family history, "The World According to Martha and Eva." They sifted through photos, watched a video made from home movies, and recounted family stories. (Inspired, a grandchild afterward computerized the family tree and sent everyone copies.) To cap off the event, a "chaircousin" was selected for the next family reunion.

Why Have a Family Reunion?

The purposes for having reunions are varied. Fifty-seven percent of respondents in a study of family reunions by *Reunions magazine* and the Hotel, Restaurant, and Tourism Management Department at East Stroudsburg University, Pennsylvania, said reunions help them keep in touch, while over 28 percent want children to learn about family heritage. Other purposes include marking a special birthday or anniversary.

Amy Barlow reports that her Mellenbruch Family Reunion started when her great-great-great-grandfather, H. F. Mellenbruch, left a letter expressing a wish that his descendants meet regularly. They celebrated their 100th reunion in 1997.

Your reunion is not at all unusual if it started at a funeral with the comment that you should all be meeting under happier circumstances. Reunions can be compared with weddings and funerals except for one important fact— those events focus on the celebration or remembrance of just one person. Reunions celebrate the whole family.

Not every family member may be ready for a reunion. If so, don't give up, just delay the idea for a while or, better yet, continue planning a reunion with willing members.

REASONS FOR REUNION

Ione D. Vargus, Ph.D., founder of the Family Reunion Institute at Temple University, Philadelphia, Pennsylvania, and director of the African American Family Reunion Conference, outlined several reasons for having family reunions in a *Black Enterprise* magazine article. She says reunions "give us the chance to celebrate heritage and kinship, cherish our elders, and strengthen our sense of belonging to family and community. It's where values are transmitted. It provides a sense of identity, belonging, and concern, along with educational activities and support of an extended family. Family reunions spanning generations help revive the role of extended family."

People are increasingly inspired to organize reunions. Is it worth all the hard work? After a resounding sigh of relief when it's over, there is the joy of having reunited the hearts of so many loved ones, as well as all the warm and generous memories.

Magda Krance in *Parenting* (September 1992) shares these insights about reunions:

> *Whether down-home or ritzy, intimate or huge, a reunion re-ignites family spirit. First reunions are a lot like blind dates—fraught with hope and uncertainty. There's something powerful about looking at others and realizing your lives are all interwoven. Reunions are the perfect opportunity for some intergenerational cuddling. Just because you're related doesn't mean everyone is going to love each other, or even like each other. But even with all the work and occasional tensions, family reunions are absolutely worth it.*

* *Dena J. Dyer of Granbury, Texas, says, "We don't have a perfect reunion, of course, just perfect enough for us. So, for as long as we can, we'll keep trekking to Sedona, Arizona, every two years to reunite."*

* *According to Mary Cooley of Juntura, Oregon, the most important reason to have a family reunion is to draw a once-close family together again after years of separation. "And more important, to keep that family in touch periodically." For over thirty years, Cooley's Ayers Family Reunions have offered attendees the chance to explore new locations in the western United States.*

* *Karen Sanders of Liberty, Indiana, says a feud kept her family apart for many years, but a funeral made them realize how much they needed each other. "With the way our world is today, a strong sense of family is needed for support," writes Sanders. She helped plan the first reunion in over fifteen years.*

* *Belzora Cheatham of Chicago, Illinois, declares that the purpose of the Brown Family Reunion is "to encourage our children to spend time together, because when children spend time together, they will grow up caring about each other." Cheatham planned the three-day celebration for Lodi, Texas, on land owned by the family since 1880. They had a fish fry on Friday, a barbecue on Saturday, and church services on Sunday. The highlight at the Saturday barbecue was*

"Brown's Trading Post." Each participant brought something from home to trade, including makeup, jewelry, cookbooks, and fishing gear.

* Alexandra Walker Clark of St. Augustine, Florida, observes that the world is hectic, demanding, and often unfriendly. "Family has always been a fortress; strong and undivided walls, secure shelter from the elements and a harsh environment. We Walkers are many, diverse, and scattered—but family, and not likely to forget it. Our reunion will long stand as a loving reminder of this truth."

REUNION FORMATS

From an afternoon picnic in a park to a week at a resort or even a cruise, the possibilities for reunion formats are endless. There is simply no set rule. Each reunion should be carefully tailored to the needs and desires of the majority of its members—though not without first considering all the possibilities.

After interviewing dozens of families about their reunions, Jean Timpel discovered that reunions have personalities. Reunions reflect the special character of each family. A successful reunion reflects what's important to everyone.

* The Evan Jenkyns Family Reunion of Canada meets every three years for sports and fun. Randomly chosen teams wearing colored ribbons to identify themselves participate in races, tournaments, and family history trivia competitions on a life-size game board. Each branch hosts a social hour during the four-day reunion.

* The Weidmanns, spread out all over the United States, picked a ski weekend in Colorado for one reunion and a resort stay in Arkansas for another. Neutral territory, they say, sparks frank family discussions.

* Bigelow reunions began in 1887. Family members meet at small colleges, where they rent dormitory and auditorium space. They stay in touch with a quarterly journal.

* Descendants of James K. Polk and Lydia (Hamilton) Matlock camp at the family ranch or stay nearby. Traditional Native American lodges and teepees set up by tribal cousins are popular places to sleep. Flags on a family standard indicate the states represented at the reunion.

* Descendants of Andrew and Lula Polk enjoy singing, dancing, rapping, and poetry reading. A member, who is a Baptist minister, formed a family choir

to sing at a special service in his church and declared the day Polk Reunion Sunday.

* The descendants of John and Maria Smith of Ireland camp out every five years at a relative's farm. They enjoy an auction of family mementos, heirlooms, and beloved gag items. Personalized balloons festoon the event.

* Sally Keenan Bauer of Chicago, Illinois, so loves the Edward and Lucy Keenan family reunions that in 1990 she married fiancé Joseph Piotrowski at one. Keenans conduct a theme contest, like a fancy-hat competition, with a prize, for example, the best reminder of a relative. Sharing heirlooms generates discussion of family history.

* In 1986, Lettie Sabbs of Chicago, Illinois, founded the Veal, Thompson, Carter, and Williams National Reunion, since grown to over two hundred. One reunion in Indianapolis started Friday night with a banquet, and talent and fashion show. Saturday morning a member led a tour pointing out where members of the Indianapolis branch lived and worked in the early 1900s, followed by a big picnic and attendance at the Black Expo of Indiana. Sunday the family worshiped together at Indianapolis's Emmanuel Baptist Church.

* Mrs. Irving Pransky of Stoughton, Massachusetts, reports that the Prensky/Pransky family performed a miracle when it pulled together 342 cousins from the United States, London, Israel, and Rome in just nine months to celebrate a family line that began in Nieswiez, White Russia (now Byelorussia). Members received books complete with family history, anecdotes, stories, artwork, poems, and a directory. Each branch wore T-shirts color-coded to an original descendant. A 25-foot wall display mapped out the family history and allowed attendees to trace their roots back through generations.

* Descendants of Simon Gay gather for reunion from as far away as California and England. Their two-day celebration in Moultrie, Georgia, began with hayrides and face painting, a cake walk, and a fish fry. A color guard and "presentation of the colors" began Sunday's activities joined by a family member attired in the Scottish highland dress of the Clan Gayre.

* One family of Killoughs was massacred by outlaws in 1838. Their burial spot, outside of Jacksonville, Texas, was declared a state historical site during the 1930s; a monument was erected by WPA workers. Twenty years later, John A. Killough was appalled to find monument grounds overgrown and hardly distinguishable from the surrounding forest. While clearing the cemetery, the idea of a reunion was born. The first one took place in 1955. According to Juanita Killough Urbach, on reunion Sunday a procession winds along a narrow blacktop road to the Killough monument. At this hallowed spot, state historian and

honorary Killough, Jack Moore, recites the story of the Killough massacre. Upkeep of the cemetery is the responsibility of the family corporation whose perpetual fund assures its future. With such foresight and commitment, Killough history is sure to survive.

* A survey generated enthusiasm when Colleen Tracey Simmons and her cousin, Ruth Butts, planned a reunion in Sioux Falls, South Dakota, for the 150th wedding anniversary of their paternal great-grandparents, William and Mary Treacy. Soon a plan "was hatched to bring cousins from Ireland." Despite successful fund-raising, a death in the family postponed the visit. A Friday evening party welcomed everyone under a big top—useful when it rained. Saturday's farm trip enthralled city dwellers. Everyone's picture and signature transformed the guest book into a souvenir scrapbook. The oldest living relative was unable to attend but sent an audiotape, making everyone "feel like Oliver was there."

* The Buffum family has documented its reunion in a brief history of the first seventy-two years. The pamphlet documents the social changes in America through the eyes of one family according to family historian, Delores Richter of Eden, New York.

* Harry Kellogg of Atherton, California, planned a surprise family reunion in Santa Fe, New Mexico, where, fifty years earlier while working during World War II on the atomic bomb project, he had met his wife, Kate. He swore their three sons and daughter to secrecy. One son explored the possibility of repeating their vows in the same chapel, now a museum. Another son assigned recitations of the original wedding readings to each sibling. A third son, a tenor, sang selections from the ceremony. The daughter planned a gala anniversary dinner, wedding pictures adorning the walls. During a day trip to Los Alamos, the children were fascinated to visit the same places their grandparents had lived in secrecy in wartime.

* Forgotten inheritance is one of the more unusual reasons behind a family reunion. The PSE&G Estuary Enhancement Program wanted to protect native habitat and fish in 20,500 acres of New Jersey and Delaware wetlands and marshes. Eight acres were divided among the many descendants of the four children of Levi Turner. Signatures had to be obtained from Turner descendants, who either didn't know or had long ago forgotten about the property. The utility provided a pig roast for a Turner reunion.

* Almost 500 Clausings visited the eight-sided barn that bears the family name at Old World Wisconsin, a living history museum west of Milwaukee. They came from as far as Australia to mark the sesquicentennial (150th) anniversary of the arrival to Wisconsin of forebears, Dorothea and Friedrich Klausing, who

settled 320 acres and grew a family of 1,200 known descendants. Souvenirs included T-shirts, cookbooks, and commemorative Christmas tree ornaments. Many took the family heritage tour—including a visit to Friedrich's grave, a sunken tombstone between two lilac bushes, which they plan to restore with souvenir profits.

✱ Alexandra Walker Clark's grandfather, Robert Sparks Walker, was a noted naturalist and author whose Chattanooga, Tennessee, birthplace is now Audubon Acres, a wildlife sanctuary. The Chattanooga Audubon Society helped Clark retain Audubon Acres for a reunion. Sixty Walkers attended, including an abundance of children and one remarkable 90-year-old cousin, who drove two hours just to be in the family picture and say howdy.

✱ "The Bullock Family Reunion started as a backyard picnic. Twenty years later it has evolved into a phenomenon!" So concludes the reunion history by Sheila Linton that includes a directory of over 700 descendants of George Bullock Sr. and his fourteen children with wives Sallie Jones and Fannie Anne Wooten. Activities include talent shows, tours of local points of interest, boat rides, and banquets. The family annually awards a scholarship. Each reunion features souvenirs that incorporate a family crest designed by a then-sixteen-year-old family member.

✱ When 250 descendants of George Washington's right-hand man, General "Mad" Anthony Wayne, held their first Iddings Family Reunion, ages of attendees ranged from 3 to 101-year-old Nadine Iddings of Asheville, North Carolina, who did not miss a single activity. A tour included visits to Iddings family homes and Wayne's birthplace. The focus was to engage the young in particular with Wayne's colorful history. According to historical records, Wayne's bones are buried in the family plot at old St. David's Church cemetery—which they visited—while the rest of him was laid to rest in Erie, Pennsylvania. The kids agreed that the details of Wayne's internment were definitely "cool."

✱ Some of the 400 Klessig Family Reunion members toured Saxonia, a seventeen-room inn, post office, and store built in Fillmore, Wisconsin, in 1855 by forefather Ernest Klessig, who later added a brewery that became the center of social life. The building was for sale and of interest to developers. Family members wanted to buy and restore the property, but no one individually had the money. They subsequently formed Friends of the Saxonia House, achieved tax-exempt status so that fund-raising could begin, and had their offer to purchase accepted. Their goal is to create a living history museum by resurrecting Saxonia as a bed and breakfast.

✱ *For over 300 years, Windmuellers lived in Germany. Hitler's rise forced them to leave. Members gathered from one to ninety-seven years came from Australia, South Africa, Portugal, Israel, Brazil, and thirteen U.S. states. They related escape and survival experiences in concentration camps and stories of starting over in different parts of the world. There was a memorial service for the 173 Windmuellers who perished in the Holocaust. One family member summed up afterward, "it was the experience of a lifetime for us."*

Reunion Who's:

Who's Family? Who's in Charge?
Who's Invited?

WHO'S FAMILY?

Whom do you claim as family for a reunion? Is it everyone with the same name? The descendants of a common forebear who immigrated to America? A grandma and grandpa and their children, spouses, and grandchildren? Cousins of a single generation and their families? Siblings whether by birth, marriage, or adoption? Probably the best way to define *family* for the purpose of reunion is "a group of people with the desire to spend time together."

The number of people who attend a family reunion depends on several variables. These include how far back on the family tree you look for a common ancestor, how successful you are in locating family members, and how widely your family is scattered. All reunion organizers agonize over the young, unmarried adults who as a group simply do not attend reunions. All is not lost, however, because as soon as they marry, and definitely after the birth of their first child, their interest in family intensifies, and you have a new generation of reunion members.

For a reunion to be truly family-based, you must invite everyone concerned—even the black sheep and eccentric old aunts.

Jann Mitchell in *Home Sweeter Home: Creating a Haven of Simplicity and Spirit* writes:

> *No matter where we grew up, whether we have loads in common or would never have picked one another as pals, the family members we meet at*

reunions are invariably a gift. We learn different things about ourselves from each one depending on their age, personality, and circumstance. These gifts include the following.

Context. Family is more than the group we grew up with; we are also nieces and grandsons and cousins—and eventually great-grandparents. We are descendants of those in fuzzy photographs and will be ancestors to those unseen. We come to understand our parents better—even if they are dead— by hearing aunts or uncles discuss their childhoods. The grandparents we knew simply as loving old people become rounded as we hear their life histories unraveled by their now elderly child. Shared anecdotes cast people in a whole new light.

Recognition of patterns. Alcoholism, sarcasm, bull-headedness? It's hard to blame someone when you see where they got it. Or a great sense of humor, artistic talent, the gift of gab. We see how we become our parents, for better or for worse—and how we can shuck the less desirable traits if we identify and understand why they didn't work then and won't work now. We may have inherited our way of smiling, but we can correct our tendency for put-downs.

Correct misconceptions. Because we got boxes of hand-me-downs and were taken out to dinner when well-to-do relatives visited, we felt like the poor, inferior relatives. Comparing childhoods with cousins, we learn how lucky we were in many ways. We understand that all families have problems, some more evident than others. We see the sad, isolating trap of playing "look good."

Continued connection. As we laugh and cry and remember and catch up, those who have gone feel close. Surely they are just in the next room. We who loved them best can offer a toast, knowing that death does not diminish love.

Solved mysteries. There are your son's ears on your uncle! and you learn that your great-grandfather, a doctor, wasn't shot in a cemetery but in his own home office. And yes, that gray-haired lady, Aunt Hazel, was the baby with whom great-grandmother was pregnant when great-grandfather was shot. A reunion's a good time to gather family facts and stories. We all hold a piece of the puzzle called family.

Brenda Kellow of Plano, Texas, recalls some relatives saying they would not come to a reunion if others were invited, but they showed up anyway. Once they got reacquainted, they seemed to enjoy themselves and continued coming each year. These people had not seen each other, in some cases, for sixty years. Once they did, animosity melted away.

Many families find embarrassment among the leaves of the family tree. Yet most secrets eventually become public knowledge: a birthdate too close to a wedding date, a divorce, or even murder. A generation or two later, a family scandal may even become the stuff of legend.

According to Los Angeles clinical psychologist and marriage, family, and child therapist Barry Sloan, if information about family scandal is kept secret or ignored, it limits what family members can talk about and "reduces communication."

Reunions are all about communication. Don't restrict yourselves. Share stories—tragedies, comedies, triumphs, and, yes, failures—freely throughout your reunion.

WHO'S IN CHARGE?

If you are reading this book, you're probably either in charge of your reunion or are thinking about organizing one for your family. One person often generates the idea for a reunion, and as others become involved it becomes important to identify who will take responsibility for decision making. If that is you, be sure you share as much of the load as possible.

On the art of delegation, Rosa Thomson of Estes Park, Colorado, feels it's important to share the joy of doing and feeling of belonging. Thomson's attitude is that the reunion organizer's job is to *lead,* not to *do* everything. For it truly is the family's—not the organizer's—reunion.

Rosa admits her family is blessed with talent and believes it's more fun to be a participant than a spectator. A son in Colorado created the announcement. A brother in Arizona printed the mailing list. A son in Washington designed a neat logo and printed the newsletter. A niece in California planned a shower for newlyweds who were spending some of their honeymoon at the reunion. A sister in New York collected family anecdotes. As a solution to the "I won't know anybody" lament, a seventeen-year-old granddaughter in South Carolina asked each kid in a letter to send a favorite picture, and then she created a poster to mail out so that names and faces would be familiar by the time of the reunion. The young Colorado moms baked cookies, and Thomson said there was still plenty left for her to do.

In the East Stroudsburg University/*Reunions magazine* study of family reunions, more than 32 percent of respondents organize each of their reunions; 22 percent or more rotate the leadership role; and more than 14 percent have a new volunteer for each reunion. In addition, over 12 percent of all reunions are organized by the person who initiates the idea.

Reunion Leadership

It's best *not* to go solo. Although there is evidence one person can organize a reunion alone, does that generate the greatest possible commitment? One person must be the leader, yes, but if that person can delegate tasks and inspire lots of volunteers, there will naturally be more interest in and ownership of the reunion.

When delegating, make sure each volunteer understands the purpose of the task. If necessary, write out instructions, read them together, and then ask questions to make sure the job is understood.

Delegating is easier within the extended family structure, where individual talents come to light. As relatives come to know one another, they learn to mobilize resources within the family itself. They discover how to draw on the skills and expertise of other family members.

Anyway, it's lots more fun when you share the work as well as the worries. Involving others as early as possible means help ranging from moral support (no small thing!) to taking charge of details, large and small. It also means defraying start-up phone, printing, and postage costs.

Reunions are best when ruled by consensus—equality and ownership are great group motivators. Every member has a voice—those who choose not to use theirs make the choice to enjoy what others plan.

If your reunion is not the gift of one person to the family (and even if it is), start building a consensus from the beginning. Knowing that everyone's desires and concerns are being taken into consideration is a smart way to instill reunion ownership. It also generates ideas that might not otherwise have come to light. For example, an older generation might not on their own plan for swimming. But if they realize they can count on some time to enjoy one another's company with a minimum of hassle because the kids are happily engaged in swimming, such facilities could be arranged.

One reunion, which numbers about 500 annually, has a standing committee of seven permanent members, one representing each of the patriarch's children. Cochairs include one appointed each year, the other providing continuity and acting as a guide. Cochairs select committee members. This system ensures constant involvement of new people.

Share Planning Tasks

Here are a few important volunteer positions you might want to consider for a successful reunion.

Organizer/chairperson/angel/leader

Must be willing to nurture and gather a crowd of people who share a past. Able to harness pesky details. Capable of comprehending and settling conflicts. Able to act on gut instinct. Diplomatic to a fault.

Treasurer

Collects and spends the reunion's second greatest asset: money. Manages budget, books, and bank account. May handle reservations, registration, and purchase of reunion keepsakes.

Secretary

Develops and maintains member/mailing lists. Writes and distributes invitations, newsletters, and registration materials.

Program chairperson

Must be creative. Able to identify family members' skills and talents. Capable of planning and organizing memorable activities for participants of all ages. Also selects entertainment. May hire photographer. Arranges setup and cleanup.

Historian/genealogist/griot/storyteller

Shares a passion for research and reveres the past. Collects and archives family history. At the reunion, displays family tree, historical wall charts, yearbooks, memory books, albums, historical documents, computer printouts.

Committees

Committees are not only crucial but also add to the fun and ownership of reunion organizing. Committees share planning, generate and implement ideas, and inspire attendance.

Many large families form boards of directors, who appoint a reunion committee, chaired by a board member. Careful notes are kept from one reunion to the next.

At an initial meeting, a task list is often made to aid in forming subcommittees. Subcommittees can vary from reunion to reunion. Myron R. Halpin of Bloomfield, Connecticut, reports that to keep enthusiasm high and others involved in the Full-Fledged-Rahm-Family-Reunion, subcommittees were formed for children's games and favors, sports tournaments and other activities, for family memorabilia displays, and *The 100 Year Book,* a keepsake of photos and information about everyone in the family.

Although distance affects how committees are structured, it shouldn't keep members from participating. Communication can be done by phone, fax, letter, or E-mail. Three-way calling, now available on most residential phone lines, can help with decision making. Distant members can help with correspondence, searching, ordering, and, of course, many tasks at the reunion. Appoint advisers from past committee members, people with a particular area of expertise, or those physically unable to help.

Remember, new people mean fresh ideas. Avoid burnout by sharing the workload.

Beth Gay of Moultrie, Georgia, suggests meetings every month, Sunday afternoon being the best time. She advises calling everyone about the meeting beforehand. Better yet, send reminder postcards. The greatest thing gained at meetings, Gay says, is becoming better acquainted, and all your work, planning, and caring will show at your reunion.

Consider the following list in determining committees for your reunion:

- *Accommodations/housing* Selects site, makes reservations and site arrangements, and welcomes members.

- *Fund-raising* Develops long-range fund-raising projects and plans and stages reunion day fund-raisers. Selects and purchases personalized souvenirs. Collects and organizes items to sell, auction, or raffle.

- *Program* Plans and coordinates reunion day activities. Arranges for event facilities or sites. In charge of entertainment, sports events, games, and icebreakers. Books the band or DJ and arranges for a public address system, if necessary.

- *Food* Plans, chooses, and provides food or works with a caterer or banquet manager.

- *Transportation* Sends directions and maps, and lists accommodations and restaurants along the way. Sets up airport pickup, along with arrangements to shuttle members during the reunion (for example, hotel to picnic, tours).

- *Registration* Recruits a welcoming committee, checks in new arrivals, makes and distributes name tags, and collects money from last-minute arrivals.

- *Photography* Hires professional photographer and/or videographer and arranges payment, or locates willing family members with the proper equipment and expertise.

- *Awards, scholarships* Sets criteria and supervises judging, recruits judges, orders honorary plaques, and presents awards.

- *Worship fellowship* Plans and conducts rituals, ceremonies, memorials.
- *Setup/cleanup* Works hard on Reunion Day!

Beth Gay offers these additional committee ideas: A *Decorations Committee* to make the place festive and welcoming. A *Signage Committee* to make the reunion easy to find. (Don't worry about perfect lettering—just use bright colors and make everything large. Try to arrange for a highway sign near your meeting place. Consider renting a sign with moveable letters and an arrow pointing the way.) A *Scrapbook Committee* monitors local papers for any mention of family members. A *"Medic"* Committee, especially useful at outdoor events, organizes the first-aid kit and locates the nearest phone and emergency numbers.

For the Will Family Reunion, Melenda Gatson Hunter of Lathrup Village, Michigan, broke a huge challenge into manageable tasks and assigned/cajoled family members to jobs appropriate to their talents: chair, cochair, treasury, hospitality, registration, souvenirs and T-shirts, and tour. Hunter, a family historian with high-tech computer skills, took on program planning.

A more informal organization may serve some families well. For example, O. John Taylor worked on genealogy lines for years and eventually established newsletters that evolved into *The Peach Tree* and *Taylor Talk*. These, in turn, led to reunions. Donations support activities; there are no dues. Newsletters hold everything together.

Family Associations

If you want your reunion to evolve into a family association, first check Everton's *Genealogical Helper* and similar periodicals to discover if an association with your surname already exists. If not, there are many reasons you may want to start one. Christine Rose, C.G., F.A.S.G., in *Family Associations Organization and Management: A Handbook,* suggests some: to gather data for the future; research common ancestry; preserve ancestral homes, cemeteries, or other family assets; publish a family history; and organize reunions.

Forming a family association is a commitment not to be entered into lightly. Discuss advantages and disadvantages before making a decision to incorporate. Family associations cannot receive tax-exempt, or 501(c)(3), status but can be nonprofit, or 501(c)(7). While restrictions and other conditions about asset distribution exist, there are postal breaks for associations who mail over 200 pieces of mail at a time.

In 1913, several relatives formed the Bunker Family Association of America (BFA) in Gloucester, Massachusetts, "to collect, verify, and preserve family history, heirlooms, and historic sites, hold annual reunions, and publish a history and genealogy of the Family in America." Their objectives haven't changed though the scope of the association has. The BFA is incorporated and has grown from thirty-six members to hundreds of families. President Gill Bunker charts two periods of association growth. The first, in 1971, followed publication of a family newsletter, *The Bunker Banner*. The second, since 1987, began when the BFA started holding reunions at sites around the country instead of only in Durham, New Hampshire.

If you want to incorporate, recruit an accountant or lawyer from your family to help. Anyone can file to incorporate, but it takes expertise to master IRS requirements and analyze restrictions.

Then plan for the election of officers. Certain families elect the entire slate annually, others biennially. Some elect half the officers each year for two-year terms to ensure continuity.

Hold annual association meetings at your family reunion. Since board members may be scattered around the country, some families, like the Bigelows, hold board meetings on the days before and after the reunion.

The Bigelows held their first reunion in 1886. Almost 100 years passed before the reunion was resurrected in 1972. The Bigelow Society, incorporated in 1975, has since added another level to their structure: representatives who serve as liaisons to members in their respective states or provinces.

WHO'S INVITED?

Because there are so many definitions of *family*, each reunion must make its own decision in the matter of who to invite. Would that be the descendants of a couple who arrived in America in the nineteenth century? We know of one such family who, tracing its ancestry to Germany, now has 3,100 known descendants in the United States, and counting. Or would it be cousins who grew up and went to school together but have since scattered around the country? We know of one such group who get together every five years at grandma's homestead, bringing their own children along. The choice is up to you!

Reunion Record Keeping

Record keeping is the bane of most reunion organizers. Nevertheless, it's crucial, and no reunion could happen without it. The membership or mailing list for many reunions is still penciled in notebooks, jotted in address books, or filed on 3-by-5-inch index cards. If it works, no need to change—unless you want to make it easier.

Computer databases can easily and efficiently keep track—datawise, anyway—of your entire extended family. If no one in the group has access to a computer, check local printers, who frequently rent time on their computers, or your local library.

Be sure to find or else adapt a database software program that suits your needs. Each entry should include fields for the following: name, address, phone number, spouse and/or children, years attended reunions, volunteer history, special talents or skills, and vital statistics: birthday, education, career, and hobbies.

It's a good idea to choose a database program with the capacity to sort information by fields, for example, FileMaker Pro 3.0. Information can then be sorted alphabetically or numerically to generate a list by name or family decent, or by birthdate or zip code. You can extract and sort all kinds of lists to, say, create mailing lists or to make name tags and tickets.

The primary benefit of using any database is that you can generate up-to-date lists without having to retype, rewrite, recode, or "re-" anything by hand. Using a system of databases for your reunion is a way of fitting pieces of the puzzle together. For example, you can link the registration database to a meal database that lets cooks or caterers know how many vegetarian or other special meals are required. You can also link it to a housing database to manage requests like a first-floor room or a specific roommate.

In addition, establishing a reunion database ensures continuity as well as a permanent record. It can be used to create lists for a directory or memory book, retrieve editorial material for newsletters, and maintain payment and registration records.

If your list is still on index cards, however, try color coding cards to designate branches or generations. For example, if the family is everyone descended from the five offspring of one couple, use a different color to designate each sibling's descendants. (And don't forget to create a master card that explains what each color signifies.)

Searching for Members

On the subject of searching for family members, we defer to the experts and will only scratch the surface here. For genealogy, we direct you to your local genealogy society; the many family history branch libraries around the country; and countless genealogy publishers, publications, and their Web sites. The Association of Professional Genealogists offers a pamphlet with valuable tips on locating and evaluating a professional researcher, typical costs, and evaluating the results.

For current, twentieth-century searches, the Internet is made for you. You'll find Web sites as well as chat rooms and search engines to help locate people.

In fact, the computer brings a whole new dimension to searching. There are CD-ROMs, for example, containing millions of phone listings in the United States and elsewhere.

Whatever technology you use, however, the reliability of the search depends on the accuracy of the information you start with. A wrong birth date, incorrect city, or misspelled name will waste hours and even dollars.

Persistence and patience are also crucial to a successful search. You'll want to be sure, too, to involve as many people as possible. Instill an element of curiosity so everyone will have their eyes and ears open to possible leads.

Genealogists can tell you there are endless sources for serious searchers. For starters, there are real estate transactions, ownership and tax records, drivers licenses, and change of address files.

The easiest way to locate anyone, according to Lieutenant Colonel Richard S. Johnson, USA, Retired, is by using a Social Security number (SSN). With an SSN, you can access addresses from national credit files, most government records, all military records (active, reserve, National Guard, or retired), most state drivers license files, and college and university student tracking systems.

When you do find someone, remember to record the source of your information. For example, the person who supplied information on John Doe is the best possible source to "refind" John Doe if he gets lost between now and the next reunion.

There is a cost to searching—a cost of time, effort, and money. If a professional does the searching for you, you'll spend more money, but your expenditures of time and effort will be less. If, on the other hand, you do some or all of the searching yourself, the money you invest decreases while your investment of time and effort increases.

To reduce your overall cost, know what you're doing. Train yourself. Seek advice from experts.

Steve Schultz of Seekers of the Lost in Vancouver, Washington, offers these search tips. Assume the missing person is still in the same city where he or she was last known to be. Call there for directory assistance, trying maiden as well as married names for women. Request that the operator expand the search to the whole area code. Then ask for the person's spouse, parents, siblings, or other family members. Repeat those steps everywhere there's a connection: college town, hometown, wherever family has had homes or land.

Sometimes searches can be completed with a single phone call, letter, or computer search, though it usually takes more effort to locate missing people. Costs associated with searches include long distance phone calls, genealogical research, postage, and miscellaneous administration charges. The good news is, a well-planned search that fully considers the costs of time, effort, and money is usually successful.

Help for Reunion Organizers

Organizing a reunion does not *have* to mean "do-it-yourself." Help is readily available from convention and visitors and tourism bureaus, travel agents, destination managers, facility staff, conferences and workshops, and, of course, bookstores, libraries, and the Web. In fact, discoveries you make and things you learn—as well as people you meet—along the way are some of the greatest rewards of reunion organizing.

CONVENTION AND VISITORS AND TOURISM BUREAUS

Working with a convention and visitors and tourism bureau (CVB) is like telephoning savvy relatives who can tell you what's best about their city. CVBs know their area intimately.

CVBs (discussed at greater length in chapter 6) can help in countless ways. Typically, they have area information and contacts with facilities, attractions, and activities. In your favor, your reunion, in travel parlance, is a group and thus subject to added consideration.

CVBs are the answer to a question from Ivan R. Scott of Columbus, Ohio, who asked if it's possible to plan a reunion in Reno, Nevada, without ever going there beforehand.

TRAVEL AGENTS

Choosing a competent travel agent is vital. A good agent can provide a cost analysis of several destinations, set up transportation for site inspections, and negotiate with carriers for discounts. He or she will search for the lowest airfare, negotiate group fares, and arrange hotel space and banquet facilities.

You'll want to consult an agent who specializes in groups or, best of all, reunions. Judi Galst of Rosenbluth Vacations points out that, as experts, travel agents assist in selecting destinations and accommodations that best meet your group's needs. They consider whether there are children, special needs, and budget constraints. If you are planning a golf reunion, for example, golf destinations with tee times, along with social events and accommodations, can be handled by an agent. If your travel agent is a cruise specialist, you'll receive guidance in selecting a ship, mailing reunion announcements, taking care of prepayments, and arranging shipboard meetings.

DESTINATION MANAGERS

In some areas, independent destination managers stand ready to see to details during your reunion. They can make local contacts for additional services you may require, including transportation, sightseeing, meeting places, and speakers. In some cases, their focus is on tours that may also interest your reunion.

SPECIALIZED FACILITY STAFF

A hotel, resort, or other facility is very interested in hosting reunions if they designate a specialist to serve you. Here's an opportunity to gain from the experience of others, as the reunion specialist has learned what works—and what doesn't—for reunions.

PROFESSIONAL REUNION ORGANIZERS

While the cost of a professional planner may be a deterrent for most family reunions, professional reunion organizers do exist, most notably members of the National Association of Reunion Managers, who specialize in high school class reunions. They charge a per person fee based on a percentage of the total cost. Alumni associations organize college reunions, and there are individuals who specialize in military reunions.

WORKSHOPS AND CONFERENCES

Each year many new workshops and conferences are offered on how to organize or spice up your reunion. They are typically sponsored by genealogy groups, churches, community colleges, universities, and extension services.

Some workshops are sponsored by convention and visitors bureaus, such as the Kissimmee-St. Cloud, Florida, Convention and Visitors Bureau reunion planners workshop, a two-and-a-half day hands-on workshop usually in February. *Reunions magazine*, along with its Web site, lists workshops and conferences as they become known.

Genealogy societies often include a reunion workshop in regular meetings or conferences—for example, The Patricia Liddell Researchers of Chicago, Illinois, which holds an annual reunion workshop in January. Brenda Kellow of Plano, Texas, offers a reunion organizing segment as part of her college genealogy course. In late spring and autumn, workshops are offered by Myra Quick in Tennessee, at the University of Memphis.

For ten years, the African American Family Reunion Conference, open to everyone, has been sponsored by The Family Reunion Institute at Temple University, Philadelphia, Pennsylvania. Institute founder Ione Vargus, Ph.D., believes passionately in the extended black family and sees reunions as one way to strengthen them. The conference follows a three-day plan not unlike many family reunions. It opens on Friday evening with a welcome reception. Saturday is packed with speakers, workshops, cultural programs, a luncheon, trade show, and exhibits. It then culminates on Sunday in a moving ecumenical worship service.

Many subjects are offered at conferences and workshops. Writing newsletters; optimizing the frequency and duration of reunions; calculating how much to charge each member; involving teenagers, children, and spouses; scheduling enough but not too many activities; storytelling to spark memories of past family events; methods for building family trust; and skits and games to strengthen family friendships are examples.

Treat yourself to a refresher course, or if you're just beginning, make the investment in your strength as a reunion organizer. If you're a reunion chairperson or committee member, you should seriously consider attending a workshop or conference. The training they offer helps you focus, stay on schedule, and manage your time and resources effectively.

A bonus is the opportunity to meet other reunion organizers and learn from their experience. Reunion organizers love to share information and the excitement of their successes.

Any opportunity you have to attend a workshop or conference, be there. You'll benefit from the exchange of ideas as well as interacting with other participants who are similarly committed to their families.

BOOKS, MAGAZINES, AND THE WEB

Reunions are growing and so is the volume of materials to aid reunion organizers. The bibliography in this book provides a comprehensive list of books currently available on the subject.

Reunion information on the Web is rapidly proliferating. The keyword *reunion* will get you new information almost any day. Some sites contain precisely the information and ideas you're looking for to aid in organizing your reunion. Many others, which are for individual reunions, display reunion plans and programs and serve as a message center for family members. You'll certainly want to visit some of those Web sites if you're planning one of your own.

Finally, *Reunions magazine*, a quarterly, is the only periodical available both for learning and sharing geared to persons organizing reunions. Primarily reader-driven, it is a great place for your family reunion to be featured or to announce your reunion in the RegisTree directory (also on the Web) and also to find hundreds of reunion-friendly businesses. On its Web site, www.reunionsmag.com, you're literally a click away from resource links, so you can directly "visit" a hotel in Florida or a ranch in Colorado. The magazine also publishes the annual *Reunions Workbook and Catalog*, which outlines the steps you need to take to organize your reunion.

Reunion resources are there to help you. Just ask!

Let's Make a Reunion Date

C hoosing the reunion date is a critical step. Once the date is set, stick to it and establish a timetable to count down to the event. The importance of deadlines cannot be stressed enough.

WHEN?

Set your reunion date to attract as many people as possible. Advanced planning maximizes the number of people who can schedule vacations and make arrangements to attend. Bob Aguas of Arlington, Virginia, for one, felt that two years was not too far ahead of time to start planning the Espina Family Reunion, since "two years is not that far away at all!"

Particularly if you want to hold your reunion at a popular location, it's essential to begin making arrangements years in advance. Or, if the idea of a reunion is new to a family, distant members need plenty of lead time to start saving up vacation time as well as money for the trip.

The dates of many family reunions fall between June and August for the convenience of families with school-age children. Other dates may coincide with special events and milestones, off-season school holidays, or three-day weekends that take advantage of special promotions.

Many reunions are established to honor a special anniversary or birthday and simply continue on at those times out of habit. One family still gathers for their long-deceased parents' anniversary in October, limiting attendance to adults, which suits them perfectly.

Holiday weekends, meanwhile, tend to be popular because most families have an automatic extra day. By far, the most popular reunion holiday is July Fourth, when millions of Americans celebrate their national family as well as their personal one. The Tommy and Joe Shields Family Reunion, for example, is held July Fourth every five years in the Clarkfork/Hope, Idaho, area. The Nichols Family Reunion and Heritage Day celebrate the nation's birthday along with the anniversary of the arrival of forefather Robert Nichols to Maryland in 1635. The Dixon Family Reunion meets for a full week around Independence Day every other year. Decorating boats for a patriotic boat parade is an activity enjoyed at the Zeigler Family Reunion, which meets every July Fourth weekend in Rockford, Alabama.

Other holidays are also great choices for family reunions. McGinity Family Reunions, according to Ken McGinity of Carmel, Indiana, meet every three years at Thanksgiving in a different part of the country. The Corrigan Family Thanksgiving Reunion at the Williamsburg Inn started as a one-day trip to Colonial Williamsburg, Virginia, over thirty years ago. The Lambert family's seven branches boast large attendance at their reunion every fifth Thanksgiving because everyone has time off and the weather is lovely there in Louisiana.

Teresa Lilly says Santa understands that those at the Lilly Family Reunion celebrate Christmas at Thanksgiving. They decorate a Pilgrim tree with colorful Thanksgiving-themed ornaments, then use brown butcher wrapping paper that kids decorate with crayons, leaves, and Thanksgiving stickers to wrap presents. Santa leaves Turkey Bags or brown paper grocery bags stapled closed and, making use of construction paper heads and tails, decorated to look like turkeys. Santa hides them while everyone enjoys Thanksgiving dinner.

Or how about Christmas reunions? Michele Hendricks of Loveland, Colorado, reports that the Newton family, holding their first reunion at Christmas, discovered the joy of simplicity and doing for one another: a hike in the woods to cut the perfect Christmas tree, making gingerbread cookies, stringing cranberries and popcorn, creating personal Christmas cards.

Or follow the example of the Ray/Clark Family Reunion, which, in July, celebrates the Christmas in Beech Mountain, North Carolina, they can't spend together in December. When Vivian Anderson of Lincoln City, Oregon, turned eighty, the family planned a reunion with a Christmas theme in July at Fogarty State Park near Newport, Oregon. They drew names for gifts, and Anderson herself knit thirty red stockings for "stuffing." A son-in-law caught salmon for a Christmas barbecue.

There's nothing sacred about summer reunions. Kids have three- and four-day weekends in winter—perfect times to get away and enjoy the company of extended family. There are lots of benefits to winter reunions, not the least of them off-season prices. Some resorts feature up to a 50 percent rate reduction in winter, as well as specials including children staying for free.

Or how about fall? The prolific Andrew Elton Williams, starting around 1822, fathered 10 children by his first wife and 13 by his second. These 23 children produced 145 grandchildren, and by 1990 more than 70,000 descendants of Andrew could be traced. The first Williams reunion was held in 1903 at Reddick's Mill, Florida. Everyone wanted to meet in autumn, after crops were in. Discovering that in the almanac there had been no rain on the first Thursday in October for fifty years, they selected and stuck with that date until 1963, when it rained. Since then the reunion has been held every year on the first Saturday in October.

Many reunions designate the same day year after year. The third weekend in July has been etched in stone for the Seideman family for over sixty-five years. Another family uses this formula: the Sunday closest to July 15th every even year.

Having a consistent, fixed reunion date has an advantage, especially for families who find it difficult to get everyone together. After children are grown, you can't always expect all of them home for the major holidays. Once they marry they have obligations to in-laws. But you can expect them for a reunion.

While surveying your group may seem the most democratic way to pick a reunion date, do so with a plan in mind. The larger the group, the more structured you'll make the survey. For example, pick several dates to list, and then ask, Do you prefer date one, date two, or date three? Of course, in large, extended families it's rarely possible to accommodate everyone's schedule. You'll need to choose the best date for the most people.

HOW LONG?

The length of a reunion will depend on your own family's preferences. Over 70 percent of respondents to the East Stroudsburg University/*Reunions magazine* study reported they devote two or more days to their reunion.

While many reunions are still only a single day, more and more last from Friday through Sunday, and some families gather for even longer. An entire week is not unusual. If members travel any distance, a longer stay makes the effort worthwhile. The occasion of cousins visiting from Italy generates weeklong reunions of Nicolo and Felicia DePronio's descendants in Toronto, Canada. Similarly, the descendants of Amalio Rodriguez travel from several Midwest states to meet in Puerto Rico and celebrate the weeklong *La Festa Patronales*.

HOW OFTEN?

Frequency is also a matter of family preference.

Neal D. Wintermute, president of the Windemuth Family Reunion, wondered how many years between each family reunion would work out best. One family quite happily scheduled reunions every five years until they realized how quickly the list of deceased grew and decided to meet more often. Almost half (46.2 percent) of all families have reunions annually, according to the East Stroudsburg University/*Reunions magazine* study. I myself regularly attend—along with 400 to 600 family members—an annual reunion that is always at the founder's family homestead and dairy farm.

Other choices for reunion frequency, according to the above study, are every two years (28.2 percent) and every five years (10.4 percent). Every two or more years gives everyone a chance to save for a grand reunion vacation. Such an interval also allows the reunion organizer some breathing room!

REUNION TIMETABLE

This list is good for checking your progress or for considering as agenda during committee meetings.

Twenty-four to Eighteen Months Before . . .

- Determine interest.
- Talk to other reunion organizers.
- Attend a reunion organizing class, workshop, or conference.
- Start mailing list.
- Form reunion committee(s) and establish responsibilities and schedules.
- Set up record-keeping system.
- Develop budget and bookkeeping system.
- Contact convention and visitors or tourism bureaus.
- Scout locations, facilities.

One Year Before . . .

- Set date(s).
- Choose location.

- Send first mailer; include tentative reunion schedule and plans (tours, souvenirs, memory books), theme, and approximate cost.
- Hire entertainment, caterer, photographer, videographer, printer.

Six to Nine Months Before . . .

- Send second mailer; include registration and souvenir order forms and cost.
- If you wish to have your reunion listed in *Reunions magazine*, send announcement.
- Schedule events and activities: program, speakers, awards ceremony, tours.
- Reserve block of rooms.
- Begin souvenir directory/list of attendees, memory book.

Five Months Before . . .

- Confirm reservations, entertainment, photographer, caterer.
- Choose menu.
- Announce event to local news media.

Two to Four Months Before . . .

- Meet with hotel staff; visit facility with reunion committee.
- Select decorations, signage, banners; order printed items.
- Reserve rental equipment.
- Submit personalized souvenir order (T-shirts, mugs, caps, etc.).

Six Weeks Before . . .

- Complete directory/memory book; deliver to the printer.
- Prepare checklist for reunion tasks.
- Designate assignments for reunion volunteers.

Two Weeks Before . . .

- Purchase incidental supplies.

- Reconfirm meeting, sleeping, and eating arrangements.
- Review final checklist.

The Day Before . . .

- Determine hotel or other staff contacts.
- Solve last-minute problems.
- Review final details with reunion committee.

Reunion Day(s) . . .

- Set up registration tables, rental equipment, displays.
- Juggle details: volunteers, food, photographer, games, entertainment.
- Decorate.
- Enjoy.

Afterward . . .

- Reflect and evaluate—note what worked, what didn't.
- Complete bookkeeping; settle accounts.
- Write thank-you notes to volunteers, hotel staff, caterers.
- Start planning your next reunion.

Finances and Fund-Raising to Pay for Your Reunion

Once you've decided what kind of reunion you're going to have (an afternoon picnic? three-day luxury weekend? weeklong camping trip?), you must be prepared to discuss how to pay for it. You'll need to be sensitive to financial considerations as they affect everyone in your family. Don't book an expensive resort hotel when most family members won't be able to afford it. After all, the point of a family reunion is that as many as possible take part.

If yours is a multigenerational family, be ready to face the full range of income levels, from tight budgets and fixed income to those whose finances allow almost any indulgence. For a high attendance rate, either keep expenses reasonable or be prepared to provide for certain family members. The generosity of some might help others afford to attend.

HOW MUCH DO REUNIONS COST?

Reunion costs range from little to lavish. Options run the gamut from a covered dish casserole at a Sunday potluck picnic, to a buffet brunch on a cruise ship, to a formal black-tie banquet in an elegant ballroom. Larger, formal reunions require hotels, catered meals, advance registrations, and lots more. Add tours and entertainment and you begin to get the idea.

You and your committee must match dollars to objectives. Budget properly and you'll save time, money, and potential embarrassment. An assumption that gets many first-time reunion committees in trouble, particularly when making facility guarantees, is that everyone will attend.

Along with overestimating your attendance, you'll want to avoid underestimating your budget, or you'll find yourself with reunion bills and no way to pay them. Enlisting an experienced budgeter is always wise. It's also advisable to work closely and cooperatively in putting the reunion budget puzzle together.

REUNION FINANCES

Typically, to get the ball rolling, the person who comes up with the idea of a reunion pays initial out-of-pocket expenses, including printing, postage, and long-distance phone calls. In that first communication, be sure to bring up expenses. State clearly that generally, people will pay their way. Or notify family members that after expenses are totaled, everyone will be expected to pay an equal share—determined by the number of people attending or the number over a certain age. One reunion, for example, appoints a treasurer who tallies food and rent receipts and divides by the number over age twelve attending. The willingness of younger members to sleep on couches or in sleeping bags greatly affects expenses.

Set financial goals. For example, do you want to break even or make just enough profit to pay start-up costs for your next reunion? Some reunions have legitimate moneymaking aims, such as scholarships, investments, or group business enterprises.

Income

Unless the reunion is someone's gift to the family, income sources include contributions, donations, fees, dues, keepsake/memento sales, tickets (meals, tours, activities, entertainment), corporate sponsorship, raffles, and auctions. Reunion organizers and committee members must assess which have the best potential and how to implement them. Raising money can in fact be a significant part of the reunion fun.

Funding Associations

Many families establish formal associations to collect and administer funds for reunions, newsletters, research, scholarships, and service projects. Two philosophies determine the approach to financing associations. One is that everyone is a member and should not be required to pay to join. People are instead encouraged to make free-will offerings to support association activities, so donations become the primary source of income. This philosophy encourages endowments. The widespread Bigelow family, for one, follows the donation philosophy. They publish a newsletter, *Forge,* and fund research from voluntary contributions. Contributors donate $5 to $100 a year and must renew annually to continue receiving the newsletter.

The Hudson/Smith/Lillard Family Reunion was the idea of the eleven children of Octavius and Lizzie Ella (Smith) Hudson originally from Dyersburg, Tennessee. Their reunion fund-raisers have included a fish fry, barbecue, and candy sales. They require $20 dues monthly.

The other philosophy is that the funding association serves a specialized function and people pay to be part of it. This involves setting up a membership fee structure with categories based on the amount of the contribution. Options include Individual, Couple or Family, Sustaining, Contributing, or Donating, which is open-ended to encourage liberal giving. Names of large contributors are published in the association newsletter to recognize generous support. The Tacketts of Pike County, Kentucky, use this system, but offer free membership to all family members over the age of seventy—extending a gesture of appreciation for family elders while ensuring that relatives on limited income are included.

One idea is to designate family boosters, members who cannot attend the reunion but are willing and able to send money to help defray costs. Be sure to acknowledge boosters at the reunion as well as in your newsletter.

Once you estimate how much income to expect, you can begin planning activities. Balance high-cost/high-risk with low-cost/low-risk events. Determine a fair and reasonable price but be sure to cover your costs. Calculate cost, break-even point, and number of people who must sign up for each activity to make it worth implementing.

A good example is hiring a bus for a city tour. The bus will cost about $300 whether it carries one person or forty-five. Monitor registrations to cover the cost of the bus or, if necessary, reserve more buses.

As you create your budget, keep a list of your estimations, considerations, and calculations. Note estimated and actual expenses and the difference between them. You'll want to analyze the data later to find hidden costs to be better prepared for future reunions.

Of course, it's best to try to do it right the first time. Failure to include everything in your budget could cost you dearly after the reunion. Always allow a margin for the unforeseen.

Whether this is your first, fourth, or twenty-fourth reunion, the process is the same. *You must do your homework*. Many first-time planners get into trouble calculating costs. Obtain an accurate estimate and periodically review the numbers.

Dodi Mace of the Robinson Family Reunion says a small treasury rolls over from year to year. The treasury is built by generous contributions from individual family members. Each family, meanwhile, is assessed a registration fee, which covers mailings, supplies, decorations, and deposits. The "Big Event" dinner is charged on a per-person basis, and other events (sightseeing tours, golf outings) are paid by individuals. Shortly after the reunion, the outgoing chairperson delivers all monies, address lists, and pertinent information to the new chairperson.

It is wise to set up a separate checking account to keep a permanent, legal record of reunion income and expenses. When setting up the account, mention the reunion and ask for small or no-service fees and/or free checks. (A budget worksheet can be found in Appendix B.)

More Budget Tips

Recruit a treasurer to whom all registration fees are sent and who pays the bills. In *How to Have a Successful Family Reunion*, Elsie G. Holloman suggests that the planning committee set up an account at a bank or credit union with two people required to sign for transactions. If you have a large number of people or an expensive reunion paid for in installments—a cruise, for instance—this is a must.

Another must is establishing procedures to handle cash, checks, and deposits. Set up a system to track who paid how much and for what. Emma Wisdom in *A Practical Guide to Planning a Family Reunion* stresses the importance of keeping everyone informed about exactly what you're "going to do with all that money, for example, making regular financial reports in newsletters." She also suggests requiring payment ninety days before the reunion so you'll have the money to work with.

Another of Wisdom's books, *Family Reunion Organizer*, recommends offering prizes to the first people who send in registrations. Or offer a discount to everyone who registers by a certain date. After all, isn't a discount for being early more motivating than a penalty for being late?

Many people now own computers or have access to one. You may already use financial software that can be adapted for your reunion budget. If you don't, Quicken by Intuit is inexpensive and easy to use. Its budget capacity allows you to track and compare actual expenses. For tying loose ends, Quicken also has a reports menu for financial reports.

What Can Be Done by Volunteers?

Don't spend money on services, skills, or talents that volunteers can perform. Is there a family artist willing to design invitations? Can someone provide and arrange flowers? Would a talented cook help cater a picnic? Might a computer whiz be willing to input and maintain your mailing list?

As reunion organizer, you are the main volunteer—share the joy. Get others in on the action. Ask, beg, demand, cajole, plead—whatever it takes to involve others in your success. And don't forget to salute volunteer service at the reunion and mention it in your newsletter.

REUNION FUND-RAISING

Paying for your reunion may be among your most creative challenges. Planning fund-raisers, for example, requires adequate lead time to develop properly. The good news is that when done well, fund-raisers can be entertaining as well as profitable.

If you're considering souvenirs or mementos, you'll also want to start early. Consider reasonably priced, functional items, like coffee mugs, paperweights, coasters, T-shirts, or key chains. You may choose to build the cost into your reunion price so that each person who attends gets one. You then order as many units as you have reservations or maybe a few extra to sell for additional funds. Or you can take orders and produce only those paid for in advance.

Never set prices too high. Some people buy regardless of cost because they want to support the cause, while others need to feel the price is reasonable. You want to promote good will and member support.

Keep in mind that while it is important to plan and execute fund-raising with all the vigor and commitment of the Red Cross or United Way, your reunion fund-raising is geared to a limited market: your family.

Reunion Fund-Raising for Charitable Activities

According to Nina Welding in *Grit Magazine,* charity reigns at the reunion of descendants of Simon and Lida Slaubaugh's largely Mennonite family. Nine years after reunions started in 1972, auctions were launched to raise money for missions. The 1993 auction raised $3,200 from 123 attendees. Auctioned by the Slaubaughs are lots of handmade items snapped up by younger members as keepsakes. With recipients decided by a vote, many charities have benefited from Slaubaugh auction proceeds. In addition, some funds have assisted family members with major medical expenses and helped others in the aftermath of natural disasters.

The Camilla and Zach Hubert Family Reunion incorporated as a nonprofit

(501C-3) foundation to conduct charitable projects. They have established book scholarships at Spellman and Morehouse Colleges and donated money to Springfield, Georgia, the community of their forebears.

The Simon Gay Family Reunion "store" sells caps, family histories, calendars, and cookbooks. The reunion committee agreed to send 100 pounds to the Nigg Old Church Trust Fund in Ross-Shire, Scotland, and to give $125 to the Ellen Payne Odom Genealogical Library in Moultrie, Georgia, to purchase a book in honor of recently deceased family members.

Other families are thinking about what they can do to develop themselves. The Dow family noted that they had reached a certain point and it was time to put something back into the community. The Washington/ Bonaparte family plans to build a retirement home for aging family members. One of its fund-raising activities is the King and Queen Dinner Dance. Each year at Thanksgiving, the Booker Family Reunion in Medford, Massachusetts, makes a contribution to a Medford organization that serves needy families and children.

Some families develop scholarship programs or emergency funds to help their own. Augusta Clarke, a Philadelphia city council member, asks attendees to put $30 in the pot when they arrive at the reunion. The Lowe family assesses each local chapter in building their emergency fund; each time a baby is born, everyone sends $1 to start an account in the child's name. Another family provides $2,000 from the national chapter toward funeral costs when a member dies.

The Rashid Family Reunion sells T-shirts, hats, and knickknacks; carries program ads; and raffles merchandise to meet reunion expenses and provide scholarships and a welfare fund. The scholarship fund currently offers every high school senior $200 toward a higher education. Funds are also sent to a Maronite Catholic Church in Lebanon, the Rashids' country of origin.

Long-Range Fund-Raising Projects

Long-range fund-raisers are those that can take a year or longer to produce. Among the most common are quilts, cookbooks, memory books, directories, and customized souvenirs.

Quilts

"We are proud of our quilts and pleased they allow us to encourage our young to pursue higher education." So wrote Opalene Mitchell of Palo Alto, California, whose brainchild resulted in such overwhelming family involvement that the Carter-Jordan-Pennington Family Reunion was able to raise $3,000 for scholarships. Although only one quilt was planned, enough painted, appliqued, embroidered, computer-scanned, cross-stitched squares were provided to make six! Reunion area chairpersons distributed and collected squares for assembly. Accompanying each quilt is a record of who made each square and what it commemorates—generally some event, experience, or person. Design elements include a family cake recipe, doilies brought along by passengers in the underground railroad, infant handprints, buttons from a grandmother, and an award emblem from an early space shuttle mission. In addition, the quilts were photographed to produce stationery, puzzles, and posters to sell.

Cookbooks

Many families publish their own cookbooks, which is often a family history book as well. Cookbooks are a lovely way to not only share some of life's pleasures but also to preserve cherished family recipes for future generations—and to raise money.

Cookbooks individualized for your reunion draw from many contributors, most of whom will buy a copy because their recipe is in it. Plus, people are always looking for new recipes.

Spiral-bound cookbooks cost between $2 and $5 each to produce, depending upon size and quantity. On one hand, the more recipes you include, the higher the cost per book. On the other hand, the more contributors you include, the more potential customers you'll have.

A cookbook publisher's experience and large printing capacity can reduce prices to as low as $1.75 each (with a minimum order of 200 books). You suppply recipes, along with cooking tips and reminiscences, acknowledgments, history, or a family tree.

You can order an information packet from a specialty cookbook publisher to help in collecting recipes. Many offer workbooks containing recipe collection forms as well as guidelines, sample pages, recipe category dividers, and suggestions for distribution and how to increase book sales.

Each company offers cover design choices, or you may use your own drawing or logo on color stock. A color photograph on the cover costs extra. Other options include colored paper, colored ink, and laminated covers. Weigh each option carefully. Decide if the enhanced look is worth the extra cost.

Recruit volunteers to collect and input recipes, reminiscences, traditions, and tips. Specify a deadline, and follow up regularly. Sort recipes and reminiscences into folders, one for each food category. Eliminate duplicates and make sure recipes are easy to follow. Standardize measurements and abbreviations. Proofread every word—more than once and by more than one person.

Printing, assembling, and binding books takes two to three months after the company receives your material. You are responsible to check proofs before the cookbook is printed. Payment is due thirty to ninety days from shipping.

All companies allow reorders. One company guarantees you will sell enough books to finance your order if you charge a given minimum price and have included a minimum number of contributors.

One family who published a cookbook reported they "really lucked out" with a publisher whose minimum order was only 100. The cookbook took a couple of years to complete "but was well worth the time and effort."

To self-publish, you'll need to answer some questions. What are the specifications: size (standard is 8½" by 11"), cover (softcover or hardcover), font, binding (plastic comb, wire, softback)? How much do you want to spend? How many will you print? How many can you (realistically) sell? Where will books be delivered and stored? How will you promote and sell them?

Mary Barile's *Food from the Heart* is a workbook designed to help you produce your own cookbook, independent of one of the professional companies. Barile includes instructions and blank forms to organize and collect recipes. She recommends asking for recipe origins and such extras as tips and variations. She explains obscure ingredients and how to translate antique recipes. The advantage of writing and publishing the book yourself, says Barile, is that it increases your flexibility so that you can include more stories and background to ensure a keepsake that preserves your family's heritage.

Memory books

Memory books are avidly read. And the more input you get from reunion members, the more avidly your memory book will be pored over! Send an open-ended questionnaire to solicit stories, reminiscences, and reflections about the past. Request pictures and news clippings too. Follow up with a postcard to those who miss the deadline. Be sure not to forget a memorial to the deceased. You may even want to ask a historian or genealogist for an historical sketch of your family beginnings.

It takes a willing volunteer editor who will solicit contributions and provide overall direction. Additional volunteers are needed for book design, layout, production, and distribution. Most of the work can be adapted to suit volunteers' schedules and talents. Volunteers don't even need to be in the same city. They can keep in touch by phone, fax, mail, and E-mail.

Keep memory book expenses low by selling advertising space. The advertisers are your members. Those who own businesses welcome the promotional opportunity. Offer several ad sizes, including simply reproducing business cards (1/12 of a standard 8½" x 11" page). Encourage newlywed congratulations, birth announcements, and welcomes to persons who've never attended before.

The Allen family, whose members are mainly in Florida and the Bahamas, developed a reunion memory book that included family history, old family photos, a current family directory, and a "who's who" to document members' accomplishments. The book was paid for largely by ads bought by family-owned businesses and memorials for deceased family members.

The Owens Family mission statement opens their memory book. The values they cherish are demonstrated through an illustrated family tree, vintage photos, and treasured recipes. Their Tallahassee, Florida, reunions are archived in a banquet program, order of worship, and memorial to the family's deceased. Committees are recognized and a family directory included. The book is saddle stitched at a local print shop.

The Hudson/Smith/Lillard family of Milwaukee, Wisconsin, preserved their reunion memories with typewriter, clip art, and copy machine. The family emblem adorns program notes, a map showing the clan diaspora, a memorial page, songs, and greetings from reunion organizers. Copies, collated and bound in Mylar covers, are prized mementos.

Genevieve Carlisle of Shreveport, Louisiana, reports that the Carlisle Family Reunion added a special touch when members presented a special keepsake album to their eighty-nine-year-old matriarch. Each person contributed something: a poem, letter, footprint, even a sonogram.

Reunion directories

Because there are 600 of them, the Slaubaughs have two kinds of family directories. Nelson and Vivian (Slaubaugh) Martin create one main directory for the whole family and small reference booklets for individual families. The main directory lists, by sibling, addresses, phone numbers, spouses, children, and grandchildren. Individual family booklets include addresses, phone numbers, birthdates, and anniversaries. Booklets are sold for the cost of printing and a small honorarium to the Martins for their time and effort. Information stored on computer is updated quickly and easily for the next reunion.

Some considerations are common to all publishing projects. For example, small quantities are more expensive because preprint preparation is the most costly step—therefore, the more copies you order, the lower the price per copy. To make money from reunion publishing projects, you set the price and keep the profit over the production cost.

Customized souvenirs

There is a veritable plethora of customized souvenirs to commemorate reunions. Among the possibilities are T-shirts, sweatshirts, caps, mugs, Frisbees, key rings, belt buckles, stuffed mascots, pens, pencils, and umbrellas.

It's a good idea to consult others who have ordered imprinted items. Phyllis A. Hackleman in *Reunion Planner* suggests asking these questions when ordering. Are there charges to screen artwork or for more than one color? Will the manufacturer guarantee colors? Does it cost extra? Will the manufacturer share a proof before production for you to verify the product you want? Are you obligated to pay for an overrun of more than the exact number you order? Who pays shipping charges?

Avoid disappointment by allowing plenty of time for order and delivery of customized items. Always give the company time to fill your order properly. Nothing is worse than a wrong or incomplete order or one that doesn't arrive in time. All companies claim quick delivery, but if you don't allow enough lead time you may pay more for a rush order and delivery charges.

T-shirts are the most common customized reunion souvenir, probably because they present a variety of selling strategies. They can be sold in advance or at the reunion or included in the reunion cost. Imprinting the same design on different-colored shirts for different branches of the family makes for a truly "colorful" reunion and one where relationships are readily visible. Be sure to offer size choices. An order blank may be included in newsletters or in the invitation. Your goal is for each attendee to have a T-shirt. Print extras if your budget allows. Also, save money by omitting the year. You may have supplies left to sell at a later date.

You don't have to settle for shirts with plain block printing. Reunion T-shirts aptly reflect the diverse personalities of reunions. The descendants of Bryant and Letitia Andrews in Mississippi and Wisconsin put their family tree on their T-shirt. An artist cousin of the Bickels inscribed a favorite Bible verse on theirs. Holcomb Family Reunion T-shirts boast "An Original Holcomb" or "I married an Original Holcomb."

Some families have a design contest. The Evan and Grace Jenkins family of Canada, for example, chose a family logo from contest entries and use it for each triennial reunion, printed on a different-colored shirt. Be sure to commend the winning designer at the reunion.

Many silk screen companies design T-shirts. They deal daily with such requests, and their charges are usually reasonable (and sometimes even free). Send photocopies or sketches of what you envision.

Large numbers of reunion T-shirts should be ordered from a vendor. Small orders, however, are often too expensive per shirt. Philip R. Henningsen of San Francisco, California, whose family is small (fifteen), found one shop willing to talk about four-color separations that estimated $25 to $30 each for twenty T-shirts.

Many copy stores use a process different from silk screen, used by large-volume printers, to make custom T-shirts. They photocopy the original color artwork onto an "iron-on transfer" similar to a clear transparency, then use a heat transfer press to "iron" it onto the T-shirt. They can use any original artwork, photograph, or photocopy, and can enlarge or reduce it. Using good-quality white T-shirts and his own artwork, Henningsen's price was $15 each, including one small (8½" x 11") transfer, or $20 each, for one large (11" x 17") transfer.

You can expect a discount if you supply the shirts. If not white, use light pastels. Do a prototype, then hand it to the production people with the simple instruction: "I want nineteen more, just like this, in these sizes."

A note about T-shirts: Henningsen related that he and a dozen or so family members wearing T-shirts visited the National Aquarium in Baltimore and got separated in traffic. When he went scouting to find the others, a guard said, "They went that way." T-shirts were also a great icebreaker for meeting strangers in waiting lines.

Auctions and Raffles

Auctions and raffles are a theme for which there are dozens of variations. Many reunions solicit items in promotional materials, then in later mailings include a list of items donated to serve as an incentive for more donations. Members who own businesses often donate professional services or products. In the case of raffles, it is wise to check any local and state regulations that may apply.

Linda Johnson Hoffman and Neal Barnett in *The Reunion Planner* suggest raffles to make up budget shortfalls. Solicit dinner donations or theater tickets for two and offer to mention donations in your memory book/program. The mechanics are relatively simple: Sell tickets before and during the reunion; then draw the winner's ticket with much fanfare, including salutes to the donors. You can also raffle or auction centerpieces.

Emma Wisdom in *Family Reunion Organizer* suggests raffling a family heirloom, rare portrait, or handmade quilt. Consider, too, special local or regional products if your reunion draws from a wide geographic area—for example, regional foods (Vermont maple syrup, Cajun spice blends, Wisconsin cheese, California champagne).

---

* *The Bichko Family Reunion creates theme baskets to raffle, such as baskets of car-wash and gardening supplies and gourmet kitchen items.*

* *The descendants of John and Maria Smith add gag items to their auctions.*

* *The Warner Family Reunion held a Chinese auction to increase their cemetery fund and finance future reunions. Everyone was encouraged to bring lots of quarters and something to auction. Items included a handmade birdhouse, a*

set of pillows, and a paint set. These were arranged with labeled bags in front of each. Bids were made by dropping 25¢ tickets in the appropriate bags. At the end of the day, winning tickets were drawn. As an incentive for those who donated, the winners of the top-three bid items also got cash prizes. Sonia Croft of Jennings, Florida, says that with so many ways to win, the Chinese auction was a real hit.

✱ *Vickie Everhart of Red Oak, Texas, makes her Pounders Family Reunion auction a real event. The meat bill for one reunion was only 67¢ after all the leftovers were auctioned off. Family members are "strongly" encouraged to donate handmade auction items—a top-selling recent item was a nostalgic painting of the family homestead. Special auction items are recognized in their newsletter, and even members who could not attend sent auction donations.*

✱ *Tammy L. Davis of Lindley, New York, organizes the Jewell/Felker Family Reunion. Auction earnings help pay reunion expenses and purchase U.S. savings bonds for newborns and high school graduates, and a penny jar collection usually covers postage costs. The $2.50 registration fee for the reunion's horseshoe tournament is split evenly.*

Picture-Perfect Fund-Raising

People always want photographs or videos of their reunions. Hiring a professional ensures the best product but is also the most expensive option. If you have a willing, experienced photographer or videographer in your family, you can actually make instead of owe money. Take group shots—for example, the entire family, each branch, each generation—and try to set up the shots against attractive scenery.

Offer pictures for sale prepaid, with print size options at different prices. Take orders for videos at the reunion so you know how many to print. Charge enough to cover costs, including packaging and postage, and allow for a modest profit. You may want to follow the example of the reunion that charges double for videos to persons who do not attend, while they have a "reunion attendee discount" for those who do. In any case, don't forget to offer pictures and videos for sale in your newsletter.

CREATIVE REUNION FINANCING

✳ *Tyrone Dumas of Milwaukee, Wisconsin, occasional organizer of the Scott McNair Brazil Family Reunion, is a master at corporate fund-raising. For one reunion, a well-conceived letter about his family convinced the Coca-Cola Company to provide a sizable contribution, which covered the cost of the reunion banquet, T-shirts, banner, and, of course, a supply of soft drinks. For a later reunion, Dumas managed to secure a gift of two round-trip Southwest Airlines tickets. The tickets were auctioned off to aid family scholars.*

✳ *Vincent Beauford of Lithonia, Georgia, then president of the biannual reunion of George Schultz and His, Inc., challenged his family to save pennies. They did! At their next reunion, emptied piggy banks yielded $999! The money assured payment of incidental reunion expenses.*

✳ *The Jewell/Felker family calendar fund-raiser presupposes that participants have loose change. Each day the specially printed calendar instructs you to, say, donate 10¢ if you watched TV or drove your car that day or 25¢ if you have brown eyes (blue, green, and gray eyes have their days too!).*

✳ *The Seidemann Family Reunion has a kuchen (coffeecake) contest, with no lack of judges to sample entries. After prizes are awarded, kuchen leftovers are auctioned—some to flatteringly high bidders!*

✳ *One family sponsored a weekend trip (open to anyone), chartering a bus for an overnight Atlanta to Biloxi package and charging $68 per person. Passengers departed late Friday night, partied on the bus, arrived in Biloxi Saturday morning, spent the night, and returned to Atlanta Sunday. Adding $20 to the trip's cost enriched reunion coffers.*

Finally, there is the very unique way that the McConnell Family Reunion funds its one-week, biennial meetings, according to Cheryl Laufer of Chesterland, Ohio. Half of the family lives west of the Rocky Mountains, and the other half lives east. At first, they alternated meetings between east and west.

As families grew, they agreed to meet throughout the east and Midwest where the larger families lived. As compensation for the increased travel expenses for "West Coasters," the "East Coasters" pay for all the rental expenses in whatever facility they rent. Food and other expenses are divided equally.

There are many ways to support reunions. Just find those that best suit your family . . . and have fun doing them.

Reunion Sites

The world is your reunion oyster. A suitable reunion site can be anywhere from a backyard to a cruise ship to lots of venues in between: hotels, resorts, ranches, condos, bed and breakfasts, inns, houseboats, and campgrounds.

For our discussion, the word *hotel* means "facility" and can refer to any meeting venue. The word *location* refers to place, city, state, region.

Family reunions take place where the family originated, or where many members live, or a central location for widely scattered families. The original homesite is especially good for a first-time reunion because it stirs interest in members to discover their roots. Subsequent reunions may then take place at other locations significant to the family. According to Tim Adell, the Adell Family Reunion meets at a place with historical resonance, one that conveys the sense "this is where we came from." Some families rotate reunions among locations close to groups of family members—a good way to share reunion planning. Or you may wish to rotate around the country, moving from one coast to the middle of the country to the other coast to ensure widespread attendance. For example, Dodi Mace of Marietta, Georgia, reports that the Robinson Family Reunion, meeting for many years in their hometown of Jesup, Georgia, then tried new locations and were surprised with increased attendance.

Some choose to make reunions into family vacations at an exotic locale like a dude ranch or resort. Other alternatives are resident camps or condos that can be leased for one or two weeks. For a rustic camping adventure, try a national or state park where cabins or camping facilities can be rented. A more ambitious plan is the international reunion bringing together relatives from different countries.

If you are looking for a new and exciting place to gather family, contact your travel agent for suggestions. If you have an idea of an area you'd like to visit, contact the convention and visitors or tourism bureau. Most states and cities publish travel guides. If this is your first reunion, start such enquiries at least eighteen months to two years in advance.

Until the early 1990s, hotels depended on business travelers for their major source of income. Then came a recession and a rise in telecommuting, and hotels suffered some fallout. With a lower rate of weekday occupancy, weekends became crucial. Looming as a lucrative source of weekend business were reunions. Many hotels have since eagerly courted reunion groups with designated staff and many of the same fine services that business travelers have come to expect. Fortunately, hotel services for reunions often include programs for kids, as one stress factor for planners and attendees alike is to assure activities for children.

Be sure to shop around. If your group meets annually or biennially in the same location, offer that as an incentive to the hotel manager. Some facilities provide a free hospitality room if you reserve a minimum number of sleeping rooms. The earlier you make arrangements, the more negotiating leverage you have.

While the hotel industry has targeted family reunions as an emerging new market, "down home" reunions still appeal. Paula Sheagley planned her large family reunion at a beautiful Colorado camp and conference resort—complete with cribs for babies! For those who drove RVs or preferred to put up tents, campsites were available just outside the lodge. The property was chosen because of its reasonable cost, excellent accommodations, and willingness to personalize dinner menus. It also offered a large all-purpose room that easily transformed from a formal meeting area one minute into an indoor volleyball court the next.

The East Stroudsburg University/*Reunions magazine* study found that in choosing the site for a reunion, convenient location is the most prominent factor (19 percent), followed closely by reasonable lodging cost (18 percent), reasonable travel cost (16 percent), and available recreation activities (14 percent). Other factors include the familiarity of the same place every year, variety of accommodations and activities, and destinations that match a theme.

In settling on a site, size *does* matter. Reunions that number in the hundreds meet comfortably in hotels, vacation condos, resorts, and even on cruise ships. The large number of people can bring down individual costs significantly. Smaller groups may be more comfortable at inns, ranches, condos, villas, or campgrounds for tents and RVs. You may even consider private homes.

* Karen Robertson of Wildomar, California, writing about the Brolra Family Reunion, says the Brolra cousins have a secret meeting at each reunion to decide where the next one will be. They choose the general area together, then take turns finding the site and planning. They agreed long ago that the reunion would never be near anybody's home so everybody can travel and see new sights.

* T. R. (Dick) Wood, a retired Corning Glass ceramics engineer, organizes and hosts his family reunion every other year. Between reunions, everyone explores their own territory, looking for ideal sites. A popular evening activity at reunions is showing slides from those independent forays. The family has so far stayed at ranches in Montana and Arizona and rafted the Rogue River in Oregon. Dude ranches seem to have been a good choice for pleasing three generations.

* Charles Kuykendall II of Cleveland, Ohio, says the Brooks Family Reunion holds every other reunion in the city where their board president lives. Family members vote on additional locations two reunions in advance (their reunions take place every two years). Since they bestow an award on the best host city, members outdo themselves vying for the honor.

* Cyndi Johanneck of Westerville, Ohio, says most of her Hanson/Steele family members live in the Pacific Northwest. They therefore try to locate sites halfway between southern Oregon and northwestern Washington, and also alternate sites so that one group is not always doing all the traveling.

CONVENTION AND VISITORS BUREAUS

Relax, reunion planning is not as cumbersome as it sounds. Once you know your destination, the rest is fairly easy. Helping to make it easy are convention and visitors bureaus (CVBs). CVBs are service organizations funded by grants from departments of tourism, membership dues from hotels/motels and attractions, or a portion of hotel/motel taxes. Donald Family Reunion organizer Brenda Donald of Stone Mountain, Georgia, reports that the DeKalb (Georgia) Convention and Visitors Bureau found hotel rates and planned a welcome dinner, special reception, African-American Heritage Tour, and picnic all within her budget. The Kissimmee–St. Cloud, Florida, CVB, meanwhile, was instrumental in managing details for the Haeberlin Family Reunion.

What a Resource!

CVBs are probably the best resource for information about places that conventions, visitors, and, yes, reunions want to go. Someone in Hawaii can contact a CVB in Wisconsin and save a lot of time getting information about accommodations, restaurants, attractions, recreation and leisure activities, historic or special interests, maps, and transportation. Here's even better news: Because the purpose of most CVBs is to encourage you to visit their area, many CVB services are provided at little or no cost. Let the CVB sell their area to your reunion.

When you first contact the CVB, introduce the history and purpose of your reunion, anticipated reunion dates, number and ages of members, budget range, number and type of rooms (approximate, if exact number is unknown), and special needs (handicapped access, no smoking space, special diets, or recreational requirements). Request references as well as a site inspection/familiarization trip. Besides brochures about area attractions, tours, and restaurants, check if they have promotional items (mugs, T-shirts, tote bags, or key chains) available for visitors.

CVBs effectively serve as liaisons between reunions and hotels and other visitor services and vendors. In other words, they facilitate partnerships between reunion organizers and segments of the local hospitality industry. They can help determine your itinerary and assist novices or volunteers with legal issues such as host alcohol liability, insurance, and permit requirements. One thing they cannot do is recommend one vendor over another. Nor can they negotiate room rates. In fact, they are required to provide impartial information, so you can be confident they will fairly represent all hotels, tour companies, attractions, and restaurants.

Some CVBs will help you develop a request for proposal (RFP) and distribute it to area facilities for response either to you directly or through the CVB. Your RFP should include the same basic information you should have at hand when contacting the CVB.

Complimentary familiarization tours (FAMs) as well as site inspections of hotels and attractions can be arranged by some CVBs. FAMs encompass numerous attractions, hotels, and restaurants. Many CVBs conduct several FAM tours annually and are always looking for invitees who meet certain criteria. Take advantage of this opportunity!

Be aware that some CVBs charge a deposit, which is refundable for those who do attend the FAM. Deposits ensure that invitees are seriously considering the city as a possible reunion site.

In reality, a FAM is an oxymoron: a working vacation. Your job is to ask lots of questions and get lots of answers. Be satisfied that you know everything you need to know about your destination.

To sum up, CVBs help take the hassle out of planning. They assist with

- *Publications.* CVBs offer brochures, guides, and directories highlighting area restaurants, attractions, events, and facilities.
- *Registration assistance and supplies.* CVBs provide assistance before, during, and after your reunion as well as supply such items as typewriters, name badges, and program covers.
- *Tours and entertainment.* CVBs arrange tours and entertainment for an entire reunion.
- *Contacting dignitaries.* City officials may be available to make welcome speeches, present keys to the city, or give proclamations.
- *Membership referrals.* CVB staffers can inform reunion organizers of businesses catering to visitors.

When working with a CVB, remember that they represent all hotels, restaurants, and attractions equally.

Testimonials from previous reunion organizers are often available. If there is a problem, CVBs want to know in order to solve it immediately.

SITE SELECTION

The necessity to decide upon and reserve space *early* often catches first-time reunion organizers by surprise. Many reunion places are popular. If you have a special place or date in mind, eighteen months to two years may not be too early. Don't wait and have to settle for anything you can get. The longer you wait, the less choice you have and the more you may have to pay.

Jacalyn Eis's family wisely forms a site-finding committee early. Family members investigate promising locales. They take pictures and collect maps and brochures, including ones for nearby recreation and entertainment, and make extensive notes of their impressions. There is no substitute for visiting a site before making a decision.

In addition, talk with friends and acquaintances. You probably know people who have attended or planned family reunions. The benefit of a word-of-mouth referral is that you learn much more about a site. Eis says if it's your first reunion, you should make your site decision by meeting with key family members.

One mistake new reunion organizers make is to reserve too many rooms or forget to ask for deposits. Don't reserve a hundred rooms when only forty are needed. Make sure you understand cancellation procedures and follow them exactly.

Many young families struggle to get time off from work and save money to attend the reunion. Choose a site within their budget. You're counting on younger members to perpetuate the reunion tradition. Don't assume their parents will or should pay their way. Such assumptions cause family problems. Scheduling a reunion at a site only a few family members can afford is a sure way to guarantee failure and cause hard feelings.

Avoid inconvenient locations. If family members all live on the East and West Coasts, meeting in the Midwest ensures that everyone's reunion costs are more or less equal. An alternative may be meeting on the West Coast one time and the East Coast the next.

Among the resources that exist to help reunion organizers find a location is *Reunions magazine*, where hundreds of listings appear in each issue and are linked on the World Wide Web. You'll also want to look through the conference sections of classified ads in travel magazines and church publications. Nearly every denomination has a newspaper or magazine that advertises retreat or conference centers. Most welcome families of all faiths.

If your family chooses a picnic, reserving park facilities is crucial—often a year in advance for popular locations or dates. When selecting a park site, consider its facilities: restrooms, water fountains, barbecue pits, playground equipment, ball fields, swimming/boating facilities, and shelters. Many facilities at recreational parks and lakes have buildings to accommodate your group in case of rain.

If you are looking for a place for just one day, Beth Gay advises you check with civic clubs, women's clubs, schools, churches, or the park department. Compare prices and features.

Be sure the facility is large enough to hold your family comfortably. Is it air conditioned? heated? ventilated? Does it have smoke-free areas? Are there tables and chairs? refrigerators? ice or soda machines? bathrooms? Is there a stage? Is a sound system furnished with the rental? Can the space accommodate the physically challenged?

When you do find a place that fits your requirements, reserve it immediately! Don't take a chance it may be available later.

* *Ayers Family Reunion sites have included ranches, national parks, resorts, and private homes in Idaho, California, Washington, Oregon, Arizona, and Oklahoma. Relatives come from all over the United States and abroad.*

* *The Slaubaugh Family Reunions are scheduled every three years. The family votes on the general area and time frame and on the committee chairperson for the next reunion.*

* *Madge Bodtke, her five children, and their spouses and offspring chose Christmas week at the Club Cozumel Caribe for their first family reunion in eight years. Many members are scuba divers and the others wanted a place where they could swim, sun, sail, and relax. The resort offered supervised games, snorkeling, and sailing for children, which allowed family members to pursue separate activities because parents were assured their children were in a secure environment.*

* *The Maxon family enjoyed several exciting transcontinental reunions, then returned to their hometown of Olean, New York, for a nostalgic journey to their past. They visited the homestead, alma maters, old haunts, and the family cemetery plot.*

GETTING THERE

* *Carole Byrd organized The Great Byrd Migration, a caravan of relatives driving through Virginia on their way to New Haven, Connecticut, site of a Frank Byrd Family Reunion. Byrd notified all relatives living in places south of Richmond to meet and start the reunion a day early!*

* *The Taylor Family Reunion, alternating their reunions between the Buffalo, New York, and Chicago, Illinois, areas, hire a bus to transport the visiting contingent and then have transportation throughout the entire reunion. The cost per person is better than any other form of transportation either for the long distance or local trips.*

First, determine the type of transportation you'll need: to and from the airport, to and from special events, a shuttle between hotels and activities, allowance for persons with special needs. It helps to plan the reunion somewhere within 100 miles of a major airport.

You'll also need to estimate the number of people requiring transportation for each event, and establish pickup and drop-off sites. Will members be moved in one trip or many?

Request information about ground transportation operators from convention and visitors bureaus or hotel staff. Consider: How long have they been in business? What is their specialty? Do vehicles have air conditioning, seat belts, rest rooms, a public address system? What is their safety record? (Contact the Department of Transportation, Office of Motor Carrier Federal Highway Administration; 1-800-832-5660 or www.safesys.org). When they quote costs, do they include fuel, equipment, maintenance, union fees, state and local taxes, surcharges and tolls?

The American Automobile Association (AAA) offers these tips for family reunion planners. Select a centrally located reunion site convenient to highways, railroad stations, and airports. Look for discounts on group fares to a single destination. Coordinate air and rail arrivals and departures to save time.

If you're taking your reunion abroad, consider the following: Allow extra time for foreign mail—several months for handwritten correspondence. Coordinate telephone conversations with time-zone differences. Arrange for a historian to travel with your group as part of the tour package. Inform your tour company ahead, and they can often comply with requests to include the "special places" members want to see. Learn as much as possible about the country's local customs, including tipping practices. Memorize a few key words and phrases of the local language, and keep a pocket dictionary handy.

HOTELS AND OTHER FACILITIES

Consider the other side of the hotel sales desk. Hotel sales managers are very busy. You'll get their undivided attention at a scheduled appointment in person or by phone.

Bill Masciangelo, a longtime reunion advocate and trainer, notes that hotels are in business to make money. To successfully negotiate hotel rates, know what your reunion is worth: $5,000? $15,000? $30,000? Check your records from previous reunions. List how many rooms you rented and how much you spent on meals. Be accurate—hotels check. You're in a better position to negotiate if you have a solid track record.

When you are ready to make a deal, put the hotel space on tentative hold. Other salespersons, especially in large hotels, are trying to sell the same space. Be flexible about dates. Finally, avoid settling on any facility without a site inspection. If you absolutely can't visit, ask for references and check them.

Introduce Yourself

If you're doing your planning long-distance, send a picture of yourself to the sales manager. It helps to personalize your relationship and gives sales managers the opportunity to match a person with the voice.

Introduce your family. Who are you? What do you like to do? Provide as much information about your reunion to the hotel as possible. It will help the hotel staff better understand your expectations.

Site Inspection

When you've narrowed your list of venues to those that meet your maximum requirements for sleeping rooms and meeting space, it's time to make a site inspection. Meet as many of the hotel staff as possible. If the sales manager doesn't make introductions, ask to meet key staff. Hotel turnover is often high, so if your sales manager leaves, you've at least made the acquaintance of others at the hotel. Check assigned meeting rooms, because printed space information may not always be accurate.

Be prepared. Show staff you're organized and know what you want. Approach your inspection as if considering buying the hotel! The site inspection checklist provided here will help you evaluate and compare venues and also come in handy during the negotiating process.

Site inspection checklist

General observations:

- How are you treated?
- What about cleanliness?
- How would you rate security and safety systems, including fire exits and sprinkler systems in rooms?
- Do you find the decor pleasing?
- Is the size of the registration area adequate?
- Is there access to public transportation?
- Is there sufficient, convenient parking?
- Are ice machines conveniently located and do they work properly?

- Do employees take pride in their work?
- Are they cheerful and helpful?

Does the hotel offer the following:
- In-house movies?
- Gift shop?
- Bell service?
- Safe deposit boxes?
- Barber/hairdresser?

Note the following about rooms:
- Are there king-size beds, doubles, singles, suites, or a mix of sleeping room types?
- Are special rates available during certain periods?
- Are registration and reservation systems automated?
- Will reservation cards be provided for your group?
- Is audiovisual support available? If so, at what cost?
- Does the hotel offer shuttle service? If so, at what cost?
- Is around-the-clock room service available?
- Can you bring in your own liquor? If so, is there a "corkage" fee?

If you really want to be thorough, ask to see the kitchen and engineering facilities, such as the heating and air conditioning units. Also ask for copies of the facility's complimentary room policy and menu selections for meal functions.

NEGOTIATING FOR SPACE

To successfully put on your reunion, you must negotiate, or you and your members may pay a stiff price with few, if any, extras.

First, do your homework. Know the facts to get the best value for your reunion dollars. Then, take notes—and take your time. Rushing through the negotiating process can cause careless mistakes. Show the sales manager you mean business.

What Are Your Strengths?

Remember, you are *selling* your family. Stress the economic impact of your family's business on the hotel or venue. Supply documentation from previous reunions. What will you spend on food and beverages, meeting space, and shopping? Are you able to make a large deposit or pay in full at checkout? Is there the potential for future business with them?

Shop around—and tell them you are. Don't settle on a venue just because it offers the lowest price. You may not get the level of service you want if services have to be cut back to meet a price.

If you really like a venue but the price is out of your range, tell them so, and ask if they could try to accommodate you. They just might. Of course, they also might not.

Hotel rates are as complicated as airfares. The principle of supply and demand prevails. Expect to pay top dollar at popular destinations during the summer. Check for dates when rates are lower, called low, off, or soft periods. These vary from place to place and season to season and can occur more than once a year. If you're flexible, you may be able to save 50 percent or more off published rates.

Always ask for complimentary items or reduced rates—because they will not be offered, you must ask. Here's a list of things you should discuss. (If this is your first reunion, don't expect to get all of them!)

- Complimentary welcoming cocktail party.
- Free recreational activities.
- Upgraded amenities for guests.
- Complimentary room(s) for your hospitality suite.
- Free parking.
- Early check-in, late checkout.
- Signs for your registration area.
- Special menu items.
- Flowers and table decorations.
- Free storage for supplies and materials shipped ahead.

After Negotiation

When you finish negotiating, you will receive a written contract. Read the contract carefully and critically. Ask questions if there's anything you don't understand or if something does not agree with your notes. Once signed, the contract is legally binding on both parties. A good contract or letter of agreement ensures that you and the hotel will meet your obligations.

Take nothing for granted. Everything you've agreed to should be listed, from any extra promised service, however small, to the type and number of rooms and for how long they're blocked. Also check these contract details carefully: requirements for deposits, reservations, meeting space, complimentary rooms, suites, facilities, check-in/checkout times and dates; taxes, transportation, master accounts, services and equipment, cut-off dates, and cancellation clauses. What happens if the hotel is overbooked?

Always return signed contracts by certified mail. Once the contract is signed, you and the hotel become a team. You are both working toward the same goal: a truly great reunion.

Countdown As the Reunion Gets Closer

It's the sales manager's job to ensure you a great reunion. Make his or her life easier by communicating frequently and meeting reservation, guarantee, and deposit deadlines. If attendance is lower than you expected, release sleeping rooms you blocked. If necessary, move your banquet to a smaller room. It shows courtesy and consideration, not to mention saving you lots of money.

Finally, keep records and get everything in writing.

FINAL INSTRUCTIONS TO HOTELS

As your reunion date draws near, clear and concise instructions are crucial! Communicate your specifications to the hotel and suppliers in as much detail as possible. You also may wish to address comments to the controller, front desk supervisor, and bellhop staff.

Your final instructions should include, but not be limited to, the following:

- Introduction and purpose of the reunion.
- Authorized signatures with samples.
- Schedule of the day-by-day program.
- A list of all suppliers providing services; bus/tour company, florist, caterer, entertainment company, photographer, registration company, press, speakers.
- Hotel room assignments. Daily pickup schedules for bus trips and other events.

- Any VIP or physically challenged persons who may require special consideration.
- Room setups with drawings to show how you want rooms arranged.
- Audiovisual instructions: easels, risers, lectern, extension cords, lighting, electrical hookups, props.
- Food and beverage instructions: selected menus, bar arrangements, type of service, meal tickets. Room service should be notified if you expect to use it heavily.
- Any extra requirements for souvenir sales and photographer.
- Miscellaneous equipment: coat racks, wastebaskets, typewriters.

Some Final Thoughts About Instructions

Don't allow specifications to get lost in translation. At a prereunion conference, review details one more time. Ask to see a copy of the hotel's version of your final instructions in sufficient time to make corrections.

Provide detailed instructions, too, to your suppliers. Give the bus company specific pickup and drop-off instructions. Let the disc jockey know exactly what songs you want played. Prepare a written script for ceremonies. If you are having a cake or wreath made, provide a picture of what you want.

Be sure to share details of the arrangements with committee members and volunteers. You cannot provide too much information, only too little.

RANCHES

Ranches evoke an image of adventure and certainly guarantee a memorable reunion. A ranch reunion means incredible scenery, good food, action, cowboys, horses—and hot tubs. Families can truly share new experiences and tackle challenges together.

What time of year suits your reunion? There's a ranch available for it. Northern ranches and those at higher elevations sometimes close for winter, while others offer winter sports. Many Arizona ranches are open all winter but are less active during hot summers.

Some ranches have extensive family programs or provide baby-sitting; others prefer children old enough to ride, or cater to adults only. Typically, larger ranches offer more organized activities and scheduled entertainment. Smaller ranches focus on personalized services.

Although ranches center around horseback riding, programs differ. Some ranches offer only walking rides, while others allow trotting and loping. Wrangler supervision varies from spread to spread. Working ranches encourage guests to assist with chores or moving cattle.

Ranch accommodations range from a simple room in a historic ranch house to stunningly decorated cabins with rock fireplaces. Most offer private baths, daily maid service, and delicious home-cooked meals.

You can use the Internet, ranch association directories, advertising, word of mouth, and *Reunions magazine* to find ranches. Ask ranches for their brochures; many offer videos. When you've found a perfect match, don't delay reservations. Many ranches book a year or more in advance.

One of the great advantages of ranch reunions is that there are no hidden costs. With the American plan, meals, lodging, horseback riding, use of facilities, and supervised activities are all included in the price. The package price will depend on family size, children's ages, length of stay, season, and type of accommodations. Additional charges may be assessed for airport transfers, optional off-ranch activities, and bar tabs.

The cost for ranch reunions ranges from economy to luxury. Some offer five-day midweek specials for less. Reaching remote ranches adds to the cost, either in long drives or premium fares to small airports.

Consider these practical advantages to a ranch reunion. First, most ranches are small, which encourages more intimate reunions. Second, you are often the personal guests of the owners. Third, your family may be the only guests and therefore receive the full attention of the staff.

Ranch Choices

- *Working cattle ranches.* Rise early. Join the cattle drive. Mend fences. Western-style relaxation—rodeos, square dances, hayrides—a timeless way of life.

- *Dude/guest ranches.* Often hosted by owners, ranch activities forge lasting friendships. Many guests return year after year.

- *Resort ranches.* Traditional ranch activities plus golf, tennis, swimming, spa, mountain biking, hiking, skeet shooting, and children's programs.

- *Specialized ranches.* Along with horseback riding, there may be fly-fishing, cross-country skiing, stargazing, white-water rafting and kayaking, or bird-watching.

Most ranches are located in western states and Canadian provinces, though you can also jump in the saddle (and lifestyle) in unexpected places like New York, North Carolina, Pennsylvania, Iowa, or Arkansas. Location will determine other potential adventures, such as national parks, geological formations, Native American ruins, old mines, ghost towns, and abandoned forts. The Internet is a great place to compare ranches. To link directly to many ranch choices, check Reunion Resources at www.reunionsmag.com.

* *For the fiftieth anniversary reunion of Jim and Miriam Herr of Nottingham, Pennsylvania, thirty-five Herrs commandeered Hidden Creek Ranch in Harrison, Idaho, for a week. Miriam shares a lovely, lingering memory of her family riding together into a daisy-filled meadow for a champagne breakfast.*

* *Seventeen members and three generations of the Wood Family Reunion hung their Christmas stockings on a giant agave plant at Grapevine Canyon Ranch in Pearce, Arizona. They were celebrating their semiannual reunion (with kids twelve and older) by taking over the entire ranch—working cattle ranch complete with riding and roping.*

* *James G. and Phyllis Schneider of Kankakee, Illinois, vacationed at Lake Mancos Ranch in southwest Colorado when their children were young, so to celebrate their fortieth anniversary reunion they hardly considered any other destination. The appeal of the ranch is its utter lack of regimentation. Horseback riding and savory, homestyle meals are the only things scheduled. A ranch counselor showed the under-six crowd a nonstop good time with games, fishing, feeding livestock, and lots of breaks for cookies and lemonade.*

* *John and Pat Lopez gather their family at Wonder Valley Ranch Resort in the foothills of the Sierra Nevada. Riding, waterskiing, tennis, and arts and crafts keep multiple generations, even toddlers, happy.*

* *Before families arrive at White Tail Ranch in Ovando, Montana, phone calls and questionnaires make the fit perfect. Cincinnati, Ohio's Jim and Peggy Bridgeland and their family looked forward to the informality once they'd settled in at the ranch, tucked against Glacier National Park. Jim and son John, avid birders, glimpsed ospreys and golden eagles. Granddaughters Caily, six, and Fallon, four, had their first riding lessons with experienced wranglers.*

REUNIONS ON WATER

Cruises

Highly responsive to family reunion travel needs is the ever-expanding cruise industry. Many cruise ships cater to families and provide special prices, services, and programs to attract reunions.

In just about a decade, cruising has evolved from a vacation affordable only for the few to one of the best value alternatives in the leisure industry. All-inclusive pricing covers meals, accommodations, and entertainment. In addition to visiting exciting ports of call, many activities are offered to satisfy different age groups and interests.

Contact a travel agent who knows group travel planning as well as family reunions. Tell the agent when and where you would like to take your cruise. Estimate the number of cabins you'll need and list attendees' points of departure. The agent will do the planning for you.

For the best ship availability, make reservations nine to twelve months in advance. Also, the earlier you book your cruise, the less it will cost. Deposit the full amount early so cabins can be confirmed on deck and near each other. Conference facilities can be reserved on some ships. Most cruise lines will also set up public rooms for a group, if reserved in advance. Depending on the number of people booked, the reunion organizer may travel free. Group discounts range from 5 to 30 percent.

Kari Satterfield's family celebrated their parents' fiftieth anniversary reunion with all the children and grandkids on an eleven-day reunion cruise through the Panama Canal. No worry about how to occupy the children. They were kept entertained with scavenger hunts, puzzles and games, arts and crafts, playdough parties, a talent show, swimming, and ice cream socials. Stops included Cozumel, Mexico; Cartagena, Columbia; and Huatulco and Acapulco, Mexico. Satterfield of Roseburg, Oregon, says the reunion cruise was "a wonderful gift my parents gave to all of us!"

Margaret Malsam's family reunion was aboard a dazzling Carnival ship noted for its fun-filled cruises. It lived up to its reputation. Malsam of Westminster, Colorado, offers the following tips for a successful family reunion cruise:

- Look for flyaway packages, which include airfare. Consult travel agents who specialize in cruises to secure bargain group rates.

- Try to get everyone's room on the same deck.

- Arrange dinner seating together at one table or, for larger groups, several tables clustered together.

- Don't assume everyone reads the instructions provided by the cruise line. Brief everyone about tipping, ordering from the menu, and optional shore excursions.
- Ask for special menus for anyone who is on a restricted diet.
- Read daily bulletins placed in your room to keep informed.

Here's another tip. Consider cancellation insurance. Otherwise, you could lose all your money for a last-minute cancellation. Insurance, based on total cost or a flat rate from some cruise lines, is purchased when final payment is made.

Riverboats

Cruising on a luxury barge on rivers and canals in France or on a paddle wheeler or steamboat on the wide Mississippi offers a very different experience than cruising on an ocean liner. Riverboat cruises provide intimate, mile-by-mile views of the river and landscape, as well as entry into small ports and through narrow locks where bigger ships can't go.

Luxury barges, traveling through some of Europe's most picturesque scenery at a leisurely pace, offer gourmet meals and the chance to tour villages, vineyards, and local fairs along the way. Never far from shore, you can hop off to walk or bike down a towpath. (Barges usually have bicycles on board for your use.) Barges with full crews can be chartered for a reunion or booked by the cabin. Prices are all-inclusive (meals, beverages, sightseeing, and bicycles). For larger groups, it's advisable to charter two barges (traveling in tandem). On riverboat casinos, meanwhile, gambling afloat means you don't need to go to Nevada or Atlantic City to roll the dice.

Houseboats

Houseboats are available for rent by the weekend or longer. Many sleep up to ten, while groups over ten rent several houseboats to form a "fleet" and meet at secluded coves, beaches, or inlets. Houseboaters learn basic rules of operation in a brief orientation session. Family members take turns at the helm while others relax, bird-watching or daydreaming, while hamburgers sizzle on the craft's outdoor grill. Be aware that some lakes and rivers are too cold for swimming.

Most houseboats have safety-conscious railed walkways and, along with a gas grill, are outfitted with utensils, stove, refrigerator, drinking water, shower, and life jackets. Some provide a microwave, TV, radio, stereo, and hot tub. You may need to bring along groceries, a cooler, fishing rod, camera, binoculars, and insect repellent. In some cases, you may also need to supply linens and bedding. Consider renting canoes or fishing boats to tow alongside and use for narrow, inaccessible waterways.

Divided by ten people, a houseboat reunion can be very affordable. Be sure to look into off-season rates, which vary depending on location and climate. The off-season cost of a seven-day houseboat rental can be $1,000 plus the cost of gas, insurance, and possibly motor repairs. Ask enough questions to determine the total cost before signing up. A nonrefundable deposit may be required.

A Floating Hotel

The Hotel Queen Mary, a 1930s luxury ocean liner, is now a floating hotel in Long Beach, California, with 365 first-class staterooms, meeting rooms, restaurants, shops, and lounges.

REUNITING WITH HISTORY

Reunions are the perfect occasion to explore areas steeped in history. Historical places often relate well to what children are studying in school or may have some connection to family forebears. Visiting such places makes history come alive. Gathering in places of historical significance adds depth to the reunion experience. Here are a few suggestions.

Connecticut

Mystic Seaport in Mystic, Connecticut, as it recalls a bustling 1870s sailing village, is a veritable maritime museum—prepare to hear seafaring songs and tales of a bygone era. Many reunions have been held at this colorful 17-acre waterfront village, dotted with shops, tall ships, historic homes, and maritime trades buildings.

Iowa

Visitors from all over the world come to Living History Farms in Urbandale, Iowa, to learn about the heritage of agriculture in the Midwest. A tractor-drawn cart takes visitors on a journey to the past as historical interpreters perform the daily routine of early Iowans at this 600-acre outdoor museum. A self-guided woodland trail connects a Native American village of 1700, a pioneer farming settlement of 1850, a farm of 1900, and "the farm of today and tomorrow."

Kentucky

Shaker Village in Pleasant Hill, Kentucky, is a national historic landmark. Located on 2,700 acres of bluegrass farmland, it boasts over thirty restored buildings. Costumed interpreters demonstrate coopering, quilting, spinning, weaving, broommaking, chairmaking, silkculturing, and sheepshearing.

Massachusetts

Hancock Shaker Village in Pittsfield, Massachusetts, also welcomes reunions.

Michigan

At the Henry Ford Museum & Greenfield Village in Dearborn, Michigan, visitors witness changes that transformed America from a rural, agrarian society into a highly industrialized nation. More than eighty historic structures have been relocated here. They include Ford's childhood home, Thomas Edison's Menlo Park laboratory complex, the bicycle shop where the Wright brothers built their first airplane, a 1950s drive-in movie theater, and four period kitchens (from the colonial era through the 1930s). Tinsmithing, blacksmithing, pottery making, printing, and milking are demonstrated.

Virginia

In Colonial Williamsburg, Virginia, the eighteenth century lives on. "Character interpreters" attired as townspeople, crafts workers, shopkeepers, servants, balladeers, and fifers and drummers present Williamsburg as it appeared on the eve of the American Revolution. The historic area bustles with carriage rides, militia drills, and live drama. Enjoy a folk art center and decorative arts gallery, candlelight walking tours, concerts, an eighteenth-century play, tavern dining, and colonial "gambols," or games.

Real Frontier Reunions at Old Army Forts

The American landscape is dotted with forts abandoned by the Army. Historic preservation has well suited them to reunions. They offer sports facilities, hiking trails, and cultural events as well as a wide variety of accommodations and meeting facilities. The Eis Family Reunion has enjoyed two reunions at restored Army forts: Fort Robinson, Nebraska, and Fort Worden, Washington. The sense of history there, Jacalyn Eis reports, was captivating as each hinted at what life was like generations ago.

Fort Robinson, Nebraska, eighty miles north of Scottsbluff, offers the experience of life in an authentic Old West atmosphere without commercialism. The fort is a great choice for families in the Midwest and for African-American families; it served as home to the renowned all-black Ninth and Tenth Cavalries, known as the Buffalo Soldiers. After World War I, it also became the world's largest remount station, specializing in horse breeding.

Accommodations for reunions include camping, lodging in historic officers' family housing, and dining in Comanche Hall, once the bachelor officers' quarters and now fully equipped with a modern kitchen boasting several refrigerators and a commercial-size stove. The dining hall seats all sixty-five guests at once and adapts well for meetings and games.

Fort Robinson considers your horse part of the family. Stabling is available for a nominal fee, and the 22,000-acre state park provides many scenic trails along the Pine Ridge Escarpment. Activities are either free or reasonably priced. Throughout the fort, there are historical museums and displays.

Fort Worden, Washington, is at the northeast tip of the Olympic Peninsula. Accommodations include restored Victorian houses, original officers' housing, camping sites, and dormitories. Dorm rooms include meals served at the dining hall. A gourmet restaurant and catering are available too. Featured are museums; a summer stock playhouse; and the Marine Science Center, with aquaria, touch tables, shells, fossils, and a variety of other exhibits.

CONDOS, VILLAS, AND VACATION HOMES

Many smaller reunions do perfectly well in condos, villas, or vacation homes. Dan Proctor, his brother, and sister, for example, planned a two-week family reunion as a Christmas present in early December in the Bahamas. Fourteen family members, including several children under twelve, fit comfortably in three condos.

Steve Carr of Yorkville, Illinois, arranged his dream family reunion for thirteen over Christmas in Orlando, Florida. The family had two door-to-door condos, each with two bedrooms, two baths, sofa beds, kitchens, and lots of amenities. Carr described accommodations as "awesome and marvelous." The family cooked most meals, carried snacks to Disney World, and returned to the condo for dinner and a rest before attending evening fireworks.

The availability of fully equipped kitchens can certainly be a plus. Making some of your own meals helps lower costs and provides opportunities for more group interaction while chopping and dicing. And while you can still eat out occasionally or have meals catered, you'll probably eat a lot less fast food.

Having a kitchen on hand is especially ideal for early morning starts to the golf course, theme park, ski slope, or hiking trail. Along with dishes, cookware, oven, and stove, many condo kitchens have a microwave and dishwasher.

Condos are in fact fully furnished. Plus all have towels, linens, and a TV; many have a VCR.

There are several service options. Daily maid service is often included in the price. Or a cleaning fee is charged, which usually means arriving to a clean condo which is then cleaned again after you leave. Any variation on these options is usually available upon request, daily or midweek.

Condo costs range from budget to luxury. You can rent in a building with a few units, a giant complex with hundreds of units, or a stand-alone cottage or villa. In fact, condos can be counted on to provide the benefit of more space at a price comparable to or less than a standard hotel room stay. Because there are often special offers that further lower the price, condos are ideal for families splitting costs for additional savings.

Karen Orloff of Hopewell Junction, New York, organized the Kaufman Family Reunion at Myrtle Beach, South Carolina. The family rented a vacation house that had lots of privacy, plenty of bathrooms, a nice large living area ,and was just a few steps from the sand.

Condo resorts provide a full range of recreational activities. Many condos have pools, Jacuzzis, hot tubs, gyms, tennis courts, and either onsite or nearby golf courses. Some offer organized childrens' and family activities.

Jon Welsh of Windsor, Connecticut, and brother, Chris, of Boise, Idaho, are true believers in condos. After family skiing reunions in Teton Village, Wyoming, and Park City, Utah, they rave about accommodations, activities—and convenience. Many ski areas provide airport transportation, grocery stores often deliver, and nightlife is close by. The Welshes "practically skied out the door to chair lifts." They recommend booking well in advance for optimum slope locations—the payoff is big in fun and value.

Condo reunion rentals are best booked through travel agents who specialize in them. Specialists have access to condos throughout the United States, Canada, Mexico, Hawaii, and the Caribbean. Many condos are in resort destinations, running the gamut from full to minimal services at more remote locations.

The condo agent will need to know your reunion dates, number of people expected, budget, preferred destination, special needs, and how much flexibility you have. Most condos require a deposit, and many require full payment for the entire stay in advance of your arrival.

Some condos require a seven-night minimum stay. Supply and demand regulate minimum-stay requirements, so in some cases, one, two, or three night stays are possible. Condo consumers almost always benefit by special weekly rates versus the more expensive nightly rate.

Some ask that if condos offer all the advantages of home, why leave? But when your home is land- and freeway-locked, it's a pleasure to step out onto your condo balcony to the crash of waves on a Gulf shore, or to listen to a loon call outside your North Woods door, or to feel the kiss of a fresh mountain breeze.

CAMPING

Camping offers fresh air, open space, and plenty of activities, all at bargain prices. It's perfect for nature lovers who enjoy fishing, hiking, and bird-watching.

First choose a campground. Ask any state tourism department for a list; then contact individual parks for more detailed information. Local chambers of commerce or park departments have information about county campgrounds, many of which offer group discounts. The federal government also manages many properties, ideal for camping reunions. There are also thousands of private campgrounds to choose from. These are often more flexible than state- or county-run facilities bound by legislative restrictions.

The Amerling family holds its reunion Memorial Day weekend at a county park in Fond du Lac, Wisconsin, that offers swimming, hiking, playgrounds, ball diamonds, and several covered pavillions. Like most county campgrounds, although they do little advertising, they offer great accommodations at a reasonable price.

The Ready Family Reunion was rescued by an accommodating private campground in Morgan Hill, California. Organizer Pat Anthony of Fort Collins, Colorado, had reservations a year in advance at a campground that suffered severe flood damage. Imagine thirty eager campers and no reunion place! Frantic last-minute calling around found a sympathetic campground owner who made room for them. Like most private campgrounds, this one held lots of events to entertain visitors, including dancing, swimming, and games of horseshoes.

Church and YMCA camps are also ideal places for reunions. Bridgette Fisher and her aunt, Barb Daley, are on the planning committee for the Hamilton Family Reunion at Camp Hemlock, a church-run facility in Michigan. The reunion started as a weekend gathering in 1990 and has grown to a five-day event.

Teresa L. Wolff's Fehringer Family Reunion is held at a youth camp in western Nebraska not far from the family farm in northeast Colorado. An uncle bought the grandparents' farm so the home place is still in the family, but even that big rambling farmhouse, the source of many childhood memories, cannot hold all the aunts, uncles, and cousins who flock from both coasts. The camp is close to the homestead, has RV hookups, cabins, a large recreation hall equipped with necessities for meals, and plenty of room for many outdoor activities.

Camping reunions are a great way for families to get together at just a fraction of the cost of staying at hotels. A little extra planning is essential, but it pays big dividends.

DORMITORY LODGING

Some families take advantage of inexpensive dormitory space at colleges or universities, available just when you need them: in summer. These offer scenic locations as well as exciting urban settings. Meals are often conveniently provided in the on-campus cafeteria. Guests at these facilities also usually have access to sports facilities, libraries, theaters, and cultural events. Private bathrooms or linens and towels may or may not be available.

Advance registrations are essential and advance deposits required. Specify your preference of dates, but be flexible. Be sure to inquire about cancellation policies.

The Adell Family Reunion has met at Bethany College in Lindsborg, Kansas. The college has no summer session, so the Adells had the run of the place, which created a sense of family unity. When they played basketball, the gym was all theirs. And everyone was housed in one dorm, which made visiting simple.

BED AND BREAKFASTS

Many people who've traveled in Europe have experienced the enchantment of bed and breakfasts. While abroad B&Bs are often a bargain, that is not always the case with the growing number of charming and often historic accommodations in the United States. Many B&Bs have fascinating tales to tell and are often located in unique settings. They provide personal attention and serve a range of fine food from gourmet fare to hearty country cooking. B&Bs are, of course, very special retreats for more intimate reunions of small families or segments of families.

RESORTS

Most resorts, like cruises and ranches, offer the advantage that costs are usually inclusive. Some activities might incur additional fees, but meals and most activities are all included in the one price.

The Hotel del Coronado specializes in family reunions. Southern California's legendary beachfront resort, built in 1888, has a history of hosting family reunions that goes back more than a century. The Del's Family Reunion specialist oversees every detail, works within your budget, and no extra charges are added for the service, which includes a complimentary family portrait. Actor Dick Van Patten and his real-life family have enjoyed reunions at the Hotel del Coronado since their children were young.

The McWilliams Family Reunion chose The Outrigger Beach Resort in Fort Myers Beach, Florida, for its beachfront location and ability to accommodate everyone's budget. A special sand wheelchair allowed the eldest family member to enjoy the warm white-sand beach.

Some families have thirty-year reunion histories at Sunrise Resort in Moodus, Connecticut. Cindy Lespier, who started coming to Sunrise as a child, now hosts the Pastor Family Reunion there.

RETREATS AND
CONFERENCE CENTERS

Colorado

YMCA of the Rockies is a very popular reunion site. They host over 650 family reunions each year at two locations on opposite sides of the Continental Divide: Snow Mountain Ranch near Winter Park on the west and Estes Park Center on the east.

Accommodations include meals, or you can choose space with kitchens. Your family can even take over an entire lodge. Large cabins accommodate twelve to seventy-two persons. The Pattie Hyde Barclay Reunion Lodge is especially designed for family reunions. Amenities include full kitchens, a paved basketball court, playground, and gas-heated barbecue grill. A resident host attends to special group needs or requirements.

Has the need for kidney dialysis kept someone from your reunion? The Marcia Murphy Lorscher Vacation Kidney Center of the Rockies is a joint project of the YMCA of the Rockies, the National Kidney Foundation of Colorado, and Denver's University Hospital. Located at Snow Mountain Ranch, it accommodates both children and adults. How often has the patient in your family undergone treatment with a full view of the majestic Rocky Mountains? Arrangements can be made by calling the Nurse Coordinator at 1-800-578-5432.

California

Carol Schneck reports that the Zweigle family chose an Episcopalian conference center at Oakhurst, California, near Yosemite National Park for their reunion. Over 100 descendants of the original Zweigle brothers incorporated a ninetieth birthday celebration into the three-day festivities.

New Mexico

Glorieta, located in Santa Fe, New Mexico, and operated by the Sunday School Board of the Southern Baptist Convention, welcomes family reunions of all faiths. Cottages, owned by individual churches, are available for reunion rentals at specific times of the year. A great nonsectarian spirit exists here, making it a welcoming site for interfaith families. The Glorieta area is ideal for hiking, and in fact two of the Sierra Club's highly recommended hiking trails begin on Glorieta lands. Winter reunions offer downhill or cross-country skiing, sledding, and snowboarding in the mild Southwest climate.

Florida

Camp Weed and Cerveny Conference Center in Live Oak, Florida, is a nonprofit facility located on 500 acres of rustic beauty, with a 140-acre, freshwater lake, canoeing, fishing, bird-watching, volleyball, baseball, swimming, and nature trails. Accommodations include a lodge with motel-type rooms, cabins in dormitory setups, tents, and RV camping. Food service is in a family-style cafeteria. Camp Weed staff can help organize your reunion.

A SAMPLING OF REUNION VENUES

Alabama

The beaches of Mobile/Gulf Shores offer surf, sugar-fine sand, palmetto—and excellent swimming, fishing, and tennis. Golf is played on award-winning courses.

California

San Diego is a mecca for reunions, with its mix of perfect weather, sightseeing, culture, and outdoor activities. Visit the San Diego Zoo and thirteen museums and galleries in Balboa Park or revisit San Diego history with restored Victorian structures, the old military post, and the site of Junipero Serra's first mission—so influential in shaping early California—all in Old Town and Presidio Park.

Colorado

Winter Park is an ideal spot for summer family reunions. Fish, golf, or relax in the shadow of the Rocky Mountains while your children enjoy playgrounds, a recreation center, and an alpine slide. River rafting, golfing, Jeep tours, horseback riding, and a rodeo are also available.

Ellis Island, New Jersey

Here's a trip to generate family memories or teach members about their heritage. Between 1892 and 1924, 12 million immigrants passed through Ellis Island. Visitors can trace their connections to the island at the Family History Center. Typing a name into the computer there will call up an image of an immigrant forebear.

Georgia

Helen, Georgia, offers a bit of Bavaria. Oktoberfest features dancing, German bands and ethnic singers, food, beer, and wine.

Islands

Islands are great for reunions—tropical islands in winter or islands closer to home in summer. Some are highly developed communities, while others are remote havens, accessible only by boat. Some possibilities: Santa Catalina Island, California, twenty-six miles off the southern California coast accessible by boat or by air; Sanibel/Captiva, Florida, some of the best shelling beaches in North America; Jekyll Island, Georgia, whose restored Jekyll Island Club Hotel was once the private retreat of famous families like the Rockefellers, Morgans, and Pulitzers; Mackinac Island, Michigan, where only horse-drawn carriages, bicycles, and your own two feet are allowed.

Kentucky

Otter Creek Park, a 3,000-acre park owned and operated by the city of Louisville, offers a nature center, wildlife, hiking trails, swimming pool, horseback riding, fishing in the Ohio River or Otter Creek, picnicking, biking, and cave exploration.

The Poconos

The natural attractions, historical sites, and museums of Pennsylvania's Pocono Mountain region are ideal for reunions. Accommodations include resorts, conference centers, campgrounds, and picnic areas. Most Pocono facilities are family owned and operated. Pocono innkeepers delight in unique reunions, such as the three honeymooning couples who met in the area in 1961, kept in touch, and in May 1991 reunited where their friendship was launched.

South Carolina

Reunion-friendly Charleston has risen from many disasters, including war, fire, earthquake, and hurricane. Patriot's Point has been dubbed the "world's largest naval and maritime museum." Its centerpiece is the aircraft carrier USS *Yorktown*, a stationary museum offering six separate tours. Reunion groups can even arrange banquets and parties onboard. Nearby plantations, meanwhile, display beautifully preserved architecture and artifacts in guided and self-tours. Many plantations are privately owned and may be expensive to visit, though the historic lesson is worth the investment.

Texas

Many elegant restored homes in Galveston are open to tourists. Charter a fishing boat or visit the *Elissa*, a restored nineteenth-century square-rigger. The annual spring sandcastle contest features more wondrous architecture. Or you can trace your roots—thousands of immigrant entries have been recorded here.

Washington, D.C.

The nation's capital hosts many free military bands and other concerts as well as ethnic and folklife festivals. Washington, D.C., is truly an exciting city to visit, from touring the White House to browsing the Smithsonian Institution.

Wisconsin

Milwaukee celebrates its rich ethnic heritage, music, food, and good times all summer long on the Lake Michigan shore. Celebrations throughout the summer include the Asian Moon Festival, Greek Fest, Bastille Days, Festa Italiana, German Fest, Great Circus Parade, African World Festival, Mexican Fiesta, Irish Fest, Indian Summer Festival, Arabian Fest, and Summerfest's Big Gig. In winter, the city features Winterfest's Big Cool.

Location, location, location is as true for reunions as other things in life. The right combination of comfort and fun, exciting activities goes a long way to ensuring the success of your reunion.

Reunion Communications:

Building Anticipation for Your Reunion

COMMUNICATION

Family reunion planners and participants communicate in many different ways: by phone, newsletter, flier, invitation, E-mail, round robin letter, or on the Web—as in the case of the Bean Family Reunion, which established its own Internet chat room. Your choice will depend on the time and money you can budget as well as on family preferences.

A formal reunion notification should be sent about a year in advance. You can save postage by asking one generation to notify its progeny. Or you can form a "phone tree" and assign names for others to call, for example, each branch notifies its own members. An increasing number of people are finding E-mail an efficient way to communicate.

Audience

Reunion organizers know their members better than most writers know their audience, so determining how they'd prefer to be approached should be fairly easy. If a lengthy newsletter would get little more than a quick glance, keep it to a single page. Emphasize important information, like deadlines and requests for deposits, with bold letters. Consider more frequent mailings or a mix of announcements, postcard reminders, and brief newsletters.

Mailings should be planned carefully to meet specific needs. Early mailers generally deal with prospective plans and requests for assistance and ideas. The Gibboney Family Association, for example, uses a questionnaire to determine when and where to have their next reunion. The Mixon Family Reunion questionnaire asks, among other things, for family tree updates, authorization to publish personal information in a family directory, and also solicits volunteers.

Bear in mind that for each mailing, someone must produce the printed material, such as surveys, registration forms, and programs; someone must address, stuff, stamp, and seal envelopes; and someone must keep track of responses. The Sappingtons do a first mass mailing of about 1,500 and then later send more detailed information to those who respond.

Sample Mailer Information

When using a regular business-size envelope (#10) for a mailing, choose a #9 SASE (self-addressed, stamped envelope) for the return; there's no need then to do any folding, and it's infinitely easier to stuff.

First mailing

Provide news about members to spark interest. Also solicit ideas about sites, dates, and activities, and enlist help to produce a program, memory book, or family history. Mention "missing persons" and deadlines.

Carole E. Neal says she maps out her Seals Family Reunion mailings before starting to send them. The goal of her first mailing is to get an idea of how many people are interested in attending. She includes a "save the date" notice, along with forms for general responses and family directory information.

Second mailing

Note plans, including when, where, and who's volunteered to do what, and summarize responses from the previous mailing. Provide a list of who's still missing, a registration form with prices and information about accommodations, a memento/T-shirt order form, and a reminder about deadlines.

The second mailing to the Seals family includes updates, forms for registration and T-shirt/cap orders, budget, schedule of events, and lodging information.

Last mailing

Generate excitement and enthusiasm. Ask for memorabilia, including old photos. If it's not too long, provide a list of confirmed attendees. For families with children, emphasize activities and child care. For elderly members, highlight meeting special dietary or medical needs. Offer details about accommodations, as well as a map and directions, a list of who's still missing, and deadline reminders.

For her final mailing, Carole sends Seals attendees a final update and some helpful details, such as information about climate and a list of eating places.

After the reunion

You'll want to have a follow-up mailing. Thank everyone who made the reunion possible—and enjoyable. Include budget details, including how much the reunion cost and plans for leftover funds. If you don't do a formal evaluation, request feedback, including improvements for next time and activities that the family would like to do again.

Registration Details

The registration form should provide space to indicate arrival and departure time, who's in the party, choice of activities and sightseeing tours, participation in tournaments and other competitions, and dietary or disability needs. The form should clearly indicate the cost of each function so that accurate payment accompanies the form. The deadline for preregistration should not only be highlighted but also repeated.

Make information easy to read. Keep sentences short, and never use a long word when a short one will do. Use checklists, outlines, bold headers, and brief, easy-to-read paragraphs.

Deadlines looming and you don't have enough of a response? You or your reunion committee must be prepared to prod family members along. Try sending another registration form, maybe accompanied by a handwritten note. Older generations are the key to making your job easier—if they're excited about the reunion, ask them to help, for example, by making a friendly call.

A conscious effort to look and sound different may not hurt. Experiment with colorful confetti, available in card shops. It comes in many shapes: letters, numbers, hearts, palm trees, stars, suns, moons. You can be sure your reunion message will be noticed when confetti falls from the envelope!

INVITATIONS

No single item preceding a reunion is as important as the invitation—whether as a separate communication, part of a newsletter or other mailing, or by phone or E-mail. Its purpose is to announce that something big is being planned.

Besides clearly stating the reunion's location, dates, and activities, an effective presentation invites family members, that is, makes them eager to attend. Use humor. Be eye-catching. Incorporate a logo that expresses something special about your family. The McMichael Family Reunion logo, for example, represents the proud history of descendants of the fourteen children of Jasper McMichael and Frances Handy of Wolfston, South Carolina. Choose brightly colored paper and provide a user-friendly response form. Don't let months of planning wind up in the recycling bin. Reunion success depends on an innovative invitation.

Karen Luna Ray of Hugo, Oklahoma, hooked members of the Luna/Looney Family Reunion with a uniquely worded subpoena. It worked! Reunion attendance was 99 percent. The Schmitz Family Reunion has used a WANTED! poster idea, as have the Wilke family.

Richard Duncan of Greenville, North Carolina, had an ingenious idea to keep family members from tossing out reunion invitations unread. He had a rubber stamp made so that each envelope was stamped WEST GREENVILLE REUNION in bright red ink.

O. John Taylor of Fowler, California, included activity leaders' names and a brief family tale on invitations to the Peach Family Reunion. "Naming names fixes responsibility, gives recognition, and lends the flavor of familiarization to the event," Taylor says.

Other invitations fuel the competitive spirit: *Last time the Mosers showed us all up. Let's see if we can get another branch of the family to show* them *up!* Ethel J. Davis of Compton, California, had the idea of offering an award for the first person who submitted a completed reply/registration with full payment to the Mixon Family Reunion.

Invitations also need to communicate information concisely. Food, fun, recreation, and official meetings are predictable aspects of reunions, but attendees should know all the details in advance, and you need to know how many people to expect using some of the devices described by the families whose inviting ideas follow. For example, the Barthmes Family Association Reunion provides an information sheet, registration form, and how-to-get-there map all in one. Everything is economically presented on two sides of a single sheet of paper. The top half is a "keeper," while together the front and back of the bottom half comprise a "mail-in-coupon" to return. Making it easy to respond in this way will also boost reunion attendance.

Another design to consider is a perforated double postcard, one-half containing all the pertinent information and the other serving as the response form.

Postcards are a very useful reunion communication tool. Because they're small and carry limited copy, they make a point quickly. They're also cheaper to mail. You can buy preprinted cards or make your own, using sturdy 65- or 80-pound paper. Four cards can be made from an 8½" x 11" page. For a dollar or two more, ask your copy shop to cut your cards—they'll look more professional.

Reunions magazine sells bright red cards that shout, "Save the date." You add the date, address, and postage. They also have a reminder postcard that declares, "Time is running out."

Lloyd Dean of Morehead, Kentucky, uses a custom-made stamp on his Dean and Creech Family Reunion reminders. The stamp features the reunion name, city, state, and zip code, which remains constant, but leaves a blank space for the date, which changes from year to year. The date is then added by hand—the perfect recyclable reunion notice!

Theresa G. Gold of San Antonio, Texas, was frustrated by the number of returns from her 3,500-piece newsletter mailings for the Hoelscher/Buxkemper Family Reunion—which bills itself as "The Biggest Reunion in Texas"—because members neglected to send address changes. Her experience became the mother of invention. Trying to verify correct addresses, she developed a preprinted card about the reunion and then only had to address, date it, and add the name of the "lost" relative.

Bonnie Scherer of Billings, Montana, updates new or long-forgotten family members about current happenings by sending short notes or postcards. Remember to keep the message brief. Tidbits on hobbies, interests, and recently completed projects will help break the ice when you gather.

Sharyn M. Kuneman announced the Manelli Family Reunion on a postcard made from a picture taken at an earlier reunion. The front was the picture and the reverse side carried the message and mailing information. This is also a great way to evoke memories of earlier reunion fun and share pictures with reunion members.

According to reunion organizer Robert Newman Sheets, hiring a graphic designer was a critical element in the success of the Newman Family Society Reunion. The designer not only created the invitations but also coordinated everything from table setups to memorial floral arrangements at each of the monuments and gravesites the family visited.

NEWSLETTERS

Descendants of Arthur and Margaret Burrows Potter of Chippewa Falls, Wisconsin, hold reunions every five years. To generate enthusiasm and excitement, the first issue of the *Guernsey Grunt Gazette: The Official Newsletter of the Potter Family Reunion* was filled with puns, humor, trivia . . . and cows. It explained the reunion's purpose: "to keep the Potter family close and to build strong bonds that will keep the family together like a herding dog does a field of cows." The logo—a gentle holstein and adjacent cowpie—illustrated the reunion theme, Don't eat the pies, and was a source of puns: Send MOO-LA. MOOve to reserve rooms. Capture the MOOment. COWtail hour. MeMOO board. Featured were "Udderly Terrible Bovine Facts, Fiction, and Jokes." For souvenirs, reunion organizer Reggie Potter and her crew took advantage of the inexpensive resources of the Wisconsin Dairy Council, ordering cow erasers, cow cups, cow coloring books, and cow posters to advertise in the newsletter. Each of the four *Gazettes* leading up to the reunion encouraged readers to register, send deposits, and reserve tee times, while providing them with directions from highways, airports, and train stations as well as a growing list of people already registered.

The final issue of the *Gazette*, delivered the last day of the reunion, exhorted members, "Let us not forget, we have a very precious possession that we must tend and nurture. It is the only one that we will have in our lifetime. It is our family."

Mary Thiele Fobian of Pacific Grove, California, notes that, "like organizing a reunion, editing a newsletter requires attention to lots of details—gathering information, maintaining a mailing list, writing, typing, copying/printing, and mailing." In general, newsletters are intended to spread news about family members and provide information about upcoming reunions and other events. Wayne W. Daniel, editor of the *Daniel Family Newsletter*, says, "I greatly enjoy putting together the newsletter, since it gives me first crack at learning about what's happening in our extensive extended family." He adds, "In addition to keeping us abreast of family news, I feel that a second important function . . . is to provide a historical document that future generations may consult to learn about us, their ancestors."

Janice Tompkins, editor of *Bower Family Circle* and *Kimmel Family News,* appreciates the newsletter's ability "to enhance a feeling of closeness among [relatives] who no longer live close together."

Goals determine content and organization. The typical newsletter features regular categories complemented by special articles. Regular features might include family news (often verbatim excerpts from letters), milestones (births, weddings, graduations, landmark birthdays, deaths), reunion updates (photos, reminders), new addresses, E-mail addresses, Web locations, phone or fax numbers, and financial reports/budgets. They might also include a genealogical query/answer column and family history features.

Reunion news should always be placed on page one. Note dates, times, deadlines, location, scheduled activities, donations/contributions/fees, contact information (phone, fax, E-mail, Web site). Insert a reunion registration page on a separate sheet.

It's important to encourage everyone, including children, to contribute something to the newsletter. Most editors admit they must often call around to get material—and then follow up. Opalene Mitchell, editor of the Carter/Jordan/Pennington Family newsletter, *Flo-Line*, points out that contributors have the best intentions, "but they just don't get around to it."

Graphics

Graphics add variety and lend interest and excitement to your newsletter. Black-and-white photos and a wealth of public domain clip art are available in books and on the Internet. Consider including things like the family tree, even maps. Be creative.

Frequency and Timing

Select one of the following frequencies: monthly, bimonthly, quarterly, semi-annually, annually. Your selection will depend on your family's needs, printing and postage budgets, and the amount of time you can devote to editing the newsletter. The Guidon/Yandeau Family Reunion publishes a newsletter twice a year (semiannually), four times (quarterly) during a reunion year. If you don't anticipate any particular schedule, borrow this phrase from the *Hente Family Gazette: Published on an occasional basis.*

Form and Function

Newsletters come in many forms, from single-sided or simple letter layout to glossy, multicolumn, multicolor productions. Most newsletters are prepared with word processing or desktop publishing software. There are many software programs to automate your newsletter preparation. Print Shop Press Writer, by Broderbund, is one example. If you are laying out your newsletter in the time-honored tradition by hand, you'll find a detailed description in *The Family Reunion Handbook* by Barbara Brown and Tom Ninkovich.

Printing

Budget is a major factor in determining how you reproduce your newsletter. Two-sided printing is most economical, conserves paper, and minimizes weight to save postage costs. Some newsletters are single sheets stapled together. Others are 11" x 7" sheets folded in half to form a seamless four-page publication. The *Ilgenfritz Family Newsletter*, for one, is a 5½" x 8½" booklet with a cardstock front-and-back cover.

Color printing is expensive but can be used to great effect for special purposes. In her *Wills Family Newsletter,* editor Melenda Gatson Hunter included a bright, colorful photo of Gatson family and friends (including President and Mrs. Clinton), taken at the fortieth anniversary reunion of the Little Rock Nine who, in 1957, were the first African-American students to attend the newly desegrated Central High. An alternative approach to including a color photo was used in an issue of the *Hente Family Gazette*: A large blank space was left at the bottom of the front page to glue in a glossy print of a group photo from the family's previous reunion.

Mailing

Getting your newsletter in the mail sounds simple, but there are many considerations. Many newsletters are formatted so that folding them produces a mailing panel on the outside, with the return address in the upper-left corner. Then it's simply a matter of sealing the open side and applying address labels and stamps. Jan Tompkins says she uses first-class postage and marks her mailing pieces with *Address Service Requested* on the left side of the mailing panel. Then if the addressee has moved, the post office will provide the sender a forwarding address for a small fee. Tompkins adds that a major purpose of quarterly newsletters is to maintain a current mailing list.

If your mailing list is large, there are additional considerations. Securing a bulk mail permit qualifies you for lower postage on presorted mail. Bar-coding software reaps even greater savings but may be priced out of range of most reunion budgets. Another option is to arrange for labeling, sorting, and mailing to be done by a "presort shop."

More and more family reunions post their newsletters on the World Wide Web. The Donkersloot family's impressive Web site makes information easily available to members on both sides of the Atlantic. They even have English- and Dutch-language versions linked to specialized pages, among them a family museum (a captioned photo "gallery") and a genealogical data entry form.

The Bottom Line

Some reunions budget for newsletter production and distribution from membership dues. Others depend on income from subscriptions. In some groups, individuals underwrite or make contributions to support the newsletter. Whatever the dollars-and-cents realities, a value can't be placed on the investment made in creating a reunion newsletter, for it's clearly a labor of love.

PROMOTION

First of all, you can publish notices free of charge in the RegisTree section of *Reunions magazine* and on its Web page.

Meanwhile, the appearance of reunion announcements is becoming an increasingly common item in large and small newspapers around the country. You needn't wonder how an announcement gets in the paper: There's no more magic to it than simply submitting one. Be sure to include date, time, location, and contact information. Write in clear, concise language, including only the necessary details and, chances are, you'll see your announcement in print. If you're featuring a special guest or unique activity, send a news release to the local media. You might be able to demonstrate quilting or other family specialties on a locally produced TV program.

Libraries or the convention and visitors bureau in your reunion city have listings of names and addresses of newspapers, radio, and TV stations locally where you can send news of your reunion.

We see a growing number of groups using the "Today Show" to tell the world about their reunions. They're in the crowds that line up each morning to wave and shout greetings to the world (or at least to their mothers!). Some grab the attention of the host and get a chance to talk about their reunions.

Once the reunion is over and you're collecting your thoughts, consider submitting an article, photos, or information about your reunion to *Reunions magazine*. The magazine is, after all, reader-driven. It will take a bit of your time, but, if your family is featured, it can be a source of great pride to share at your next reunion. If you know before your reunion about a special surprise or activity or something terribly unique, notify *Reunions magazine* ahead of time. They can sometimes assign a writer. Suggestions should be made in writing well in advance.

WEB PAGE

As the popularity of the Internet grows, creating a Web page can help increase reunion attendance. Fortunately, there are many on-line resources to walk you through the process of producing a Web page. Chris B. Call of Santa Rosa, California, helped us simplify making a Web page. You will need an Internet service provider to host your pages, an ftp or telnet program (http://www.shareware.com/) to unload and modify pages and images, and a little imagination. If you already have an Internet service provider, Web pages cost only your time and commitment.

Words of Wisdom from the Voice of Experience

- There's no need to reinvent the wheel; learn from others. Conduct your own reunion pages search. If you find something you like, save it as a file and modify it to suit your needs with credit to the original site. The search engine Yahoo has an entire index related to reunions. Browse sites for ideas.

- Use free Web page design tools, including background colors, textures, icons, bars, arrows, and more. (Check out www.yahoo.com/Computers_and_Internet/Internet/World_Wide_Web/Page_Design_and_Layout/). Keep it simple, because graphics take a while to load and can frustrate a novice designer.

- Make your page easy for people to find. List it on search engines, such as Yahoo, Alta Vista, InfoSeek, and Excite. To access search engines, click *add URL* and fill in your information. Also register your reunion with commercial sites dedicated to reunions: *Reunions magazine* (www.reunionsmag.com), ReunionNet (www.reunited.com), and Reunion Hall (www.xscom.com/reunion).

- Use interactive communication tools, for example, a form page (http://www.worldwidemart.com/scripts/formmail.shtml) that standardizes responses and encourages specific information. Include space for names; street, E-mail, and Web addresses; and phone and fax numbers. A comments section allows notes. An electronic guest book (http://www.wordwidemart.com/scripts/) is a nice way to keep family members informed about others.

- Create nostalgia. Incorporate anecdotes or trivia about family members. Or offer a pictorial of members, from infancy to adulthood. Include a retrospective about what life was like twenty, thirty, or forty years ago (http://www.agloan.com/history.htm).

A reunion Web page is a very effective tool for locating members and encouraging participation. You'll want to create a Web site that's more than just a recitation of time and place. Make your browsers smile, and they'll be more likely to get involved and attend the reunion.

And after the reunion is over, the Web page can be a continuing resource for members to stay abreast of family doings.

Reunion Day:

Ideas for Your Crowning Event

Jean Timpel of Cedarburg, Wisconsin, interviewed dozens of families for articles in *Reunions magazine*. These comments are from members who found reunions worth the effort.

- "I was the envy of all my friends when I told them about the festivities. They thought it was a miracle that we could get so many families to celebrate together." *Blachman Family Reunion*

- "We went with some reluctance to the first Goddard reunion, and it was such a positive experience that we never want to miss one!" *Goddard Family Reunion*

- "What a great reunion! It was everything one could have hoped for . . . best of all, the strong feeling of being with family." *Bigelow Family Reunion*

- "I guess I'm a sentimental fool; I'm so happy everyone came." *Deschaine/ Bernier Family Reunion*

- "There is something almost mystical about meeting people you have never met before who look strangely familiar and with whom you have almost instant rapport. Genetic attraction." *Sussel/Solomon Family Reunion*

Families spend time, money, and effort creating memorable reunions. Certainly, when plans are made, all ages must be taken into consideration. Still, generally, if the kids are happy, everyone else at the reunion will be too. Effort to make sure the youngest reunion members are entertained pays off in big dividends.

Many people feel that the best part of family reunions is reminiscing. Yes, even gossiping. Everyone loves the chance to catch up with relatives they don't see often enough. And this is one time when people are delighted to let the old-sters tell their stories.

Make sure everyone feels welcome but not obliged to participate in activities. Simple, spontaneous activities are always memorable, and many transcend age differences. Try a genealogy scavenger hunt in which kids collect family facts from each other as well as grown-ups—a fourth cousin's favorite sport, the newest niece's birth weight, the name of the person who traveled farthest to attend the reunion, and so on.

✳ *Valerie Schulz writes that the "orchestra" of people she loves, from the youngest piccolo to the oldest bassoon, had "not played together for years." In the time leading up to "their reunion symphony, babies had been born, houses built, jobs lost and won, gardens planted and harvested, illness conquered, teeth offered to fairies, and many moons waxed and waned."*

✳ *Every two years, the Ratliff Family Reunion meets outside Sedona, Arizona. Dena Dyer of Granbury, Texas, plans her vacations around the reunion. There are few scheduled activities; the only requirement is to have fun. They do silly things and tease each other mercilessly. Dyer says she never laughs harder than at reunions.*

✳ *A goal of the Wheelwright Family Reunion, according to Catherine W. Ockey of Camano Island, Washington, was to celebrate the lives of Max and Ann Wheelwright—Max's eightieth birthday, Ann's seventy-fifth, and their fifty-sixth wedding anniversary. To encourage activity, score sheets were printed up to award points: ten points for making a pottery item, swimming an hour, wearing the official reunion T-shirt, identifying five wildflowers, or helping Max build his stone wall. Babies got ten points for napping.*

✳ *The descendants of Dr. Alfred and Jan Witherspoon Scott of Boston, Massachusetts, plan weeklong reunions. One memorable reunion was in adjoining beach houses in St. Croix, Virgin Islands, where their time was spent scuba diving, swimming, and boating. When they meet in California, they bring tents, rent an RV or neighboring house, and have food catered so everyone can relax. Children who go to sleep promptly find a treat of "pillow candy" the next morning. (Adults don't get pillow candy because they stay up too long talking!) Several times weddings have been timed for the family reunion, adding to the memories this family treasures.*

THE MECHANICS OF REUNION DAY

Final Details

In the final days before your reunion, you'll need to focus on details, details, details. A key element of reunion success is good communication. Hopefully, you've been communicating with hotel representatives as well as other suppliers during the long planning phase.

As you approach reunion day, ask for a prereunion conference with key hotel/facility staff. Review plans and requirements, clearly communicating your needs to your hosts.

Reunion briefings are essential. Meet with committee members daily to review every detail. Prepare written instructions explaining volunteer tasks and responsibilities and brief the volunteers before registration. Be sure to thank the volunteers for their help and motivate them to have a great reunion.

Set up a message center for attendees. A central location like your hospitality suite is a good spot. Make it a fun place to visit. The simplest message center is a bulletin board—supply it with colorful push pins. Preprinted message forms are a nice touch.

Paula Sheagley, a former professional reunion planner, cautions that you can go dizzy with many last-minute details. Certainly each one is important to assuring a well-organized and smoothly run reunion. Don't forget to cross-check each reservation with your check-in list. Ask those with a balance due to bring cash. Double-check special dietary requests with the caterer. If attendance grows, you'll need to increase catering counts (guarantees). Go over schedules, fees, and payment with all contracted outside services (photographer, memory book publisher, decorators, DJ/band, face-painting clown, caterers). Get change from your bank so you'll have plenty available to make change for your "show-at-the-door" attendees and memento sales.

In case of rain

You may feel that rain wouldn't dare dampen your reunion, but the weatherman may disagree. To be sure—rather than sorry—reserve a park shelter or arrange some kind of coverup. If shelter is not available where you plan to meet, you may want to arrange an alternate site.

Plan alternative activities too. Bring board games. A large paper banner or tablecloth and crayons or markers can entertain children for a long time. Rent a big-screen TV and VCR and encourage family members to bring videotapes of weddings; your last family reunion; and birthday, graduation, and retirement parties. Some families enjoy playing cards for an entire afternoon and never miss the sun. If there are musicians in your family, ask them to lead songs or accompany dancing.

When it comes to working miracles, Karen Robertson gets a prize. Bad weather forced her to alter plans and establish the Indoor Brolra Family Reunion Olympics. A 4-foot butcher paper scoresheet was tacked on the wall, listing everyone's name and marking off columns for each event. Teams included elders, children, and grandchildren—everyone old enough to walk was included. There were individual points for first, second, third, and fourth place, and every member got points earned by their team or representative. These are some of the indoor games Robertson devised.

- *Humming contest.* Time each person to see how long they can hum the same note without taking a breath (or fainting). Equipment needed: stopwatch.

- *Apple peeling contest.* One person represents each team to see who can peel an apple in one continuous peel. Equipment needed: apples and knives.

- *Peanut pushing contest.* Teams line up, and each player, crawling on all fours, pushes the peanut across the room with his or her nose. Equipment needed: bag of peanuts in shells.

- *Toilet paper mummies.* Each team has two participants. One completely wraps the other in toilet paper. Supplies needed: several rolls of toilet paper.

- *How much do we weigh?* The object is to guess the weight of the entire group. One person records weights to check guesses against. After all weights are collected, kids love to help with the adding and checking. Equipment needed: scale.

- *How long are we?* Participants guess how long the whole family would be if everyone were laid end to end. Someone then measures all attendees. Recruit kids to do the measuring and figuring. Equipment needed: tape measure.

- *Egg carry relay.* Each member must carry a hard-boiled egg on a spoon from one end of the room to the other and back. Equipment needed: spoons and eggs.

- *Bubble gum blowing contest.* Who can blow the biggest bubble? Supplies needed: bubble gum.

- *Thread-winding contest.* Two participants from each team unwind a spool of thread across the room. Who can rewind the thread faster? Supplies needed: a full spool of thread for each team.

Practical aspects of final preparations

If you are in a park or wilderness setting, consider sanitary facilities. You may need to provide tissue and moist towelettes. Large reunions on private property often rent portable toilets.

Pack a reunion supply box. If in doubt about an item—take it! Be prepared for anything; you won't regret it. Round up the following:

- Cash box.
- Cash.
- Name tags.
- Colored markers.
- Posterboard.
- Stapler.
- Pens and pencils.
- Glue sticks.
- Scissors.
- Calculator.
- Masking tape (check with facility manager before affixing items to walls).
- Camera, film, and batteries.
- Paper clips and rubber bands.
- Pads of paper.
- Payment checks.
- Tickets for raffles or give-away prizes.
- Baskets.
- Files containing copies of service agreements and contracts, dinner tickets, and records of reservations.

Also prepare a first-aid kit including:

- Adhesive tape.
- Antibacterial ointment.
- Antiseptic soap.
- Antidiarrheal aid.
- Adhesive bandages.
- Cold medication.

- Thermometer.
- Pain reliever.
- Cotton swabs.
- Sunscreen.
- Insect repellent.

Be prepared for emergencies

Always have a plan to cover emergencies. For example, some family members may be elderly or prone to illness and injury. An existing illness can be complicated by fatigue as well as change in diet and time zones.

Become familiar with local medical support systems. Does the city use 911? Learn the numbers for the nearest police, hospital, and dentist. Where is there a drugstore open around the clock? Check on first-aid kits. Are hotel staff members CPR trained? Are wheelchairs available? What is the hotel's emergency procedure? Alert everyone to fire safety instructions posted in rooms. Publish key emergency numbers in your program. It is always better to err on the side of caution.

One final note: Ask about the hotel's security system and services. Are security guards on duty day and night? Are parking lots patrolled?

Registration

No matter what size your reunion, find some way to acknowledge that people have arrived. First impressions are lasting ones and registration sets the tone for your entire reunion. Regard registration as your reunion welcome mat.

If yours is a very large reunion, registration must be formal to keep track of everyone. After hotel check-in, urge family members to stop next at the reunion registration desk, where they receive name tags, meal tickets, agendas, and schedules. For the Jackson Family Reunion in Dallas, Texas, people with walkie-talkies called ahead to registration as attendees arrived at the hotel so that materials were ready and waiting for them at the registration desk.

One of the simplest ways to register is with a "sign-in" registration book. Ask everyone to include their name, address, phone number, and the "original" family member to whom they are related. Registration books are the core of your next reunion mailing list.

Accuracy is an important goal. You'll need to keep track of paperwork, especially forms and money. Advance planning and "walking through" the registration process helps eliminate potential problems. Family members will generally begrudge a wait to receive registration materials. If registration is your task, see it as a challenge and make it fun for yourself, your volunteers, and the registrants themselves.

Advance registration

Advance registration improves attendance, generates cash flow, and gives you an early indication of the effectiveness of your promotions. It helps you better plan for adequate room, bus, and event reservations requiring deposits and guarantees. Incentives encourage advance registration, so consider a reduced registration fee before a certain date or a reward for initial registrants.

Upon receipt of advance registration and money, you can assemble a packet for each registrant. The packet may include a preprinted name tag, tickets for meals and sightseeing tours, reunion souvenirs, and special instructions, such as banquet seating guidelines. Assemble packets in advance to bring to the reunion for quick, easy distribution.

On-site registration

Plan registration information carefully. Design or order forms, tickets, signs, and other systems necessary to handle registration. Forms should be in duplicate, with boxes to check off answers. Tickets should be numbered.

Assemble supplies and furniture: tables, chairs, wastebaskets, pens, staplers, paper clips, signs, computers or typewriters, phones, cash boxes. Depending on the size of your reunion, plan separate areas, for example, for tours, ticket sales, souvenir sales, and transportation. Expedite the process with a special area for those who've preregistered.

Having a large, multibranch family reunion? Designate separate registration tables for different branches, with color-coded banners, signs, or helium balloons matched to the color of T-shirts. Post a message center and ask members to sign in so that persons arriving can see who has already arrived.

Welcome

Beth Gay says to make everyone welcome. So what if you've never heard of Aunt Suzie before or if forty years ago Uncle Arthur had a feud with Uncle Gilbert? Forget it. Just enjoy the day.

The welcoming committee directs arrivals to the registration table. Use this opportunity to record recent births, marriages, and deaths on forms provided by the family genealogist. The registration table, or its vicinity, is a good place to set up a suggestion box and display reunion mementos for sale.

Consider some special welcoming strategies. Deliver a personal note of welcome to each room with surprises or goodie bags. Ask the CVB for souvenirs, samples from merchants, or native foods or crafts. Check with local vendors for giveaways to promote their stores.

Engage the most gregarious, outgoing volunteers, perhaps several family elders or committee members, as a hospitality committee. Bright red vests can advertise these goodwill ambassadors. They can watch for first-timers and then introduce them around.

You can also help first-timers get to know others by involving them in reunion activities. Ask them to volunteer as candle bearers during a memorial service. Enlist their help when selecting and distributing door prizes or awards.

Of course, you'll want to make "old-timers" feel special too. Recognize who's attended often, for example, by using ribbons to identify them.

Signs

Prepare or order signs—and plan where to put them—to welcome members and for airport arrivals, parking, registration, information, souvenir sales, hospitality suite, bus identification, banquet seating, and registration. Embellish signs with your family logo or colors. If you are meeting in a rural area or at a private location, post signs and consider clusters of balloons to mark the way. Laminate a welcome banner to weatherproof it and preserve it for use at many reunions.

When Jan Bowman planned a 350-person, six-generation family reunion, she pulled out all the stops. For one week, the family took over a hotel in Athens, Texas, and every business in town had a sign saying "Welcome, Bowman Family Reunion." The whole town turned out for a parade complete with floats and a police escort!

The Lamberts were made to feel like real celebrities by Innis, Louisiana, stores and shops with window signs that said "Congratulations on your Lambert Family Reunion!" The marquee at the Lake County Fairgrounds in Grays Lake, Illinois, acknowledged the Busse Family Reunion trying to set a Guinness World Record for the largest reunion. They recorded 2,400 members for their celebration of the sesquicenntenial of their forebears' arrival in Illinois.

Name Tags and Other IDs

Make name tags, badges, buttons, or pins a big deal. The McLeod family uses matching leaves of a family tree displayed proudly at reunions for their name tags. Handmade or computer generated, the information on these IDs must be correct and readable from about six feet away. List name, family branch, and hometown. Use a simple stick-on label, pin-on style with glassine holder and cardboard insert, or printed buttons. Prepare these in advance.

Buttons can be sold as fund-raisers or used as awards or mementos. They can be personalized or all be identical and identify the reunion rather than individuals. A group button might include the location and reunion slogan or theme. Color-coded buttons can identify family branches and generations. Use name buttons as an icebreaker. Pull them randomly from a box as people arrive, pin them on people's backs, and ask attendees to find the person who belongs to the button by asking yes/no questions: Is my person male? Am I forty or fifty or sixty years old? Do I live in Milwaukee?

Regardless of how they're used at the reunion itself, buttons make a long-lasting memento. Long after the reunion, they provide a tangible reminder of good times, camaraderie, and fellowship.

Buttons are generally inexpensive, though your choices will affect the price. A quantity of identical buttons will be much less expensive than buttons personalized with names. Once you know your requirements, contact a button manufacturer or buy your own button-making machine. Powell, Ohio, button maker Rob Fish suggests that when placing a custom order, you ask about turnaround time, quantity discounts, design charges, setup fees, freight costs, taxes, procedures for ensuring all names are spelled correctly, and computer equipment compatibility (if you're going to create your own artwork or supply a list of names). If you're ordering personalized buttons, get several without names for people who don't register in advance.

Juanita Searcy reports that she made name tags in four colors for her Hughes Family Reunion in Tallahassee, Florida. She scanned an old photo of her parents and placed it in the center of the button. She also made "prize" button key rings for the oldest and youngest members and the member who traveled the greatest distance.

One reunion uses red, white, and blue badges to help differentiate reunion members. Red badges are for members who've attended all previous reunions. White ones designate at least one other reunion attended, and blue identifies first-timers. Consider using baby or childhood pictures. Include a logo or ribbon to designate generation or branch or direct descendants versus in-laws. Dr. Cecil Paul Enders Pottieger of Frederick, Maryland, says direct descendants of Captain Philip Christian and Anna Appolonia Degan Enders wear red ribbons at annual reunions, while spouses wear white ribbons. Or list relationships: *I'm Trudy's son, Christopher,* or *I'm Carol's grandson and Trudy's son, Christopher.*

Put numbers on the back of name tags for drawings or door prizes. Also consider giving two or three name tags duplicate numbers so persons finding someone else with the same number get a prize.

Clothing

Reunions typically are casual events. Everyone wants to look their best, but if this is their vacation they want to be comfortable too.

Even if you think appropriate dress is obvious, include clothing guidelines in your prereunion materials. If you're gathering at a Montana ranch in winter, you will want to be warm outdoors and comfortable inside by the roaring fire. There is little need for formal attire though attendees may want to bring some wranglin' clothes. On the other hand, a seat at the captain's table on a cruise may demand something dressy.

As always, consider your family's preferences. Many reunions feature a formal banquet to give everyone a chance to show off their snazziest duds. This is a golden opportunity for men who own tuxedos to dazzle family. Nevertheless, other families will settle themselves at or near the beach and never be out of their swimwear.

THE FUN, PROGRAMS, AND ACTIVITIES OF REUNION DAY

Icebreakers

A concern for reunion organizers expecting extended family whose members don't know one another is to have people interacting as quickly as possible. Yet even as adults we find it hard to strike up a conversation. Committee members should be prepared to circulate, say hello, and get conversations started. It won't take long before everyone's talking and having a good time.

One family starts with the oldest generation, who introduce themselves and members of their branch who are present and share any special events that have occurred since the last reunion. Then letters are read and pictures shown from members not able to attend.

Karen Robertson suggests an icebreaker where each person writes down little-known facts about themselves. Facts are listed on paper and the object is to find the person who matches each fact and get their signature. People get acquainted and learn interesting things about one another.

Another idea is to make a list of questions to distribute as family members arrive. To get answers, people must circulate and talk to others. Include one question about each branch of the family so everyone can feel like an expert. This also encourages people to seek out distant relatives. Questions could cover current news, for example, Who just got engaged in the Hansen branch of the family? or Who is retiring and moving to Arizona? Include questions about family history too. People will need to ask older relatives for answers or check the genealogy display. If there are still family members who speak it, write a line or two in the family's native language to be translated. Those who don't speak the language will have to find those who do.

Doris A. Phillips of Indianapolis, Indiana, says the Phillips/White/Wilson Family Reunion gave each of their more than 100 attendees a get-acquainted list of thirty "instructions." Some examples: Find someone who sings in the shower. Find someone who's left-handed. Find someone who's a Crazy Hat judge.

Bob Snyder writes that his Kauffman Family Reunion soon had former strangers laughing together with their version of "Whoppers." In groups of five or six, each member wrote down four alleged facts about themselves: three true but hard to believe and one false but believable. Others in the group tried to identify the "whoppers" as "facts" were presented. Points were awarded for people fooled or for every true fact correctly guessed. Discussion of real and bogus experiences and achievements continued throughout the reunion.

These icebreakers collected from the Share the Secrets Conference at YMCA of the Rockies are great ways to break down long-time-no-see barriers.

- Circulate a roll of toilet paper and ask everyone to take some squares. Then ask them to tell as many things about themselves as they've taken squares. If Auntie Erika took seven squares, you'll learn seven things about her. The facilitator should start to model what to do.

- Ask everyone to stand in a circle facing in. Explain that each person is to say his or her name and pantomime a favorite activity or hobby. For example: "My name is Patty." Everyone says, "Hello, Patty." Then she pantomimes her hobby: say, piano playing, cooking, biking, or golf. Everyone guesses until they arrive at Patty's hobby; then her turn is over. When the game is finished, everyone's name and hobby are known.

- Time to scramble! Get everyone onto their feet and moving to form groups based on things you call out, for example, everyone with blue or brown eyes. Once the groups are formed, make another call. Everyone who likes to play baseball or chess or Nintendo. Everyone who loves lasagna or barbecued chicken or french fries. Before long, lots of people know lots about lots of others!

For an icebreaker, Rosa Thomson asked reunion attendees for "This Is Our Life" photos showing their family's home, yard, activities, sports, hobbies, and pets. From these, her son created a display to help everyone get to know one another. A genealogy display including lots of family photos quickly gets members of the Guidon/Yandeau Family Reunion mingling.

At Karen Naedler's Cousins Connection, everyone taped baby pictures to a huge poster labeled "Beautiful Babies." The fun was trying to guess who was who and marveling at family resemblances. A sister-in-law spent hours making a word-find puzzle using all the cousins' names.

The Deschaines tried a humorous twist on the "Identify the Picture" contest. They took a series of torso shots at the reunion of men holding beer cans next to their navels, to be posted the next year for identification.

Maurice and Florence Krueger of Mina, South Dakota, share these successful Polt Family Reunion icebreakers.

- *Ancestor search.* Each parent/child team receives a list of forebears and has fifteen minutes to collect signatures from their descendants. The team who gathers the most signatures is declared the winner.

- *For children ten or under.* Each girl gives her name and her mother's and grandmothers' names. Each boy gives his name and his father's and grandfathers' names. Don't forget rewards for each child.

- *Timefiller.* Ask everyone to face the person to the right and give him or her a compliment.

Reunion trivia

One Kentucky family's Reunion Trivia game involves everyone from six to eighty years young. They start with questions like Who is the youngest/oldest family member? Which couple has been married the longest? the shortest? How many sets of twins are there? Then they ask more "trivial" questions. What is Unce Bubba's real name? What were Uncle Charlie's two cats' names?

They also include "bragging" questions to recognize people who are doing something significant. Who's attending college and where? Who bought a house since the last reunion? Who had a baby this year?

Be creative. Questions are limited only by your imagination. Still, keep in mind your objectives to entertain, educate, reminisce, and get everyone involved. Never ask a question for which you have no answer. A slight dose of silliness is fun, but don't go too overboard. Avoid negatives, too, such as: How many husbands did Aunt Martha have? Why did Aunt Ellen go to jail on Christmas Eve?

Be patient, understanding, and well versed in crowd control. And when calling on people, don't play favorites!

Other approaches to reunion trivia. Organize teams that include members from each generation and each branch of the family. Set out paper bags and ask relatives to deposit questions. Categories can include anything you choose: sports, geography, music. This is an opportunity to share, so welcome family stories that may interrupt the game.

Adapt historical trivia to the generations of your family. For example, starting with the oldest person present, begin: When Oma Wenzel was born, in 1903, the price of gas was ____ per gallon; first-class postage was ____; bread cost ____ per loaf; the ballpoint pen was not yet invented; credit cards did not exist; the zip code was ____ years in the future; *Life* magazine was ____ per copy. Then continue: Oma Wenzel's oldest child, William, was born in 1934, when the price of gas was ____; and so on.

Michele Beckett Hendricks of Loveland, Colorado, says Newtons play the Newton Trivia Game, a rollicking way to share family history. Everyone sends in anecdotes and tales of exploits beforehand, which are then compiled into questions.

Bingo

At the banquet of their three-day biannual reunion, Winston Family Reunion attendees of all ages indulge in a night of Bingo Madness—with much of the credit going to Andrew Walker, who constructed the giant bingo sets.

Walker shares some of his best Bingo Madness secrets: Prepare a souvenir grab bag for all participants. Solicit small prizes in advance from all branches of the family. And let winners choose prizes—they'll then be age- and interest-appropriate. Have everyone mark a "bonus number" along with the freebie on the center of the card. If the bonus number is called as part of the winning row, award an extra prize. Try a special "Black-out Jackpot" to add a little spice. Each participant pays $1 for each card they play, and the money is used for a cash jackpot.

In *Family Reunions and Clan Gatherings*, Shari Flock suggests asking each player to write his or her name on a piece of paper, then fold and drop that paper into a container. Also before the game, each person is given a sheet of paper divided into squares (12 minimum, 100 maximum). Players circulate the room, collecting a different signature in each square.

To play, names from the folded papers are drawn until someone completes a row. As each name is called, the person is asked to stand.

More games

Karen Robertson describes several games used at the Brolra Family Reunion to break the ice and barriers.

Circle tangle. Everyone forms a circle. They then climb over and under joined hands and outstretched legs. When everyone is in a huge tangle, the object is to get untangled without dropping hands. This can be done with teams so that one team tangles and the other team gives instructions to try to get untangled. Roles are then switched so the tangled team becomes the untanglers.

Shoe store. Divide into teams of ten to fifteen people. Each team sits together on the ground. Everyone then removes their shoes and piles them equal distance from the teams. At the "go" command, each team sends one person (the shopper) to the pile of shoes (the shoe store). Each person on the team shouts out descriptions of his or her own shoes (no pointing or giving directions). The team whose shopper outfits them all with their shoes first, wins.

Pattern juggling. Form circles with ten to fifteen people in each. Ask each circle to create a juggling pattern by throwing a ball back and forth so that each person has it only once. Then ask them to repeat that same pattern, but when they throw the ball, to say the name of the person they are throwing to. The person who receives the ball says, "Thank you, _____," naming the thrower. All circles repeat the pattern a few times. Then they can drop acknowledging one another to see which circle can juggle their pattern fastest. Or set thirty seconds to see which circle can do the most pattern repetitions in that time. Circles can be shuffled so that everyone learns more names and tries several patterns. All ages can play.

Trading time

Ask teenagers to come prepared to trade school T-shirts. Best are shirts that include not only the name of the school but also the city and state for out-of-state cousins.

If your reunion includes family members from all over, trade souvenirs. Encourage people to trade and then trade again. As a final activity ask everyone to show what souvenirs they've ended up with. They may still be trading at the airport on their way home!

The Barnett Family Reunion has a special trading tradition. Each child digs into his or her toy box for something to take to the reunion. Toys are then piled on a picnic table or blanket. Each child's name is put in a bag and pulled one by one to pick a "new" toy from the pile.

Sample Reunion Day Program

Large reunions need to schedule activities especially if they're fitting everything into a single day. The Seideman Family Reunions are at the family farm settled in 1848 by Fredrich and Rosina Seideman. This is a typical timetable for the Seideman Family Reunion:

Approximate Time	*Activity*
11:00	Registration begins.

12:00	Creative activities: face painting, T-shirt design, mural drawing.
	Petting pen opens.
	Watermelon seed-spitting contest.
1:00	Kuchen bake-off judging.
	Treasure hunt.
	Pie-eating contest.
	Bingo.
2:00	Storytelling.
	Tug-of-war.
	Parent and child balloon toss; three-legged race.
3:00	Clown parade followed by penny dig.
	Potato sack race.
	Adult balloon toss.
4:00	Mommy screaming contest.
	Cow-calling competition.
	Prize distribution.
	Kuchen auction.
	Annual family reunion talent/talentless show.

Some reunions post their programs on bulletin or chalk boards; others hand out programs either before or during the reunion. Carole E. Neal made a program book for the Seals Family Reunion. It included a welcome page, memorial and dedication pages for deceased family members (grouped by branch, dates of birth and death, and where they are buried), banquet program, menu and words to songs to be sung at the banquet, list of activities, poems and writings from family members, a brief family history, acknowledgment of the reunion committee, business cards from family members, and a family directory.

POTPOURI OF ACTIVITIES

The creativity of families in enhancing their reunions would seem to be endless!

* *Consider a conversation by speakerphone with family members who are unable to attend. If you're at a hotel, this can be broadcast over the public address system, with someone designated to carry on the conversaton at your end. Don't*

forget about differences in time zone, particularly on other continents. Also, you'll need to make sure your reunion site has an available phone jack, or bring a long extension cord.

* *Descendents of Dr. Alfred and Jane Witherspoon Scott of Boston have a white elephant gift exchange at each reunion. One at a time, everyone chooses from the selection of wrapped packages. Once everyone has opened theirs, they negotiate and trade. Some monstrosities reappear year after year!*

* *Descendants of Reverand Shelman and Elizabeth Campbell Vann gathered in Meldrim, Georgia, to celebrate family unity, respect for ancestral land, and special talents. The family still flourishes along winding Van Road, which blooms with well-tended gardens. The reunion, a showcase for many family talents, included ribs fresh from the hog slaughter, a fishing tournament (and fish fry), beauty makeovers, professional gospel singing, and lots of visiting. A wonderful dimension was added by Luther Van of Savannah, Georgia, whose reunion paintings and sculpture were part of an exhibit at the nearby Beach Institute African-American Art Museum.*

* *Patricia Miller and Nate Molden managed a surprise wedding ceremony at the Molden's Starling/Wilbourn Family Reunion. Miller envisioned a small, intimate wedding, but Molden wanted to take advantage of his large, scattered family being together. The reunion organizer, Molden's brother, and a family minister were pleased to accommodate the couple. The wedding was kept hush-hush so no one would feel obligated to bring gifts or be distracted from other reunion activities. The reunion program listed a "special event" between the convocation and meal—an event that was met with cheers and great happiness.*

* *As preparation for the Haeberlin Family Reunion, everyone was asked to write something to mark Cecil and Grace Haeberlin's seventieth wedding anniversary. Tributes, all placed in a special album, included poems, recollections, and pictures drawn by small children.*

Music, Songs, Skits, and Talent Shows

The menu of musical options covers everything from sing-alongs to a full orchestra. Determine your budget and the kind of music needed for each event: ceremonial, performance, dancing, background. What mood do you wish to set? Can you afford a live band? A disc jockey? Are there family members who can pitch in?

These ideas worked for other reunions. A local band played for opening ceremonies. An accordion player performed at registration. Strolling strings serenaded at a luncheon. A dance band played during the banquet. A DJ "spun" sixties, seventies, and eighties music. A singing group entertained. A rented jukebox—with appropriate records—was a unique twist.

Stu D. Baker, an entertainment consultant in Los Angeles, California, advises that when choosing musical entertainment, be sure to consider selection and presentation. First choose the type of music desired: Big Band, fifties, ethnic, rock and roll, country. Then review what experience with reunions the DJ or band has had. Check references and a printed list of available music. Also identify technical requirements, such as staging, chairs, sound system, instrument storage, unloading area, and changing room.

The contract should specify that the band or DJ hired is the same one who will perform at your reunion. Some entertainment companies switch, and the substitute is not always as capable or effective as the entertainer(s) originally requested—get who you pay for. Review the band contract for number of breaks, band attire, method of payment, overtime charge, restrictions, unions, setup time/sound checks, meals included, music selection, number of players, and rehearsals.

Four Jenkyns cousins once sported women's dresses in front and men's costumes in back for a quick turn from Barbershop Quartet to Sweet Adelines. The Jenkynses and the Smiths, too, have featured square or Western dance at their reunions. The Missouri Sappingtons end the day with a jamboree led by several family musicians; anyone is welcome to perform or just sing along. Some families polka to a cousin's accordion music or join in Mexican folk dances accompanied by guitar. Does your family include someone who plays in a band, sings with a group, plays an instrument? Ask them to perform or lead songs.

The Robinson Roots Family Reunion includes a score of music organized and directed by Doretha R. Davis. If music is going to be part of your reunion program, consider some of Davis's hints for organizing and coordinating musical activities.

- If there is a theme to your reunion or to an event or day, plan music to the theme. If there is no theme, select tunes that blend.

- If you are in charge of the music, communicate with the reunion organizer or person doing mailings to keep family members informed of your plans. Ask for suggestions, as well as names and ages of participants, and give them a deadline to respond.

- Stick to your schedule. If response falls short, make your own selections appropriate to each age group (children, teens, adults); select at least two or three songs for each. Photocopy words and music. Mail copies of sheet music and, if possible, a tape of selections to people who will be participating. If your family has groups of members who live near one another and can rehearse ahead of time, encourage them to do so. Set aside some rehearsal time at your reunion so far-flung members will be in tune—and tempo.

Carolyn Johnson says music helps make her reunion unique. Attendees spend at least one evening on a Florida beach serenading one another and anyone else who wanders by.

The Koehler Family Reunion sing-along is always a special feature. Organizer Janis Wilkens of Rock Hill, South Carolina, asks members to bring a favorite song: an old standard, something they remember grandma singing, or something new to teach.

There was a whole lot of shakin' goin' on at the Berger Family Reunion in Leipsic, Ohio. Robert Berger Jr., an Elvis impersonator, left family "all shook up" with his gyrations, sequined jumpsuit, cape, and curled lip. The performance was the highlight of the family's (so far) largest and best reunion.

Carol C. Michels of Wilmington, Delaware, says that when her Donahue Family Reunion gets together, music—and with it, magic—happens. One year they hired a Dixieland band, and another year they revived a family tradition of Sunday afternoon musical revues and had a vaudeville show to celebrate the eightieth birthdays of two favorite aunts. For their fiftieth anniversary celebration, a Murder Mystery was staged. Fifteen attendees willing to make fools of themselves were cast. Among the good sports was a Florida sheriff who shaved his mustache of twenty-six years to play Desiree Flambeau, an aging actress with an unseemly past. A grandmother needed three costume changes for her role as an international dress designer. Uncle Bunch finally found a bush jacket to go with his borrowed pith helmet as Major Barry, a very British retired officer.

A variety or talent show is a feature of many reunions. Invite everyone to perform. Children and aspiring entertainers love the chance to display their talents.

Skits are a favorite part of family variety shows. Every family has a few "hams" who don't need much prodding to perform. Family stories can more often than not be the subject of lighthearted satire.

The Adell Family Reunion staged a "No-Talent Show" in a very talented family. The idea was that everybody should do something silly or campy that wouldn't be taken seriously enough to spend valuable family time rehearsing. Two cousins who play professionally with the Atlanta Symphony Orchestra switched instruments for the No-Talent Show and performed a mock-stuffy rendition of a Bach piece meant for four instruments—and though not in the script, but totally in the spirit, one filled the other's horn with water. Another professional musician played the first piece he ever played at a recital exactly as he'd played that first time—with a dead G key. Every time he touched it, no note sounded. Everybody howled.

A fashion show can be a popular feature at a reunion. One variation has a narrator spoofing crazy outfits. Another spotlights antique clothing or fashions from the past.

Themes

Consider your reunion theme for costume party ideas. Some ideas: denim and diamonds, vintage, silly socks, hats (top hats, fedoras, bowlers, fezzes, helmets).

Everyone got into the act in Piedmont, South Dakota, for a combined Western-style reunion/fiftieth anniversary surprise party. First, Elmira Smith of Carroll, Iowa, directed kids "backstage" to pull "poppers" simulating gunfire. Next, she ran into the room, talking loudly about guns going off, and clapped her hands to sound like gallopping horses. Her husband and cousin then entered, sporting Western hats, water pistols, and sheriff's badges. They hand-cuffed and "arrested" Smith's Aunt Norma and Uncle Albert, the fiftieth-anniversary honorees.

* *Gatsby party: everything and everyone in summery white, with a gazebo close by, croquet, champagne, and a 1920s car, if you can get one.*

* *Flamenco fantasy: gypsy music, mantillas, castanets, flamenco lessons.*

* *Pirate party: eye-patches and sabers, a treasure hunt, Caribbean foods.*

* *Black-and-white night: black-and-white decorations, food, videos, and dress.*

* *St. Patrick's Day: green derbys, shamrocks, pots of gold filled with chocolate coins.*

* *Oktoberfest: a perfect theme for reunions held in autumn or by predominantly German families. You might want to scout some of the burgeoning microbreweries and sample their frothy seasonal creations. Men wearing lederhosen and women in colorful dirndls ensure a Bavarian look.*

In keeping with a Kentucky plantation theme, the Newtons dressed for a reunion in antebellum attire. Family couturiere Michele Hendricks of Loveland, Colorado, sewed old-fashioned gowns with crinolines for the Newton women with matching garters and string ties for the men. On Sunday, the clan gathered in their finery for church and posed afterward for a family portrait.

Arlene Mertens-Haraden of Farmingdale, New York, tells about the Mertens Family Reunion at North Myrtle Beach, South Carolina, with a theme party every other day. The first one was called Mingle, Mingle, Mingle. Memento books were handed out and there was a baby picture display. The next theme was a Tacky Tourist Barbecue. Family members dressed in their tackiest clothes, with a prize for the "best" outfit. Christmas in July was the third theme. Everyone created an ornament and wrote a personal description, in twenty words or less, on it. As creator identities were guessed, ornaments were placed on a Christmas tree. Everyone picked or "stole" a gift from a grab bag. The party ended with the family's rendition of "Partridge in a Pear Tree."

Holiday themes

Planning for holiday themes takes creativity—and time. Announce your theme and begin your preparations at least a year in advance. For example, if your theme is Independence Day, you'll want to take advantage of "day after" sales to shop for decorations, paper goods (plates, cups, napkins), banners, posters, garlands, and prizes.

For the Cundy family's red, white, and blue patriotic-themed reunion, Terry Hamilton crafted an assortment of special decorations, including centerpieces and party favors. Other themed decorations included American flags and Uncle Sam hats. Terry's sister, Cyndee Williamson, sewed red, white, and blue swimming suits for every child. A red, white, and blue reunion cake rounded out the patriotic theme.

Christmas. Christmas in July is a popular theme particularly for far-flung families who know they will not be able to spend the holiday together. For example, Ellen Clark of Jacksonville, Florida, planned the "Christmas at the Beach" Ray/Clark Family Reunion, held at Beech Mountain, North Carolina, for July. Friday evening, everyone helped decorate a tree by stringing popcorn and hanging family photo ornaments. Santa arrived the next day with presents for the children. Attendees sang Christmas songs, and the reunion closed with the Swedish custom of breaking and eating "peppermint pig" candy for good luck. A helium balloon Santa was released to fly back to the North Pole but needed a little help when he got stuck under the eaves.

Thanksgiving. Every reunion is a time to give thanks. Still, a Thanksgiving theme seems particularly meaningful around harvest time. The Lambert Family Reunion's Thanksgiving program was centered around the theme "The Lambert Tribe: Pilgrims and Indians Reunion" to celebrate the family's dual Colonial and Cherokee heritage. The theme was carried out in the design of the decorations and directory. Computer-generated awards included Long

Time No-See Um, Pow-Wow Chief and Tribal Generations honors. A letter of recognition from the president of the United States was shared.

Historical themes

Alexandra Walker Clark and her children wrote a skit for the Walker Family Reunion depicting Alexandra's great-grandfather's 1872 arrival by covered wagon at the old farm near Chattanooga, Tennessee. Her son, Liam, starred as his great-great-grandfather; daughters Sarah and Amanda dressed in calico and effectively re-created the covered wagon with two hula hoops draped with a bedsheet. As a result, the kids became hooked on family history.

The Robinson Family Reunion highlights different aspects of American Colonial life. They perform such reenactments of seventeenth-century life as using period surgical instruments and cooking meals in a large black kettle hanging over a fire. According to Laverne Aitchison of Phoenix, Arizona, the Guindon/Yandeau Family Reunion chooses reunion sites in Ontario, Canada, to "walk in the footsteps" of their forebears.

Glenn H. Dayley of Chubbuck, Idaho, chronicled a fascinating reunion in Grantsville, Utah. Pioneer forebears were instrumental in Grantsville's founding and development. The reunion tour included a stop on Cooley Street at the home of John William Cooley, Dayley's great-grandfather, and visits to the home of Prudence Fenner Fairchild, his great-grandmother; the Grantsville cemetery; the ranch site of James Dayley, another forefather; and historic Grantsville fort, school, and church.

At each stop "ghosts" of their forebears (uncles, aunts, and cousins dressed in period costume) told their life stories "in their own words." Tears rolled down the cheeks of "ghosts" as they related trials and hardships they endured to establish Grantsville. Even the youngest children felt the family spirit such role-playing evokes.

The street that bears John William Cooley's name, nicknamed Lovers' Lane, is lined by the poplar trees he planted. To honor him, five grandsons planted two more poplar trees.

Keith and Betty Dayley and their children organized the reunion. They traveled to Grantsville months before to research stories and forebears lives. They contacted the Grantsville city council, chamber of commerce, and local residents, and took pictures, drew maps, and wrote histories for a guide booklet. They also assigned family members to play the roles of forebears and prepared life histories for these "actors" to study. In addition, they periodically sent out a family newsletter detailing their progress. Glenn Dayley says, "An experience like this causes you to think, wonder, and profoundly appreciate the struggles and sacrifices made by ancestors who set the foundation we are building upon today."

Ethnic themes

Ethnicity flavors all our lives and should be the spice of reunions as well. Use ethnicity in your theme, entertainment, tours, and, of course, everyone's favorite: food!

Many reunions are fortunate enough to still be in touch with relatives abroad and enjoy including foreign cousins. Feature costumes, crafts, culture, and the traditions of your immigrant forebears. Exhibit family artifacts, such as a fan from "the old country."

Plan an old-fashioned Gaelic *ceilidh* (pronounced "kaylee"). This is where the phrase "to sing for your supper" originated: Everyone is supposed to take part in the entertainment with a song, story, joke, dance, or other performance. While live pipers may be hard to find, cassette tapes of bagpipe music are everywhere. Drape tables—and people—with your clan tartan.

Ruth Montgomery reports that Medicine Lodge, Kansas, was the site of an international reunion of the Lillieqvist family. Thirteen family members from Switzerland, Sweden, Norway, and Denmark joined sixty relatives from throughout the United States. Miniature flags representing each country adorned dinner tables, and the celebration included singing national anthems.

The first German/American Smyser Family Reunion in America was held in York, Pennsylvania, in 1845. One hundred thirty-three American cousins attended and resolved to hold a similar celebration in 1945—changed to June 1946 because of the war. Over 1,500 Smyser cousins attended. Activities included a reenactment of the widow Anna Barbara Schmeiser and her children—Matthias, Margaretta, and John George—arriving on the ship *Brittania* into the Philadelphia harbor in 1731.

W. Robert Jackson of Youngstown, Ohio, describes the annual reunions of The Rashid Club of America, descendants of five very young Rashid cousins who abandoned life in Judiet-Marjaroun, Lebanon, in 1896 to immigrate to the United States. The family has since grown to about 1,500 members in twenty-eight states and Canada. Their reunions, started in 1928, are held over the July Fourth holiday in major cities. The first night is Arabic Night. Featured are tabbouleh, kibbee, pita bread, stuffed grape leaves, spinach pies, and baklava—all get-in-the-mood foods.

Flora Toms O'Hagan tells of Cornish Cousins from the United States, Canada, and Cornwall, England, who gathered in Ely, Minnesota. Cousins from Cornwall shared what it means to be Cornish with a hands-on workshop to create "a shoal of fish lanterns." First, willow branches were bent and shaped into fish skeletons, covered with tissue paper, and glued. Then candles were mounted in lanterns for a "hot fish" parade in the style of an anual Cornish procession—celebrating the story of a man without kin or wife who set out into stormy waters to catch fish to feed his starving village of Mousehole. Villagers lit his way to shore with lanterns. This miracle of food is celebrated on December 23 with Starry Gazey fish pie.

As far back as 1410, Pout families lived in and around Canterbury, Kent, England. Some Pouts since immigrated to Australia and North America. Jill Nielsen of Burnaby, British Columbia, was corresponding with a cousin in Canterbury who had researched the family. Reunion plans resulted. More than 100 people attended the weeklong reunion in England. A double-decker bus outing was arranged to visit farmlands once owned or worked by Pout families. One stop was at a vineyard for cream tea—scones with strawberry preserves and clotted cream, served with hot tea. While sampling the vineyard's wares, a family trait was discovered: a taste for sweet wine.

For a Vaughn Family Reunion, Rose M. Vaughn-Mallet of Milwaukee, Wisconsin, made shirts for each family branch in separate *kinte* cloth pattern colors. The *kinte* cloth pattern, originating in Ghana, is honored in America as a tradition. Black represents people; red, life; yellow, health; blue, love and tenderness; and green/white, bountiful harvest.

Helen Cochran of Gary, Indiana, reports that the Cochran Family Reunion always includes a tour that offers younger family members opportunities to learn about and take pride in their heritage. The Cochrans' Chicago reunion included a visit to the Du Sable Museum of African-American History and Art.

John Gurda, author of fascinating family and community histories, has often written about his Johnson Family Reunions.

> *What reunions offer is a chance to renew family links, to find our places in the story that began in distant lands so many decades ago. Generations later, the story continues. At its heart is the theme that Torger and Johanne Johnson learned in the 1870s, the same theme that unites and animates every family: Life is precious. Pass it on.*

Sports, Games, and Tournaments

Sports, games, and tournaments are highlights of many reunions. They can be as simple as informal rounds of softball, volleyball, Frisbee, or darts, or as complex as three-day tournaments involving a number of teams and a variety of contests.

Games that families stage include relay, sack, and three-legged races; watermelon seed-spitting contests; peanut, penny, or hard candy scrambles; horseshoes; tug-of-war—games that kids of all ages enjoy. Be innovative. The Bickels once had a stroller race with mothers pushing their toddlers along the course.

The Newtons held an Olympian reunion at Palmer, Alaska, over the Fourth of July weekend. Opening ceremonies began with lighting the flame in the main meeting hall using an outdoor grill starter as the torch. Events included water balloon volleyball, miniature golf, and line dancing.

The Brolra Family Reunion Olympics are a tradition. Karen Robertson reports that the games have been played on the beach and in parks, parking lots, and resort courtyards. The family stages relays (Peppermint Pass, Wheelbarrow Race, Balloon Carry, Orange Pass, Bucket Brigade), tossing games (Egg Toss, Balloon Toss), individual games (Simon Says), group effort (Jump Rope, Dishpan Feet, Sand Castle Building, Tug-o-War), pure silliness (Circle Tangle, Shoe Store, Pattern Juggling), and for those who like to ante up, marathon poker games.

The Fehringer Family Reunion has been hooked on horseshoes since most were old enough to walk. The game gives them time to socialize as well as joke about their lack of skill or boast of their prowess at the toss. In keeping with the changing times, golf and volleyball are played too. For the younger children, a water balloon toss provides lots of laughs. Older kids play softball or soccer.

There's no downtime at Lindsey reunions, according to Doris Curless of Lowell, Indiana. Family members fill their day with team games, contests, and swimming. A piñata bash highlighted one Sunday picnic.

Keith Manos arranged to have his reunion honored on the scoreboard at a Cleveland Indians baseball game. I discovered that a group of twenty-five or more for a Milwaukee Brewers game must simply ask for such a recognition when making group ticket arrangements.

Golf

Golf was by far the most important reunion activity listed by respondents to a nationwide East Stroudsburg University/*Reunions magazine* survey of family reunion organizers. In fact, almost 20 percent of all reunions include a golf game.

Use the resources of the local convention and visitors or tourism bureau to find general information on golf in the area, or include golf in your criteria for choosing a reunion location. Golf course staff are usually experienced at planning tournaments. If you decide to include a golf tournament, coordinate with the golf club's pro shop such things as player pairings, rain contingency plans, even food and beverages.

Organize a golf tournament. Establish a goal for your tournament. Is it for camaraderie or competition? Are the players experts who want to be challenged or novices who perfer an easier course? Reunion members' golf skills may vary widely. Tournament organizers or golf professionals at most resorts can help you select a course that is a challenge for serious golfers and fun for others.

Book the golf course when you book your reunion. Send announcements early to get an accurate head count. Determine golf handicaps in order to match players by skill level, and find out if members need to rent golf clubs or shoes.

The Newton family teed off with a golf tournament at their Kentucky reunion. To get into the swing, participants put their names in a hat. Chance therefore determined teams, creating amusing mismatches of serious golfers with enthusiastic novices. Some returned with trophies, but all came back from the event grinning.

Match the tournament format to your family. Choose a scramble, best ball, individual stroke play with gross scoring, or individual stroke play with net scoring. The best ball format, for example, works well for players with bona fide handicaps in teams evenly divided by ability. You may want to challenge more competitive players with skill contests.

Offer prizes for everyone—the more prizes the better. Include a prize for the longest drive. For the shortest drive, a golf instruction book or a fishing kit will poke a bit of fun. Don't limit yourself to the traditional. Something-for-every-one prizes may include most balls hit out of bounds, most lost balls, and neatest scorecard. If you are a regular customer, a sports shop might donate prizes.

The Hebner Family Reunion in Michigan has established two annual awards: the William Ford Hebner Sr. Trophy for the golfer with the best score with a handicap and the Uncle Bruce Perkins Award for the best score without a handicap. Other prizes are given for Not Keeping Your Eye on the Ball, Most Improved, and Top Junior Player.

Valerie Keiser Norris of Woodstock, Georgia, describes how the Young Family Reunion features an Annual G.R.M.A. (Grandma Doughnut Open) in honor of Grandma Young's delicious deep-fat-fried, eat-em-plain-or-split-open-with-a-bit-of-butter doughnuts. About 110 people gather annually, and awards range from reunion T-shirts and golf supplies to the highly regarded, much-sought-after trophy for Best Foursome. Everyone claps politely, even when Uncles Paul and Ed win *again*.

Contests and Prizes

Contests are popular reunion activities. Some are spontaneous, others well planned. The reported highlight of an evening program at an Eby Family Reunion in Prince Rupert, Canada, was The Eby Ear Wiggling Contest. And then there's the traditional Hambling Family Reunion yummy fudge contest.

Alice Fairchild reports that contests at the Gunckel/Nelson Family Reunion have proved that yo-yos are indeed an art form as are hula-hoops. For their Prettiest Male Leg Contest, wives try to pick their husbands out by their feet alone (shoes have been removed). Everyone then votes for the "prettiest legs."

The Simon Gay Reunion's Bonniest Knees contest has all the kilted gentlemen lining up for blindfolded female judges to feel the knees and choose the "bonniest pair."

The Keenan Family Reunion conducts contests featuring designated articles of clothing, for example, boxer shorts or socks. Prizes include Most Original, Best Example of Family History, and Best Reminder of an Ancestor or Family Member. The necktie year included some wild vintage Goodwill ties, particularly impressive when worn with T-shirts. The hats theme inspired one decorated with Santa Claus and his reindeer as a tribute to forefather Edward Keenan, who for many years was Santa at a major department store. Another featured the family homestead complete with house, outhouse, and pump. Grandma's flower garden was memorialized on a hat covered with petunias.

Reunions usually mean good food. Showcase some of that fine cookin' with a contest. Have a chili cookoff or, for the children, a cookie decorating competition. Both the Polk and Seideman Family Reunions feature dessert competitions.

Turbeville Family Reunion attendees gathering at the Lakeland, Florida, home of Dovie and Bob Effinger were each asked to decorate a small cake. Cakes decorated with everything from faces, flowers, boats, and golf clubs to modern art were arranged on a truck tailgate, and family members voted for their favorite. First-, second- and third-place winners received Florida lottery tickets.

Word-find puzzles are popular at reunions. Include reunion-related words like *banquet, family tree, hugs,* and *genealogy,* as well as names of forebears.

Family honors

Consider recognizing individual attendees for some of the following:

- Oldest person.
- Youngest person.

- Longest married couple.
- Newest married couple.
- Person who traveled farthest to attend the reunion.
- Person who has attended the most reunions.
- Most children, grandchildren, great-grandchildren.
- Man who looks most like great-grandpa.
- Woman who looks most like great-grandma.

Contest prizes

Presentation can be Oscar-like, with two attendees announcing each award, thus drawing more people to the podium. Members married the longest can give the Newest Newlywed award.

One family's prizes for specially recognized persons are a dust pan with a long handle (oldest), large pack of bubble gum (youngest), and a large pack of pretzels for the long drive home (who came the farthest).

Arlene Mertens-Haraden of Farringdale, New York, offers these ideas for matching prizes with awards. Most Patriotic Award: a small American flag or a T-shirt, mug, or keychain featuring the flag. Funniest Questionnaire: a hamburger yo-yo. Best Memento Book Production Award: a rolodex file and a roll of film. Best T-shirt design: a calendar featuring famous artists.

With a bit of creativity you should have no difficulty finding organizations willing to generously donate novelty items for prizes, including key rings, cupholders, buttons, and pens. Convention and visitors bureaus can often provide things like lapel pins. Shopping malls may offer coupons for reunion members; ask for the marketing or public relations director. Be prepared to put your request in writing, as many organizations require a written request. Briefly, explain about your reunion and how donating items highlights the donors' products or services.

After your reunion, send donors a thank-you letter that says more than just thanks. Detail how many participated, how people responded to items, and why their giving was so important to your success.

Lots of things can be found for prizes as well as giveaways in party goods stores. Look for simple games and crafts that provide kids with activities at the reunion. Consider coloring books, crayons, colored markers and pencils, balloons, and stickers. Don't forget all the little samples and trinkets you receive throughout the year. Collect them in a box or bag to then raid for your reunion.

Dionne Chalmers has successfully filled goody bags with such things as calculators, calendars, cassette tapes, lotion or perfume samples, mouse pads, stuffed animals, magnets, screwdrivers or other tools, tape measures, lint removers, address books, whistles, seeds, miniflashlights, sun visors, candy, and pocket planners.

Rose Hendrickson of Park City, Utah, makes 4-inch-square muslin bags with twine drawstrings, and rubber stamps *Morris Reunion* on them, filling them with sunflower seeds to distribute at the reunion. Included is this message from Grandma Anna Morris: *The Morrises were like tumbleweeds spreading their seeds all over the West. With seedlike vigor, may the Morris reunion continue to grow and flourish.*

Storytelling and Oral History

Consider hiring a professional storyteller to dazzle your group with tales of love, friendship, and derring-do! Or schedule your reunion at one of the many storytelling festivals around the country. You can always gather around the campfire for heartwarming tales or spinetingling ghost stories from your own griot.

Storytelling counterbalances our fast-paced TV culture, creates images that linger, and honors forebears through memory. Stories connect us with our roots, binding generations and bringing new meaning to history. By listening to how others dealt with life's problems, we're given strength and wisdom to endure our own trials in life. The universal truths gleaned from stories help us make sense of the world.

Oral history and storytelling go hand in hand. Oral history is a tradition in the Walker/Jones family. The biggest reunion event is a picnic featuring storytelling by elders aged 72 to 102.

Yvonne Belden advocates capturing the personality, charm, wit, and, yes, eccentricity of your family with an oral history. You'll want to carefully choose interview locations. Focus the interview with questions and expand on the answers you're given. Encourage discussion of achievements and adventures and triumph over problems. Bring out the interviewee's unique qualities. Be sensitive to strong emotions.

Like in the game of Telephone, details can get distorted, elaborated, even eliminated as a story is passed down from one generation to the next. Sharon DeBartolo Carmack, C.G., author of *The Genealogy Sourcebook*, states that themes to common family tales include Native American descent (usually a tribal princess), siblings ("Our branch of the family began when three brothers came from the old country . . ."), and royal or celebrated ancestry. Such tales add color to family history, and it's interesting to trace their origins.

An additional value of oral history is learning about the social history of the time. Be sure to ask such questions as What were your meals like during the Depression? Did your family experience blackouts during World War II? How did your family celebrate holidays, anniversaries, birthdays? What was your family's favorite entertainment? Why did the family move to California?

Tips for conducting an oral history interview

- Prepare your questions in advance, gathering background information about your subject.

- Ask open-ended questions, such as Where did you live when you were first married, and why? Have photographs and/or artifacts available to help jog the person's memory.

- Make an appointment with your interviewee and keep it short, about an hour.

- Record the interview on video or audiocassette. Have extra tapes and batteries handy. If your subject is shy about being recorded, be prepared to take notes.

- Ask the who, where, and when, but don't forget to ask what, why, and how.

Carmack notes that one of the very best times to interview teens is during your family reunion. Suggest that when they're getting bored listening to the old folks, they can tell you things. They'll love the opportunity to talk about themselves.

Here are some questions to ask. What's your favorite subject in school? What are your ideas for a career? Who do you look up to? What's your favorite kind of music? How do you spend your summers? Who's your best friend? Why? What do you want to be remembered for? What do you think about religion? family? race relations? gangs? violence? Where do you see yourself in ten years? twenty years? when you're forty? The fun part will be interviewing your subjects again in twenty years and asking some of the same questions!

Don't neglect interviewing younger children too. Ask them, What's your favorite cartoon? Which vegetable/fruit do you like most/least? What do you want to be when you grow up? Why? What chores do you have to do? Which parent are you most like? Why?

Speakers

Some reunions include speakers as part of the program. Survey your members for those with the talent and desire to share knowledge, experience, or skills. Keep an open mind about subject matter and you may be pleasantly surprised. Make sure the speaker addresses topics of interest to your family.

If you plan to hire a speaker, do your homework before signing any contract. Interview the candidate. Ask for credentials and check references. Arrange to preview him or her live or on videotape. Be aware that some speakers expect you to pay for travel, room, meals, and other expenses. Others want the opportunity to sell books or tapes. Get all agreements in writing.

Don't forget to determine presentation requirements: audiovisual equipment, podium, microphone, water, spotlight, chalkboard, laser pointer.

Sightseeing / Tours

There are two ways to plan a sightseeing/tour agenda. You can set up area tours, booking buses and guides yourself, or you can call a local sightseeing company like Gray Line to handle all the details. You'll still need to do the promoting, though sometimes professional tour organizations help pay the cost.

Helen McArthur, organizer of a Gathering of the Clan MacArthur Society in Canada, arranged an outing to Stettler, Alberta, by Prairie Steam Engine Train. Old-fashioned train travel, a sing-along, and historical sightseeing soon made former strangers family. Ken Fletcher reports that the Crosslen Family Reunion celebrated Jean Crosslen's eighty-fifth birthday with a ride on the Platte Valley Trolley that Jean often rode from her home to downtown Denver.

An afternoon or evening at a local race track might appeal to your group. When arranged ahead of time, many race tracks will name a race in honor of a family. Family members may even be invited into the winner's circle for the winner's presentation.

Vivian Andrews Odoms of Detroit, Michigan, masterminded a trip to downtown Detroit for the Wills Family Reunion. Lunch and shopping in Canada lent international flair. A tour of Fort Wayne, a military installation, was led by one of the original Tuskegee Airmen, filling the whole family with a sense of pride.

The Jolly Family Reunion reserved Friday for a tour. From their Topeka, Kansas, reunion site they planned a day trip to Kansas City, Missouri, where they visited the Black Historic District, the Negro League Baseball Museum, and the Kansas City Jazz Museum.

The goal of a Bell Family Reunion was to meet the granddaughter of Alexander Graham Bell. Irving Bell of Springfield, Vermont, says their destination was the summer homestead—in Baddeck, Cape Breton, Canada—of one of Bell's two living granddaughters, Dr. Mabel Grosvenor. The bus trip took an entire week, starting in Portland, Maine, aboard the *Scotia Prince* for an all-night trip to Yarmouth, Nova Scotia, and many historic sites were stops along the route.

Camping Activities

For reunions spent camping, Larry Polenske in *Reunions magazine* has advocated planning activities around the campground's features. Ask the camp director about educational programs or naturalists who present programs about local wildlife and flora. Most campgrounds have nature trails. A scavenger or treasure hunt encourages members to explore trails and promotes camaraderie. Volleyball or horseshoes inspires spirited competition.

A traditional hay ride can be a fun way to tour the grounds. Check if a ride can be scheduled just for your reunion.

Be sure to include information in your reunion letter about campground activities so that members can bring appropriate equipment. Gear might include bikes, tennis rackets, hiking boots, or swimwear.

For the Giese Family Reunion, Dale and Carolyn Giese chose the city of Ely in the Minnesota Boundary Waters Canoe area. Everyone enjoyed hiking trails, fishing, and visiting around crackling campfires. The younger ones spent most of each day at the beach, their parents watching from lounge chairs. A two-day canoe trip went off without a hitch. For their final nights in Big Lake Camp, Dale Giese had brought along old-time radio show tapes: *Inner Sanctum, Fibber McGee and Molly, The Shadow,* and *The Whistler.* Every night the granddaughters asked for lights out to listen to another tape. Just as the Shadow was exploring "what evil lurks in the hearts of men," ice chests began to clatter. A bear was visiting.

Workshops

Some families organize workshops at their reunions. Computer workshops turn the tables, since kids know infinitely more about computers than most adults do. Kids and grandkids can be teachers for a change, and adults and grandparents the students. Give the younger generation a chance to shine! Ask them to demonstrate reunion-related applications: word processing (correspondence, family histories, and stories), spreadsheets (ledgers and accounts), graphics (invitations and flyers), E-mail (quick communication), and, of course, surfing the Internet (research reunions as well as family history).

When organizing workshops, you might find that family members have just the talent and expertise you're looking for. If not, use friends or resources such as a university, professional organization, or library. In the case of medical workshops, check with your doctor or the education department at a hospital or HMO.

The Burnett(e) Family Reunion held two workshops: one about financial planning and the other about family health. The health workshop used a questionnaire to collect family health history from the six represented branches. Workshop objectives included educating members about taking charge of their own health. Together, participants began diagramming family history in a genogram and tracing health issues through several generations. The workshop was so well received that it will continue at the next reunion.

Family health history is a hot reunion topic. Research has linked many diseases to genetics; diabetes, heart conditions, and some cancers, for example, may be inherited. Claude Ramsey, who's been involved with the Ramsey Family Reunion, notes that family reunions are a good time to update medical records.

Growing Your Family Medical Tree by Fran Carlson creates a "Family Deck of Life" to help you identify your health risks and develop a personal health solution. Carlson was inspired to create this method of documenting health history after discovering at her family reunion a pattern of death due to severe allergic reaction. Her coding system, which traces medical conditions back three generations, is easy to use. As a way to promote health among current and future generations, it's a great tool to introduce at your reunion.

In her upcoming book, *Reviving the Legacy: African American Family Reunions*, Ione Vargus, Ph.D., cites examples of workshops at reunions. Workshops can tackle such topics as examining values and forging economic development. Vargus, founder of The Family Reunion Institute at Temple University, Philadelphia, Pennsylvania, says workshops are an activity that hold the promise of "dealing with social issues of the day and bringing the family closer."

At the Gaither/James Family Reunion workshops, professionals have shared expertise in education planning, entrepreneurship, political involvement, investment counseling, intergenerational relationships, and family economic development. After several hours of discussion, workshop groups report to the whole family. Out of these workshops, the Gaither/James family has established investment and scholarship plans.

On Saturday morning at the reunion of Daniel Boone's descendants there is a roundtable discussion called Sarah's Circle, named for Sarah Morgan Boone, Daniel's mother. The focus of discussion is on the trials and tribulations of Boone frontier women, about whom many hair-raising stories are told.

Workshops can be used to share genealogical information and teach others how to do searches. Highlight one fascinating forebear or family branch or else a particular historical period and the family members who lived during that time. Or recount the search itself, highlight dramatic twists and turns. Make a field trip to a genealogical collection, library, or repository. Or engage a speaker with a particular genealogical specialty that will intrigue your members.

Genealogy

Do you know a better place than your family reunion to share the fruits and triumphs of your genealogical passion? Your family reunion puts you in the spotlight before the very best audience for your endeavors, your own family. Every member of every generation can relate to the fruits of your genealogical research, which, after all, constitute your family's history.

History lives

A family reunion is a living legacy. Emphasize the importance of everyone's connection, and celebrate people, history, and ethnicity.

There are many ways to make history come alive. Charlotte Johnson of Alton, Illinois, historian for the George Schultz and "His" Inc. Family Reunion, presents an entertaining slide show about the formation and genealogy of the family. The lives and adventures of family founders can be inspiring. Survival often confronted them with an urgency most of us rarely experience today. Simple necessities—food, clothing, and shelter—were a struggle, and hearing about their gift and determination can breed a sense of appreciation and family pride.

At their reunion, the Alford Family Association features a Family Forum incorporating genealogical tools to help members see how they are connected. Computers are set up at the Tackett Family Reunion so attendees can check genealogy lines.

Try planning reunions at or near places of significance to your forebears. Organize tours that include family residences and homesteads, property, and landmarks. Visit where forebears went to school and worshiped, where they worked and are buried.

Use family history and trivia to customize games to play at your reunion, including crossword puzzles or other word games, or scavenger or treasure hunts. When activities enjoyably incorporate family history, family identification grows.

Sharing your genealogical research

Wayne W. Daniel of Chamblee, Georgia, provides a Genealogy Work Table to exchange information and a Show-and-Tell Table to exhibit historical and current materials at the Daniel Family Reunion. Daniel suggests notifying members in advance to bring photos and other memorabilia.

Many families display posters at reunions, or bulletin boards of photos. A large family tree is often the focal point. Among other items to display are historical documents and papers (photocopies only, please!), maps, and artifacts.

Consider your audience. Be sure the display is accessible and easy to read. Also be selective about what you include. Don't use absolutely everything so that your display appears cluttered. This will allow you, too, to vary the display and keep your audience interested from year to year.

Trails and landmarks

All of us are touched in one way or another by migration. Use a reunion to explore those connections. Marsha Hoffman Rising, C.G., C.G.L., F.A.S.G., of Springfield, Missouri, writes that family research goes where our people have gone—over the Alleghenies, through the Cumberland Gap, down the Ohio River, up the Tennessee, across the Mississippi, or over the Rockies. Get caught up in your forebears' dreams and follow their journeys.

Powell brothers John A., Noah, and Alfred and their families left Menard County, Illinois, in 1851 and traveled by covered wagon to Willamette Valley, Oregon. Their sister, Lucinda Propst, later persuaded her husband, Anthony, to go west with their children to join her brothers. Lucinda died in childbirth and was buried on the trail near Butter Creek. A month later Anthony died. In 1916 the Powell family began having reunions, and in 1920 the Powell Memorial Society was formed. Descendants gathered in 1990 to mark Lucinda's burial site with a highway marker and later with a tombstone. In 1993 a tombstone was dedicated at Anthony's grave. Family member Jean Laws of Olympia, Washington, says these commemorations brought family members closer.

Rose Sheldon Newton of Fort Wayne, Indiana, says visits to a former homestead, cemetery, or battlefield are incorporated into Sheldon Family Reunions. Recently the Sheldons returned to the site of the Deerfield (Massachusetts) Massacre, where colonial forebears were either slaughtered or carried into slavery in Canada.

Carolyn Wilson-Elliott wrote that she combined their small family reunion with genealogy research at the Arkansas Historical Society Four Corners Ancestor Fair, a two-day event focusing on genealogy searches in Arkansas,

Oklahoma, Missouri, and Kansas. Attendance at the fair made reunion planning easy.

While at the fair, Wilson-Elliott was introduced by an exhibitor to a distant cousin who told family stories about convicted murderers and train robbers—a great hit with the kids. This cousin directed them to another relative, who had researched the family back to 1660. They all pored over photos, looking for family resemblances. An extra day was spent in Arkansas, visiting sites featured in family tales, and driving to Round Mountain Cemetery, where many forebears lie buried. At the base of Round Mountain, the White River was discovered, where an ancestor had drowned.

Cemeteries

In the dedication of her book, *How to Plan a Spectacular Family Reunion*, Geneva Turner, Ph.D., wrote: "Mountains of gratitude to Uncles Henry and Thomas Turner, who expressed a universal truism—meeting at funerals has to end." That sentiment has been, and will continue to be, the impetus for many a reunion—to spend time with relatives while you're all still alive. Nonetheless, the move from funeral to reunion is not without a stop at the cemetery, either in person, in photographs, or on video.

Cemeteries are places of enormous fascination. There, proximity to history and ancestors is compelling. Family groups often use the reunion weekend to tend to gravesites and cemetery plots or to dedicate markers and monuments. Projects range from restoration and repair to family research, data collection, and mapping. Kids love to create tombstone rubbings they can take to school for show and tell. Family members should be encouraged to share stories and reminiscences about those buried in the cemetery. Most family reunions include memorial services in their programs, which are particularly poignant when held at the cemetery.

Holding a cemetery reunion. When genealogist Sharon DeBartolo Carmack, C.G., attended the Carmack reunion, she suggested a tour of cemeteries where family members were buried. Carmack says this experience taught her more about the family than she could ever have found in traditional genealogical records. She videotaped tombstones and encouraged older family members to tell stories relating to the deceased. She learned, for one thing, that her grandfather, David McMasters, died on top of his roof during a thunderstorm, while adjusting the lightning rod!

Cemeteries are the perfect place to teach children about respect for the dead and the sacredness of the final resting place. Explain that a cemetery is a museum without walls. Many tombstones are hundreds of years old and are not to be climbed on, colored on, or knocked down.

If your reunion is not near any family plots, bring the plots to the reunion. Designate a cemetery committee—comprising people who live near forebears' graves. Direct the committee to make slides, a videotape, or tombstone rubbings, in order to present a "cemetery tour." During the presentation, encourage those on hand to reminisce about departed family members.

At one Glenn Family Reunion, headstones were dedicated for Starling and Eliza Glenn (born 1823 and 1827, respectively, in Winnsboro, South Carolina). Benjamin Glenn led a tour of the small cemetery and enthralled the grandchildren with tales recalled by family headstones.

Margaret Kaffka Garrehy of Sacramento, California, and Pat (Crotty) Glugla of Deerbrook, Wisconsin, met when Naomi Engelmann, indexer at Wisconsin's Antigo Library, noticed that both were researching the same family. What are the odds? The outcome was a reunion, the Stanislaus Glugla Connection-Greatful Dead Tour, at Queen of Peace Catholic Cemetery in Antigo. The day before the reunion, each grave was decorated with flowers. Margaret and husband Den Garrehy parked their motorhome next to the cemetery building to mount a fourteen-page, computer-generated list of descendants for Stanislaus Glugla, who was born in Poland in 1820 and immigrated to America in 1870.

Antoinette Kyle Ketner Bengtson of Lincoln, Nebraska, left a note in a bottle at the Gibboney family plot in East End Cemetery in Wytheville, Virginia. Jean Bourne, a cousin from Blacksburg, Virginia, found the note when she visited the gravesites, and the Gibboney Family Reunion found another participant.

C. Patricia Irwin Lesley recalls her dad mentioning a family reunion he attended as a boy. The reunion tradition began in 1878 when adult children of Peter Irwin met to clean up the Old Seceder Cemetery in Downington, Pennsylvania. Men trimmed grass and repaired the wall and tombstones while women and children prepared a picnic. Now at Irwin reunions, care of the Old Seceder Cemetery remains a priority. Dues of $2 per adult are used for cemetery maintenance and family records preservation.

Reenactments, style shows, and demonstrations

If your reunion date coincides with a special family anniversary, celebrate with a reenactment. Consider anniversaries when your forebears arrived in the United States or left or established themselves in a place or celebrate milestone birthdays and wedding anniversaries. Just keep in mind that the reenactment of a special event requires a script, set, and costumes. Rehearsal will probably have to be scheduled during your reunion.

If someone has unearthed trunks or boxes of period clothing, a style show is a perfect way to make use of them. All ages can participate—everyone likes to play dress-up! Remember that to younger generations, clothes from the 1940s through the 1970s are "period," and fortunately many people still have examples of those "memorable" fashions in their closets. Or rent or hunt resale shops for costumes and come as your favorite forebear.

Living museums, demonstration farms, and historic villages all feature demonstrations that will enhance everyone's understanding of history, including blacksmithing, horseshoeing, farming, food preservation, milking, and harvesting.

The Sappington Family Reunion in Moniteau County, Missouri, offers demonstrations of quilt piecing, pottery making, and whittling (bring a pocketknife!). Attendees are invited to share, teach, or sell crafts.

Organizers set up an entire museum for the annual Seidemann Family Reunion. Family antiques are arranged in a kitchen, parlor, bedroom, schoolroom, and library where genealogy materials are displayed. Display cases showcase original documentation for the homestead that remains in the family. Placed outdoors are antique farm implements and equipment.

Everyone grows on one

Everyone is fascinated by family trees. The lines that link parents, grandparents, aunts, uncles, and cousins are a clear, graphic demonstration of family. Whether a simple chart or a fancy display, elaborately illustrated, your family will delight in a family tree of their own.

Pauline Bizette Brandy of Davie, Florida, says the Lamberts use a generations-old family tree modernized with Family Tree Maker software that allows for easy updating. Carole Jones Byars of Knoxville, Tennessee, describes a "gingerbread" family tree introduced at the Clifton Family Reunions in Harrison, Arkansas. It features male and female gingerbread figures made from nonedible cinnamon dough. Each figure has a family member's name on the front and parents' names on the back. Four generations are represented, suspended by different-colored ribbons, and as children are born, their figures are added.

Sylvia Brudi of Fort Wayne, Indiana, takes family trees quite literally. She's planted seedlings in a tree mug as a door prize. A small tree in a pot that can fit on an apartment balcony or terrace also works well as a prize. Cuttings or grafts for those clever enough to know what to do with them can extend a family's connections even further. Or plant trees in the name of children, grandchildren, or recently deceased members.

The Skinner/McQueen Family Reunion planted and dedicated a tree to Margurite Tibben's parents, Bill and Leona Skinner, in the park where reunions have been held for many years. A liquid amber tree was chosen to commemorate autumn, a favorite time of year for both Bill and Leona. A red garnite plaque reads *The Family Tree, Its Roots an Ancestry, Its Limbs New Generations.* Skinner grandsons dug the hole and placed the plaque.

Preserving Reunions

The family reunion is a perfect place to bring, display, and solve the mystery of photos you can't identify. Indicate who brought each photo; then ask everyone to help solve the mystery. This will certainly put older family members in the spotlight! Also bring artifacts you can't identify.

Descendants of Gottfried and Emma Wilke set up a table for mystery photos at their reunion. Often by the end of the day an older relative surprises everyone by saying something like, "That is Aunt Kirsten, but that man is definitely not Uncle Ed. It looks like the neighbor she was seeing for a while."

Ways to incorporate photos

- Use a Polaroid camera for shots you can give out then and there.
- Feature a photo contest.
- Buy throw-away cameras and hand them out. Have shooters return the cameras and produce an exhibit for the next reunion of pictures "from the perspective of (name of photographer)."
- Spell out the family name using appropriately positioned family members. Take a photo from a high vantage point.
- Photograph generations, branches, and then the whole family. Use one-hour processing for a quick display.
- If you can get them developed in time, show slides the final night, recapping highlights of the reunion. Or open your next reunion with the slide show.
- Gather and display baby pictures.

One Lambert Family Reunion cousin is in charge of old family photos. She copies old photos, returns originals, and takes orders for reprints. New photos of the whole group and the seven family branches are taken at each reunion.

Exhibiting photos

Exhibit photos, along with videos, films, and artifacts, in a central gathering place. If outdoors, place the display under a shady tree with lots of chairs nearby. If indoors, set up in a quiet spot or hospitality suite, where people can take a break and explore the past or reminisce.

The reunion archivist or family genealogist can gather all the materials as well as display equipment. Folding tables are good for objects. Photographs can be mounted on boards—foam core boards are sturdy and won't warp. Prop up the boards on easels or attach cardboard easel backs. Materials can be found at most art supply stores.

The Bickel Family Reunion sections off bulletin boards for each family to have a place to post pictures. Some families match the bulletin-board background to their name tag, ribbon, or T-shirt colors. Group pictures taken at each reunion are also displayed so relatives can follow the changes over the years.

Another idea is to plan a slide show. Ask everyone to bring about five slides, each accompanied by a brief written explanation.

Memories on video

Some families preserve their history on video. Videos can be made by a reunion member or by a professional videographer.

A good videographer blends into a crowd. He or she should be sensitive to details and be able to work without direction. Professionals integrate artifacts, still photographs, and home movie footage with live interviews to create a lasting memory. Just be sure to ask for references. A reputable videographer will happily provide a prior client list and samples.

"Family reunion videos are most emotionally charged," explains Audrey Galex, owner of Roots and Wings—Life Stories, a company in Decatur, Georgia, that produces oral histories. "They offer an opportunity not only for family members to talk about historical facts but to share values, hopes, and dreams."

Technical considerations. A good video company uses S-VHS, HI8, or ¾-inch tape formats, all better than consumer quality. Also insist on good handheld and wireless microphones since camera microphones are inadequate.

Develop a budget with your videographer based on your production aims. Expect a complete cost breakdown in his or her initial proposal. Watch for hidden costs (additional videotaping, editing hours, graphics, licensed music, and duplication fees). Remember to ask for bulk order discounts. Bulk duplication cost and available packaging options should be included in the initial proposal. You can distribute production costs by adding a few dollars to the price of duplication so that everyone who wants a copy shares the cost.

For your protection, structure your production agreement to pay half before taping, reserving the other half until you have an acceptable product. Most videographers will not duplicate until they have full payment.

Arrange to participate in editing so you can provide input about which scenes to include. Your reunion videotape should capture key moments and memories. Intersperse comments with speeches, dances, or other events. If the reunion setting is significant—say, at the family homestead—be sure to include location shots.

If you're creating the video yourself, check your supplies; be sure to have plenty of film, batteries, bulbs, and tape. Special equipment may be rented in advance. Expect to sacrifice social time at a reunion and be available for spontaneous happenings.

Enlist an assistant. A well-organized adolescent or teenage family member could help by carrying a notebook or sheets of paper on a clipboard and checking off names of people as they are videotaped. Everyone should be included in a family video to make it a true record of the reunion. Encourage elders to tell family tales involving covered wagons, floods, tornados, births, deaths, and triumphs, or to disclose their secrets to a good life. Let youngsters speak their minds too. Kids say the darndest things, and you'll want to preserve these gems.

If your family reunion features a potluck meal, scan that groaning table—before the bidding, "Dig in!" Or take background shots in the kitchen. Audio accompaniment, including gossip and giggling, also communicates some family traditions.

Videotapes are an ideal way to share the reunion with shut-ins and relatives unable to attend. Provide a sign-up system so that people can order copies or receive forms to order later by mail. Require prepayment, including postage.

Photo CDs

Melenda Gatson Hunter of Lathrup Village, Michigan, has discovered a way to preserve photos old and new and use them in her family's newsletter, *Keeping Families Together—Gatson Family & Cousins*, and a family tree book. She has a photo lab scan selected negatives (in the order she instructs) onto a CD. She then uses word processing software to output images for her newsletter and for creating a display for the Will Family Reunion.

Reunion portraits

Family reunions are great times to make family portraits. J. R. vanLienden, of Masterpiece Portraits in Sarasota, Florida, offers these tips for photographing a large group:

- Soft, warm smiles are better than big cheesy grins.
- Ask persons not in the picture to stand directly behind the photographer. Then if those being photographed look at them, they'll be looking into the camera.

- Proper clothing can turn a picture into a portrait. One of the easiest ways to keep clothing from being distracting is for everyone to wear reunion T-shirts. When clothing tops are all the same color, attention is forced to faces. Long sleeves in particular help keep flesh tone restricted to faces.

- Choose the setting carefully. Minimize background distractions.

- Encourage people to relax. Position everyone so you can see their faces and keep individuals and rows close.

- Lighting is crucial. Avoid sun that shadows faces. Use sunlight behind subjects just after noon until about three o'clock, or else open shading from the shadow of a building or tree. Built-in flashes work well if the sun is to the subjects' backs, coming over their shoulders, and you use the backlighting mode. Use tripods if you want to make bigger prints from your photographs.

- Shoot lots of film.

- If it's in your budget, hire a professional photographer.

Time capsules

Consider a time capsule of reunion memorabilia; include videotapes, photos, and memorabilia, or make a memory book of each reunion. Rose Hendrickson of Park City, Utah, reports that the Morris Family Reunion traveled *forward* in time when in 1996 they made a time capsule to be opened at the reunion in ten years. Each member wrote a greeting, put it in an envelope, and sealed and addressed it to him- or herself. Kids were willing participants.

If the Kids Are Happy . . .

Family reunions have special significance for children meeting extended family for the first time. Plan energy-burners as well as reasons for kids to talk with "new" family members. Adrienne Anderson in *Reunions magazine* suggests these common-sense guidelines for games.

- Vary activities.

- Once rules are stated, stick with them.

- Count off randomly.

- Line up children from tallest to smallest.

- Form one big circle.

- Break the big circle in half or separate into inner and outer circles to choose teams.

When planning many games, vary between strenuous and quiet activities. Always plan more than you think you'll need—better to have too many than too few! If a game doesn't catch on in the first few minutes, abandon it and go on to something else. Also, consider having two game leaders: one to organize while the other directs a game.

We often hear the lament, "But what about the kids?" Well, what about them? Young people are bursting with creativity, initiative, and family pride. One such person is LaShonda Bennett of McDonald, Pennsylvania, who told how she (at age fourteen) became involved in the Bennett/Thornton Family Reunion and made a significant contribution to its success. She volunteered to update the family yearbook. Inspired by the theme "Holding Onto Our Heritage with Our Youth Today," she also wanted to learn about the family. She wrote to everyone asking for information. She used a previous year's book as a model and created art and titles for each section.

Feature special teen activities with trips to amusement parks, malls, a wave pool or giant slide, bowling alley or roller-skating rink. To plan exactly what the kids want to do, ask them for suggestions. The Hairston/Gallant Family Reunion has a "youth council" for just that purpose. The chairperson of the council sits on the family reunion board and offers ideas to ensure that kids will enjoy themselves. Another family has kids huddle before the end of each reunion to come up with ideas for the following year. To highlight teenagers, the Cook/Mickens/Cabbagestalk Family Reunion assigns them full responsibility for hospitality at one of their functions.

Donna Garrett of Roanoke, Virginia, wanted to be sure to involve the younger generation in the Talley Family Reunion. Using the letters in their family name, she wrote a short script about the clan for each grandchild to recite. For props, the kids made poster signs with "their " letter. Garrett taped cue cards to the back of the posters.

From eldest to youngest, each began:

> *T* is for *tolerance*—Papa Talley never saw color or wealth . . .
>
> *A* is for *ability*—Talleys can fix or make anything . . .
>
> *L* is for *love*—Love of family won out over riches and fame . . .
>
> *L* again is for *laughter*—Talleys have a smile on the inside *and* the outside . . .
>
> *E* is for *eternity*—Together, in their eternal home, Talleys will be singing . . .
>
> *Y*—*You* preserve the Talley name; some have added *Garrett, Berry*, and *Clifton*, but once a Talley, always a Talley . . .
>
> *S* is for *success*—Talley men and women are the greatest!

Everything went without a hitch until the youngest. Knowing he was supposed to say something, he just began babbling, "*S* is for spaceman, *S* is for stop," and so on. And for posterity, camcorders were rolling!

Projects for kids

Provide projects that will enhance kids' understanding of extended family.

Mapping your background. This activity makes kids aware of significant places in their family's past. Provide markers and a map of the United States or the world. Have kids mark cities and towns where their parents and grandparents lived, beginning with where they were born, where they might have next moved, where they went to school, and where they live now. Be prepared to help supply this information.

Hands across time. Families who are serious about genealogy may already have a photocopier at the reunion. If so, consider this activity. Ask kids to wash their hands, then put their hands, palms down, on the copier and press the COPY button. Compare these copies to those made in a year or two to see how much the kids' hands have grown! Make extra copies for future reunions.

Treasure hunt

Gloria Gray-Weissman of Munster, Indiana, suggests a treasure hunt where the treasure is learning about family. Give kids a list of adult relatives wearing things in a silly way. Some examples: a male not wearing shoelaces; a female wearing her wristwatch upside down; a male wearing a bobbypin; a female wearing a price tag; a male wearing his socks inside out. The kids write the name of the person they found matching the descriptions while learning more about family members.

Scavenger hunts

Ann Pelletier Strong of Barrington, Rhode Island, devised a scavenger hunt with the special purpose of getting youngsters to interact with older relatives. Scavengers received information that included physical clues (He has red hair. She wears glasses.) and a short bio (no names included) for three or four relatives. The biographical clues required the youngsters to ask questions. Successful matches yielded tokens exchangeable for prizes. The real prize, of course, was meeting interesting people who were also relatives!

Here are some tips for successful scavenging. Send adult relatives a short questionnaire asking for identifying physical attributes and a short biography. Pair younger kids with older cousins. Distribute scavenger hunt materials early so that kids can begin right away—before they've even thought about not having a good time!

Lowana Orcena offers another variation on the scavenger hunt. Make an equal number of clues for two teams; then hide the clues so that each leads to the next. Send teams, each accompanied by an adult, in opposite directions, with the last clue ending up at the same place for a surprise—for example, a treat of banana boats. (To make banana boats: Roast bananas, marshmallows, and Hershey bars wrapped in tinfoil over warm coals until marshmallows and chocolate melt, three to five minutes.)

Each scavenger hunt requires different clues. These were Orcena's examples.

1. 1, 2, 3,
   Come follow me,
   We're heading for that big tree.

2. The tree has a clue,
   What will we do?
   Go to the right,
   Check out that bike.

3. Bike, hike,
   What we need is
   A very tall light.

4. The light works fine,
   But don't turn blind.
   We have to find
   Where they dropped those dimes.

5. We all found a dime,
   Now it's time to climb.
   Let's try that great big slide.

6. Last clue.
   We're so close, you can smell it.
   Behind that building
   The secret will tell it.

We love Mother Earth

As an early arrival project for cousins, form a committee of kids to paint and decorate reunion recycling boxes. Decorations may include family trees, logos, earth symbols, or just fanciful designs. Line boxes with garbage bags and sort according to local practice: metal, plastic, glass, paper. Cash rewards at recycling centers are a great incentive and can be divided among the crew or donated to the next reunion.

"Labor day" reunions

How do children learn about parents', grandparents', and forebears' jobs or professions? How do they learn how others work and what they do to support and maintain their families? Work is part of family history. Families are built and sustained by work. But your children may not have a clear idea what a work day involves—for you or anyone.

Use your reunion as an opportunity for adults to celebrate the part of their lives that rarely includes children. Include fun tours that will educate them. Industrial/factory tours are generally available. Ever wonder how Tabasco sauce, Harley-Davidsons, or Levi's are made? Call up for a tour and go!

Potpourri of kids activities

Lively games and activities will keep kids engaged and interested in your reunion. Face painting, a piñata, or a puppet or magic show are all things that will involve kids quickly. One reunion organizer took kids to a gym with a rock-climbing wall for building teamwork and confidence. She reports that an introductory lesson and one-day pass were much cheaper than a theme park.

Wash day relay race. According to Cynthia Lee Adams, the Barnett Family Reunion has a range of active, shy, and special-needs children. This is a game that involves all of them. String a clothesline between two trees. Form two lines with an equal number of older and younger children in each. The first child gets a clothes basket filled with a pair of pants, a shirt, socks, and clothespins. The child runs to the clothesline, pins up the clothes, runs back, and hands the next child the empty clothes basket. The second child runs to the clothesline, takes the clothes down, puts them in the basket, and brings the basket to the next person. Clothes are alternately hung and taken down until everyone gets a turn even when one line finishes first. Have assistance available at the clothesline to help the small and special-needs children. Every child gets a prize but the winning team gets theirs first.

The kids take something special home from each Woodworth Family Reunion. One year it was bubbles, a helium balloon, crayons, and a custom-made *Woodworth Family Reunion Coloring and Activity Book*. The family's reunion is held at the Jack Tone Ranch in Stockton, California, famous for its Arabian horses, a location which generated a cowboy theme for the coloring book.

Crafts. Many families provide arts and crafts activities for kids. These should be planned well in advance of the reunion date since most include supplies.

Some families buy crafts kits for kids; others simply collect materials. Crafts are great for rainy days as well as on very hot days when kids may need to be a little less active.

Do crafts that will provide a lasting memory. For example, have the kids sculpt clay figures of family members. Or take Polaroid pictures that the kids will make and decorate cardboard frames for. Have them paint rocks collected from a hike in the woods or paint squares for a quilt, or make and trade friendship bracelets or lanyard jewelry. And there are always watercolors, crayons, and lots of paper or cloth.

Here are more complicated crafts to try. Make old candle remnants into reunion candles; dip wicks for tall tapers or fill cans for pillars. Tie-dye, paint, or sew grandma's buttons on T-shirts.

Joyce Wolfe of Nanty Glo, Pennsylvania, reports that kids at the Bichko Family Reunions have made sand designs in corked bottles, autographed T-shirts, and decorated sun visors, bookmarks, and cards and envelopes with rubber stamps.

Intergenerational activities. Reunions make it easy to mix young and old in sharing time together in a number of ways, including the following:

- *Cooking.* Churn butter, crank ice cream, hand down recipes and techniques. Ethnic cooking takes on new meaning as the younger generation gives it a try with help from the experts.
- *Fishing.* Anglers, share your best tricks and secrets.
- *Quilting, knitting, tatting, crocheting, sewing.* Busy fingers—and tongues—bring traditions alive.
- *Singing (or strumming).* Everyone's got a song in their heart.
- *Whittling.* Produce sawdust as well as something useful.
- *Exploring hiking trails.* All the while talk about your own family migration.
- *Playing games.* Aren't there family favorites you'd like the grandkids to learn?
- *Storytelling.* Legends, yarns, and tall tales all get a hearing at reunions. Shared stories become a priceless legacy.

Silent auction. Instead of bidding money, kids answer questions in the silent auction devised by Anna M. Miller for her family reunion. Some of her questions were:

- What do I like best about my dad?
- What can I do to help an older person?

- What three things will I do for my family next week, and why do I want to do them?
- What makes my mother special?
- What do I like best about Grandpa?
- Why do I like to go to Grandma's house?
- What funny experiences do I remember involving a relative (or relatives)?
- What would I like to do at the next family reunion?

Younger children may need adult help to write a bid (answer a question).

Enforce time limits for writing bids and for judges to reach their decisions. An auctioneer states auction rules, presents questions, and announces judges' decisions. Judges may include parents, grandparents, aunts, uncles, or cousins; five is a good number. There must be at least one prize for each child, and once all prizes are awarded, swapping is encouraged.

Nourishing the nurtured. Even if featured food isn't homemade, an ice cream social can be an event. Prepare an ice cream smorgasbord, with lots of flavors and topping choices including hot fudge, butterscotch, seasonal fruits, marshmallows, nuts, chocolate jimmies, cherries, and, to crown it all, whipped cream. Create a clown face on a scoop of ice cream and place the cone on top for a hat. "Grow" ice cream gardens: Fill plastic cups with dark chocolate ice cream (to look like dirt), top with sprinkles, and insert a green straw; then freeze until firm. Construct a blossom out of gumdrops and toothpicks and attach.

Or tailor bread making to your origins, producing cornbread, tortillas, nan, soda bread, challah, or focaccia. Kids can get covered in flour and knead and knead.

Put kids in charge of making tablecloths. Markers, poster paint, and 10 feet of wide paper (available at party goods stores) are the basics. Decorate hand- or footprints and autograph.

Recipes. Try these special "recipes" for kids, with adult supervision, of course.

Finger paints

½ cup cornstarch
1 envelope unflavored gelatin
¾ cup water
½ cup dry detergent
Food coloring (various colors)

Prepare unflavored gelatin as stated on package. Set aside. Dissolve cornstarch in ¾ cup water over medium heat until thick. Add dry detergent and mix well. Combine with gelatin. Divide into smaller portions, and stir in food coloring. Store in covered containers.

Soap bubbles

4 cups of water
8 tablespoons liquid detergent
4 tablespoons glycerine
1 small bottle of commercial bubbles
2 teaspoon sugar

Mix all ingredients. Expect laughter, fun, and smiles.

Balloon arch

Gather 11-inch balloons, a fishing line, wide clear packing tape, and helium. For a weekend reunion, have the helium tank delivered by Friday afternoon (many helium supply companies are closed on Saturdays). Make sure the tank is picked up the following Monday to avoid additional rental charges.

Tape one end of the fishing line securely to the floor at the spot where you want your arch to begin. Ask for a volunteer to hold the fishing line spool while you inflate balloons.

Tie the inflated balloon knot around the fishing line where you secured the line. Continue tying balloons to the line, and watch your arch take shape. Helium-filled balloons cause the formation to rise naturally. Once balloons are tied to the line, they'll slide easily for better placement. When your arch reaches the desired height and width, tape the other end securely to the floor. Make sure the balloons are evenly placed, allowing them to touch gently. The arch will appear to float in space because the fishing line is practically invisible.

Tailor-made programs

One effortless way to provide reunion activities and entertainment for kids is to choose a site that caters to your youngest members. Rocking Horse Ranch in Highland, New York, offers the Wild Buckaroo Day Camp program for ages four to twelve. The Wigwam Resort in Litchfield Park, Arizona, offers Camp Pow Wow for kids five and up. The Splash Club at Loews Beach Hotel, Santa Monica, California, is an on-site day camp for kids from five to twelve. Crystal Mountain Resort in Thompsonville, Michigan, offers Camp Critters (ages three to five), Camp Crystal (ages six to twelve), Piglet's Place Nursery (ages three and under), and Pooh's Mountain Midgets (ages three and four). Sunrise Resort in Moodus, Connecticut, offers kids countless activities in three age ranges from three to seventeen as well as a mentoring program where teens help with four- to seven-year-olds. Camp Cookie at the Doubletree Hotel at Lincoln Center, Dallas, Texas, is geared toward kids twelve and under.

Reunion day camp

Lucy Sankey Russell describes a do-it-yourself day camp, Cousins Camp, at the Russell Family Reunion. Cousins ages four to thirteen were divided into four groups meeting in the morning, with adults sharing the supervision duties.

Chickadees (six to eighteen months) played, napped, and enjoyed walks in strollers. Sparrows (three- and four-year-olds) hiked, explored, picked blueberries, did arts and crafts, and practiced "I'm a Little Teapot" for the talent show. Cardinals (seven- and eight-year-olds) fished, hiked, went boating, and used a telescope. Kingfishers (ten- to thirteen-year-olds) golfed, fished, and set up a family Olympics obstacle course.

Memorials and Worship

Solemn business is conducted at reunions as memorials, commemorations, and worship services are incorporated into the schedule.

Make your tribute special. Along with retracing milestones, choose songs, readings, or excerpts from letters to read. The ceremony may include music, an honor guard for veterans, or a simple wreath laying accompanied by a prayer. Whatever form the memorial takes is not as important as that it honors the memory of the deceased.

Alva L. Kennedy of Charleston, South Carolina, describes how the Roberts Family Reunion Round-Up featured a special memorial service at Lake Junaluska, North Carolina. Children ages four to twelve, dressed in white shirts and dark slacks or skirts, honored deceased relatives by each placing a white carnation at the altar of the Memorial Chapel by the Lake.

A memorial service is a regular tradition of the Allen Family Reunion, whose attendees light candles in memory of deceased family members and recall an impressive family history traceable back to the 1700s.

Memorial services are generally held during the day. For a change, consider a candlelight evening service. If the service is scheduled near a monument, light the way with votive candles in holders. Also have each member carry a candle or flashlight.

At Sunday Mass, nine huge candles representing each family unit lit the altar draped with their best hand-crocheted cloth at the Bellerose Family Reunion in Montbeillard, Quebec. Each scripture reading was specially chosen and the music led by cousins. The children of the third generation hung cut-out paper doves from a corner birch tree.

Sunday Mass at the Treacy Family Reunion was a sea of green T-shirts. A graveside service later that day included holy water from an Irish shrine.

Ross Gordon Gerhart III of Ambler, Pennsylvania, reports that descendants of Johann Peter and Elisabeth Schmidt Gerhart assemble annually at Christ German Reformed Church at Indian Creek, Franconia Township, Pennsylvania. The Gerhart Family Reunion Choir provides music for the service, and then invites the congregation to refreshments and fellowship afterward. An all-afternoon picnic follows, with games, family history activities, and a memorial program.

A Saturday evening banquet at the Owens Family Reunion featured a memorial service while on Sunday everyone attended the church where forebears George and Malinda Owens worshiped before them and where the couple's grandson preached.

The four-day Jolly Family Reunion culminates in a traditional Sunday "blessing of our family," according to Bonnie L. Graham of Lawrence, Kansas. Catherine W. Ockey reports that the culminating event of the weeklong Wheelwright Family Reunion was a church service where the hymns they sang "were in harmony with the beautiful world around them."

Reunion Meetings

Reunion business meetings are a necessary part of the program. Check the suggestion box before the meeting for discussion possibilities. During the meeting, be sure to recognize and publicly thank those who helped with the reunion. Now's the time to discuss the date, place, and frequency of future reunions and to enlist volunteers to work on the next one. Patricia Atkins of Round Lake, Illinois, reports that her Hamblin Family Reunions choose their next chairperson at the family reunion business meeting.

In addition to the treasurer's report and items listed above, some families also feature speakers; awards and presentations; and official announcements of births, graduations, honors, marriages, milestones, promotions, and retirements. The business meeting may also be a time to memorialize those who have passed on.

Families who are incorporated are required to hold annual meetings. Reunions are the perfect place for this, since you can expect the largest number of members to be present.

Kudos, Citations, Proclamations, and Greetings

Plan ahead to include public recognition of your family at your reunion. Tyrone Dumas welcomed his McNair/Brazil/Scott Family Reunion to Milwaukee, Wisconsin, with greetings on behalf of the people of Wisconsin from the governor, mayor, and county executive.

Among the many ways to honor your group is soliciting such citations. Who do you want to acknowledge your family and your reunion? the mayor? the governor? senators? congressional representatives? the president of the United States? All possible. All doable.

Here's how. Carefully craft a letter to solicit a proclamation. Include information to prepare the proclamation in this initial correspondence. Introduce your family and reunion—what's special about them? Include the date, place, and number expected. Allow plenty of lead time; six months is not too much.

Food

Families breaking bread together is a universal tradition. Meals provide continuity as well as help establish warm relationships. Food brings people together, giving them a chance to share their lives.

No matter the fare—from homey potluck to catered fare to formal banquets—meals comprise an integral part of reunions. Maybe that's because mealtime is also family time—a chance to share thoughts, news, and stories.

None of Grandma Floy Kincaid Page's five children or eleven grandchildren who ever attended a family reunion in Morgantown, North Carolina, could eat her goulash without thinking of her in the bright yellow kitchen where pound cake was always available and something was always cooking on the stove, according to Malina Wilderson Belvins of Mechanicsville, Virginia.

Hamburger hot dish is a forty-year Dotzenrod Family Reunion tradition. Diana Dotzenrod Fitch of Burr Oak, Iowa, says the recipe is easily adaptable to lower-fat meats. Best of all, leftovers improve with age—though after Dotzenrod reunions, there are no leftovers.

Passing a basket of muffins at a reunion often has a magical effect. Older family members share stories of how their mothers made bread, as far back as cooking in an open fireplace with a peat-fueled fire.

Providing reunion food does not have to mean do-it-yourself, of course. Many families would rather have meals served and spend time visiting. A catered meal, especially if the gathering is in a rented hall, makes things simple for everyone. If you choose catering, get costs in writing to include in your fees and announcements.

At Seideman Family Reunions, refreshment stands provide food for members and profit for the reunion. Hamburgers and bratwurst, ice cream, candy, snacks, beer, and soda are sold.

Pauline Bizette Brandy reports how the Lambert Family Reunion in Innis, Louisiana, contacted friends to act as amateur caterers. Coordinators for each family branch estimated attendance for a head count to set a price for the menu, which included grilled or barbecued chicken and pork, salad, sweet potatoes, and rolls. Members brought desserts.

Other families prefer to meet at a restaurant. Check the possibility of a buffet meal or of offering guests only two or three menu choices.

As for beverages between meals, many families set up a keg of beer, cases of soda, and a pot of coffee, if electricity is available. Lemonade and iced tea are also popular. Don't forget disposable cups and ice.

Reunions lasting several days often combine options. Whatever you plan, be sure your invitation includes the arrangements, costs, and other details.

PICNICS AND POTLUCKS

Americans are famous for picnics—in backyards, on beaches, at parks. Picnics have long been a favorite for summer gatherings. It seems that when families grew and moved apart, the picnic became the highlight of a visit home, and before long the picnic became a reunion.

Here are some practical ideas for dining al fresco.

- Eating outdoors doesn't have to mean roughing it. Pick garden flowers and herbs for color and scent. Use plastic tableware but consider an elegant white linen tablecloth and serve food in attractive bowls.

- Use tiny silver frames for placecards. Ask each member to select from photos of "the good old days" placed in a centerpiece tray.

- Have a rain plan. Reserve a pavilion site or rent a tent if you're picnicking in the park.

- Clean the garage if you're picnicking at a private home.

- Defy the wind. Fill a vase with marbles or pebbles before putting in flowers. Place something heavy on each of the four corners of the tablecloth or use tablecloth holders, widely available at variety and dime stores.

- Use, rent, or borrow a long table rather than lining up mismatched card tables. Place serving tables in the shade.

- Use votives or hurricane lamps for candles.

- Don't forget ice! And remember, ice cream requires dry ice to stay cold. Try freezing beverage ice cubes with surprises in them: mint, berries, slivers of citrus zest.

- Discourage uninvited flying guests. Citronella candles work well at controlling bugs if you don't want to use sprays. Or pass around soothing repellent.

Carlotta Levesque Campbell describes her family's reunion picnic in Lincoln Park, Chicago, Illinois:

Thank heaven for those huge shade trees. They managed to keep our area twenty degrees cooler than the rest of the park. Everyone brought a dish. Grills were lined up on one side and tables on the other. Big tubs of pop and other drinks were bathing in ice. There was so much joy and love around, you couldn't help but have a good time.

Potlucks with a wealth of unique casseroles and delectable desserts, not to mention the ever-present specialty potato salad, are always popular for reunions. If you want leftovers for a second meal, ask people to bring a main dish and a salad or dessert, and be sure to arrange for enough coolers and ice to avoid spoilage.

As "food forums," nothing can beat a family reunion. The competitive edge shows as family cooks try to outdo one another. And because every potluck inspires requests for recipes, request that cooks bring their recipes along. You may want to collect recipes to compile in a family cookbook or include them in your newsletter.

* * *

✳ *Theresa R. Harris of Birmingham, Alabama, describes how a gigantic fruit salad assembled at the reunion allows everyone "to enjoy time together getting to know each other and keep little hands occupied." Everyone participates, and a family ritual is remembered with the sweetness of the fruit it provides. The goal is to create a work of consumable family art. Each family is assigned one ingredient to bring—a large watermelon, cantalopes, honeydew melon, kiwis, strawberries, pineapple, chopped pecans, and poppy seed dressing. Assembly is a part of the reunion fun. Young children can seed and make melon balls, remove strawberry stems, and break pecans into pieces. Older children can peel and slice kiwi and pineapple and carve the watermelon hull. Take turns tossing the delectable mix with dressing.*

* June M. Entwistle of Treasure Island, Florida, says that chili is always a favorite at her family's reunion cookouts. As years passed, their original "blow your mind" recipe was modified to address weight problems, high blood pressure/cholesterol levels, and food allergies. Today's turkey chili is certifiably nonlife threatening.

* Karen Naedler of Hopatcong, New Jersey, planned a simple menu for her reunion's picnic: hot dogs; hamburgers; corn on the cob; gallons each of olives, pickles, and hot peppers; and a sheet cake that read Cousins Connection. A pizza parlor heard about the reunion and donated four dozen hoagie rolls. Naedler's sister-in-law was unstoppable, making a huge pot of sauce and eighty meatballs for delicious hoagie sandwiches.

* The highlight of one Paque Family Reunion was a "Spanferkel," or pig roast. Do it yourself or hire a caterer to prepare and deliver to the reunion.

* Elinor Nuxoll of Spokane, Washington, bakes an oven full of potatoes ahead of time, totes them along, and uses them for various dishes for several reunion meals.

* Judith L. Weber of Greenfield, Iowa, reports that every Weber Family Reunion gathers around a table laden with dozens of delicacies. Four ambitious Weber ladies compiled 750 recipes from descendants of Johann Conrad (J. C.) Weber into the Weber Family Cookbook. Using profits from cookbook sales, a reunion was planned around the recipes. Dishes, including fruit sticks and Pennsylvania Dutch-style green beans, were prepared and served by a caterer along with fourth-generation Weber and cookbook committee members. Each recipe was identified by name and cookbook page number. Grandma Weber's sugar cookies were served with dandelion wine for afternoon tea accompanied by Bavarian music.

* Joan E. Ebacher of Richmond, Indiana, shares her successful menu for Ebacher/Scholtens Family Reunions. For the final countdown, helpers assemble precooked and sliced pork loin, dressing, scalloped corn, sauerkraut with bacon, and green beans. Dessert pies, watermelon, and fruit salad are brought by reunion guests. Children are enlisted to set and decorate tables and gather chairs.

* For many, nothing beats fresh fish for a memorable reunion meal. Baked or grilled fish keeps calories and fat to a minimum and healthy, tasty eating to a maximum. Suzanne Deats of Albuquerque, New Mexico, remembers her Uncle Glen cooking freshly caught catfish at a 1944 reunion at her granddaddy's birthplace, Reynolds Bend, Texas. Over fifty years later, Deats remembers the noise the fish made in the fryer, the smell of them cooking, and the feel of the gritty cornmeal coating in her mouth.

✱ *Meals figure prominently at the four-day Robbins Family Reunion every four years. Most are potluck and include regional food; the centerpiece of the reunion in Maryland was a crab feast. Regional food always makes the hosts feel special. Here's an idea Robbins suggests: One night let parents have dinner out, while children and grandchildren cook out and visit. The next night, switch places and have the children go out to eat together.*

✱ *Family reunions are a long-standing tradition for the descendants of John and Clara Fehringer, who reconnect on the plains of western Nebraska to celebrate their heritage. Teresa L. Wolff says some of her earliest memories are of "aunts cookin' up a mess of roast beef, mashed potatoes, and that deep brown gravy that only comes from slow roasting the meat to well-done perfection." A big hit was always Grandma's raisin-filled cookies, baked and brought now by her oldest daughter, Sister Esther Fehringer. Reunions start on Friday evenings when hamburgers work well because they're cooked to order as people arrive. At one reunion, husbands of three cousins hosted Italian Night, dressed in Chef-Boy-Ar-Fehringer costumes. Each family unit is responsible for providing one meal, including cleanup.*

✱ *Make cleanup an assigned task so you know who will be responsible. Cleanup is a good time to help, especially for kids. Make it into a game by timing them or offer treats or prizes for jobs well done. Include recycling in your cleanup plans.*

DESSERTS

Loretta Sadler of Harrodsburg, Kentucky, reports that the Sheperson Family Reunion ranging from ninety-year-old Sam to the newest baby, annually bakes up reunion spirit with a theme. For a hillbilly reunion, the special cake was a moonshine still complete with jugs. When they went Hawaiian, a long sheet cake represented a white beach with hula dancers and swaying palm trees. There were *eight* cakes the year the Shepersons celebrated trains; seven boxcars, trimmed with Sam's and his siblings' names, trailed the "parental" engine.

A reunion cake tip for smaller families comes from Ruby Sims of Ocean Springs, Mississippi. A round cake decorated with a tree, family name, and images of forebears is centered atop a sheet cake that lists the first names of descendants.

Doris Vaughan of Columbus, Wisconsin, provides "Our Flag Pie Cake" for the Michel Hoover Family Reunion during election years or when a family member comes home from or is going into the military. At annual Bernard Family Reunions, Anne Farnese of Philadelphia, Pennsylvania, bakes a big batch of butterscotch brownies called "blondies" to remember her Aunt Hilda, whose baked goods were legendary; before she died, Hilda entrusted Anne with the recipe. Wilma Cook Collins of Phoenix, Arizona, has attended family reunions in Oklahoma since 1954, where peach or blackberry cobblers are a must.

SHARING THE COOKING

Some of the best reunion fun, says Jacalyn Eis, who cooks for the Eis Family Reunion, is preparing meals together. The best recipe is one that gets the family together to have a good time. Every reunion, the Eis family makes sure to include everyone and mixes groups by age and gender. Eis cautions, however, to designate one person to shop for basic supplies (napkins, paper towels, salt, pepper), with funds from the treasurer. Ask attendees to bring extra coolers, barbecue grills, and sharp knives.

Do yourself a favor and prepare a list of cooking teams and menus for each day. Choose one energetic organizer for each day's cooking team and avoid cliques in putting teams together. Post cooking team lists on a central bulletin board and in the kitchen. Also announce the teams at the first family meeting. For bigger reunions, post lists of contents on refrigerators: breakfast supplies in one, fruits and vegetables in another, meat and milk in still another. Display menus for all meals prominently in the kitchen, with a shopping list and pencil near the next day's menus. Direct the last person who uses up a food item to add it to the shopping list.

Each team should meet in advance to decide how they will organize the assigned meal, that is, starting time, cooking tasks, and choosing someone to check supplies. The designated shopper should check supplies and review the shopping list, then get money from the treasurer or save receipts for reimbursement. Cooking teams only cook main meals. Provide breakfast (cereal, milk, eggs) and lunch ingredients (sandwich makings, fruit, and potato chips) for everyone to prepare their own.

MENUS

Keep menus simple. Avoid meals that require elaborate written recipes. Or consider partially cooked or precooked meals. Pizza the first night is easy.

Sample menus include:

- Pizza, salad, vegetable.

- Spaghetti (use ready-made sauce), tossed salad, garlic bread.

- Canned ham, baked potatoes, vegetable, rolls.

- Grilled steaks, burgers, hot dogs, corn-on the-cob, salad.

- Baked turkey, mashed potatoes, gravy (from mix), fruit salad.

- Roast chicken, baked beans (canned), vegetable, cole slaw.

Reunion home cookin' can be done, according to Anna M. Page, who cooked for thirty for the Barnes Family Reunion. First, she advises, analyze your facilities and equipment. List equipment you have and what you'll need to prepare the type and amount of food you're planning. Most of us don't have freezer or oven space to accommodate large groups.

Arrange the menu in detail before the reunion. Plan each meal with contrasts of color, texture, flavor, and consistency in mind. Nutritionally, an ideal meal includes an entrée, grain product, and two fruits and/or vegetables, but don't worry about making sure every single meal is perfectly balanced. Plan on leftovers and fit a leftover meal in after several days of planned meals.

Home recipes can easily be modified for larger groups. Check the number of servings and multiply by two, three, or whatever you need to produce the appropriate yield.

Don't double or triple dessert recipes, however. Provide a variety of desserts and let people choose. Make cookies and bars ahead and freeze. Pies are quick with prepackaged crusts and canned fillings. Avoid desserts, such as homemade ice cream, that require refrigeration.

A trip to the wholesale club may inspire ideas. Frozen lasagna is more expensive than home cooked but beats the price of catering. Remember to read serving sizes carefully because they may not be realistic for your family; Page says her family eats significantly more than suggested serving sizes. Consider that large institutional-size (#10) cans each contain 12 to 13 cups, yielding approximately twenty to twenty-five servings, compared to home-size cans which yield four to five servings. Beverages sold in larger containers list amounts in ounces. A standard beverage serving size is 8 ounces. Realistically, calculate 12 ounces per serving.

Prewashed and cut vegetables such as baby carrots require no preparation, are nutritious, and are (almost) universally loved. Ditto for prepackaged tossed salads. Frozen vegetables require minimal preparation, and fresh fruits require none.

Don't forget to involve the kids. Mix and freeze a batch of sugar cookies beforehand to bring to the reunion. When kids get bored, get them started frosting and decorating the (thawed) batch. They'll be busy for at least an hour—and also provide more munchies for guests.

CAMPING FOOD

Outdoor writer and reunion fan Larry Polenske has these cooking suggestions for families who are camping: First off, make cooking for a large number of campers manageable by keeping things simple and sharing preparation. A campground with electrical hookups will make the job easier. Portable appliances (electric griddles, crock pots, coffee makers, even microwave ovens) can then be brought along to speed things up.

Chicken and ribs or burgers and brats are not only easy to grill but also satisfy the heartiest appetite. Plus they can be cooked ahead and kept warm in roasters.

Instead of trying to cook all the meat at one campsite, assign each campsite one menu item to prepare. Prepared food is then brought to a central location and placed in warming trays or roasters.

Alternatively, skip cooking altogether and have a caterer deliver meals. Many caterers have special menus ideal for open-air eating. For a Western theme, one caterer dressed cooks and servers like cowboys. They cooked gigantic burgers on a huge grill, handed out straw cowboy hats, and took pictures of guests standing next to cardboard cutouts of John Wayne and Clint Eastwood. Prepared food can also be picked up from caterers and served by members.

A departure-day group breakfast is a great way to end your camping reunion. Pancakes and sausage are quick and easy. Use grandma's old sourdough or buttermilk pancake recipe if you must, but a standard commercial mix is easier. One person mixing and two stationed at electric griddles can serve piping-hot pancakes in assembly-line fashion. A pastry potluck, meanwhile, requires no cooking. Each family brings its favorite coffee cake, cinnamon rolls, or doughnuts to share. Add coffee and fruit and breakfast is complete, with virtually no dishes to do.

HOTEL FOOD

The Bodtke Family Reunion package included an open bar and meals at Club Cozumel Caribe. Seven of the sixteen family members are strict vegetarians. "Actually, the Mexican cuisine is very conducive to a vegetarian diet," says Kendall Pusey Bodtke. "We worked out our menus on arrival."

Bill Masciangelo, former reunion coordinator for ITT Sheraton, suggests that good communication with the hotel's catering and beverage manager not only saves costly mistakes but also will make your reunion go more smoothly. Menu choices, number of courses, and service type (buffet style, sit-down) are important aspects of meal planning. Work closely with hotel caterers. They're up-to-date on trends—what works and what doesn't. Be prepared to inform them of your group's preferences and its budget.

In-House Dining

Most hotels require that you use their catering services. Menu options are plentiful and can be tailored to suit your needs. If the hotel cannot provide your desired menu, ask the sales manager or catering director to recommend an outside caterer.

Events at your reunion that call for food to arrange with hotel staff include a welcoming reception, breakfasts, lunches and dinners, memorial brunch, coffee/refreshment breaks, dinner dance, banquet, and picnic. Each of these requires detailed planning. Items such as count guarantee (required forty-eight hours before the event), theme, decorations, music, type of bar, seating arrangements, and cost must be considered. The most important and time-consuming event to arrange is the banquet/dinner dance, often held Saturday or the last night.

Reunion banquet checklist

- Identify the purpose of the reunion event: banquet only, awards banquet, dinner/dance, dinner/talent show.
- Select food service type: buffet style, sit-down, hors d'oeuvres, or dessert only.
- Many places offer a choice of entrées; if so, on the invitation, let attendees know they'll need to make a selection ahead of time. According to Paula Sheagley of Canon City, Colorado, if you can't decide whether to serve beef or chicken, many catering directors are willing to serve a "combination plate." In any case, sample the menu before the reunion.
- Set a schedule. Do you want a reception before food is served?
- Arrange for speakers and entertainment.
- Establish waiter-to-table ratio, which affects service speed.
- Determine what bar type best suits your needs—open, cash, or tickets—and inquire about liquor regulations.

- To establish a price, include tax, gratuities, insurance, bar setup, decorations, favors, and rental costs. Having attendees pay when they send in reservations is easier than trying to figure out who owes what the night of the banquet. The hotel manager can help. Also ask how to handle last-minute guests or no-shows.

Private as well as hotel caterers often provide extra services, such as equipment rental, decorations, linen, china, silverware, and entertainment and transportation services. They also offer special prices; for example, one hotel waives the rental fee with 250 catered meals on a Saturday night and 150 meals Sunday through Friday.

CATERING

Plenty of caterers know from experience the ins and outs of catering reunions. Some can organize every detail for you, from food to furniture and space to put it all in. The most commonly catered reunion events are buffets, picnics, and formal sit-down dinners or banquets. However, even if your reunion is at a private home, a caterer can supply a fabulous meal for every taste and style.

It's a good idea to consult a caterer before committing too much of your budget to any facility. Caterers can often help you arrange for a banquet hall or reunion site at a better price.

A full-service catering company is therefore a good place to begin your planning. Michael Goetzinger of Black Tie & Catering, Milwaukee, Wisconsin, prides his business on personal service. He will organize everything from site selection to decorations, florist, bartender, and band. Other rentals that caterers handle are tables, chairs, tents, or special equipment to make espresso, popcorn, helium balloons, or snowcones.

You can expect professional caterers to serve innovative foods with fresh, quality ingredients. In most cases, restaurant-quality meals are prepared on site. If your reunion is outdoors or you do not have access to a kitchen, food may be prepared in a mobile facility equipped with burners, grills, and warming units.

You may order catered food with or without service. Certainly one convenience of a catered reunion event is bar service. Many caterers subcontract bartenders and order liquor on consignment.

Linda Farland of Lettuce Off-Premise Catering, Chicago, Illinois, creates savory picnics. Menus range from Mexican fajitas and Jamaican drunken beans to Chicago-style bratwurst and hot dogs. Each menu can be adjusted in size and selection. Prices anywhere from $12 to $20 per person include the chef, equipment, disposable ware, linens, and a transport trucking fee. Tables, chairs, tax, and gratuity are extra.

For reunions of 150 people or less, Lettuce Off-Premise Catering can serve on *Chicago's First Lady*, a private yacht that cruises Lake Michigan or the Chicago River. Lettuce rents the yacht, arranges the entertainment, and customizes a meal tailored to your reunion.

A simpler, less-expensive, and universally available option is chicken from one of many specialty quick-service restaurants. For example, many KFCs now cater, deliver, and set up your reunion picnic. Call in advance to make arrangements.

Whatever your catering decision, there are important things to remember. Be prepared with accurate guest counts, dates and times, and know your budget. Communication is key. Convey your needs and desires in a clear, concise manner. Listen to suggestions. Ask questions. Work together. Be successful!

CELEBRATE FAMILY ORIGINS

Sharyn M. Kuneman suggests a United Nations theme as an exciting alternative to predictable potluck fare. Make a list of countries from which family members emigrated. List all countries on index cards, assign entrées or desserts, and send the cards off to members. Or you may want to assign different meals to different family units, so on Italian, Chinese, or Mexican night, everyone prepares a different dish.

Bean soup is an institution at annual Schwalm Family Reunions, which started around the turn of the century. Ann Cassar of Thornton, Pennsylvania, reports that attendance averages 350 people from all over the United States and Germany. A typical four-table picnic spread at one reunion included baked ham, ham salad, grilled chicken breast, ring bologna, venison bologna, meat loaf, cheese cubes, deviled eggs, baked beans, sliced tomatoes, macaroni salad, potato salad (German, of course), cucumber salad, raw vegetable platter, pickles, olives, pickled cabbage, pickled red beet eggs, pea salad, rolls, sandwiches, potato chips, grapes, cherries, blueberries, lemon fluff, strawberry delight, chocolate cake, angel food cake, and cherry pie. With so many culinary delights, why does the Schwalm family bean soup crew arise early to light wood fires to prepare two 85-quart kettles of bean soup, especially when the humidity and temperature can reach 90 degrees Fahrenheit in July? Because it's delicious, traditional—and reunion members count on it.

Descendants of the German Gabel brothers have met every August since 1922. Early in the morning, a tent kitchen, tables, and benches are set up.

Wherever they gather, after offering thanks, the food includes Pennsylvania Dutch bread and butter pickles.

Carmen Turner, a Key West city commissioner, reports a turnout of 518 at the Allen Family Reunion hosted by the family's Conch branch. The reunion featured "The Taste of Key West," a marvelous spread of home-cooked Key West and Bahamian foods served in a local park. Members sampled delights like crab and rice, conch fritters, pigeon peas with rice, souse, fried plantains, *picadillo* (Cuban ground beef), fried grunts, arroz con pollo, and other native foods.

The Simonic Family Reunion theme is based on their Slovenian heritage. Menus include lamb, pork, lemon chicken, sausage and sauerkraut, assorted vegetables and salads, and various desserts, including a nutroll, poppy seed rolls, and apple and cheese strudel.

Patricia L. Fry of Ojai, California, author of *The Mainland Luau: How to Capture the Flavor of Hawaii in Your Own Backyard*, offers a luau menu for 100 people that includes pineapple-shrimp *pupus*, salmon-stuffed cherry tomatoes, a veggie platter, roast pork, Hawaiian yams (cooked in the pit with the pig), fresh fruit bowl, crab rice salad, long rice (a hot dish), green salad with a sweet-and-sour Oriental dressing, and fruity island punch.

If you're having a luau, create a Hawaiian atmosphere. Ask guests to wear colorful Hawaiian-style attire. Display large potted plants, tubs of flowering trees, or bouquets of bird of paradise, cannas, iris, or bougainvillea. Also decorate with fishermen's net, wooden oars, large shells, an old boat, and Hawaiian travel posters. Supply Hawaiian music—live or recorded—and someone to teach the hula.

The African Hut in Milwaukee, Wisconsin, caters African cuisine from Kenya, Nigeria, and Tanzania, featuring imported ingredients, natural spices, and little red meat. Owner Yinka Adedokun creates meals that introduce his American customers to African culture. Ethnic catering like Adedokun's goes far beyond eating. It enlightens reunion goers by satisfying not only their appetite but also their curiosity about foods favored by forebears.

Preparing for Your Next Reunion

The wrap-up is the last stage of your reunion. Send news releases to the hometowns of individuals who received awards or special recognition during the reunion, since everyone likes to see their name in print. Do write thank-you notes to committee members and to hotel staff, vendors, or suppliers who did an outstanding job.

While you're still at your hotel or facility, pay all your bills and return borrowed equipment. Before you leave, make sure there are no unresolved problems. It's much easier to settle things in person than by letter or phone call.

You'll want to have collected data about the number of meals eaten in the hotel's restaurant and from room service, and the number of rooms used by your group. This information is invaluable in negotiating your next reunion by demonstrating the profit to the hotel. It is well worth the effort.

Tip the staff who deserve special consideration. Make it a point to write a letter to the hotel's general manager to recognize employees—by name—who did an outstanding job.

A crucial final step to all reunions is an honest, objective evaluation. Evaluation results should confirm what you observe during the reunion.

All the information you collect—positive and negative—will help you plan future reunions. Each reunion presents new challenges, and an evaluation prepares you with ideas and suggestions. In fact, remind everyone to share their opinions and observations every chance you get. Make it clear that the voice of each family member is important.

EVALUATION

The purpose of an evaluation is to help improve your next reunion. Be sincere about wanting to hear what people have to say. In your introduction to the evaluation form, stress that opinions and ideas are important to help plan future reunions. Ask members to be candid, assuring them that responses will be kept confidential. Be sure to indicate where to return completed evaluations.

It's best to get evaluations done on the spot. Collecting them before family members go home saves postage, and impressions are still fresh. Remember to include evaluations in reunion packets. To analyze results for reunions over 100 people, it is advisable to use a computer. The evaluation form should therefore not only be easy to complete but also to tabulate.

You'll want to be thorough and do two evaluations: one for attendees and one for committee members who helped organize the reunion. Following are two sample evaluations, one for each. Personalize them to fit your needs.

ATTENDEE EVALUATION

1. Is this the first time you attended the _____ reunion?
    Yes ____   No ____

2. How did you get to the reunion? Car ___ Airplane ___ Train ___ Bus ___
    Other _____

3. Were the instructions clear for getting to the
    A. City/location?   Yes ____ No ____
    B. Hotel/lodging?   Yes ____ No ____
    C. Reunion activities?   Yes ____ No ____

    If not, please explain. _____

    _____

    _____

4. How convenient was the location for you? Circle one:

Not at all		OK		Very convenient
1	2	3	4	5

5. How convenient was the date for you? Circle one:

Not at all		OK		Very convenient
1	2	3	4	5

6. Were fees for registration and events affordable? Circle one:

A. Registration fees were

Not at all		OK		Very affordable
1	2	3	4	5

B. Activity fees were

Not at all		OK		Very affordable
1	2	3	4	5

7. What was the best aspect about the reunion for you?

_____

_____

8. What was the most disappointing aspect of the reunion for you?

_____

_____

9. How likely are you to attend the next reunion? Circle one:

Not at all	Likely	Very likely	Definitely
1	2	3	4

If you circled 1–3, what would make you decide to come to the next reunion? _____

_____

10. What ideas do you have for the next reunion?

A. Site? _____

B. Activities? _____

C. Ways to improve? _____

11. Please rank each of the following (circle one):

	Awful		OK		Exceeded expectations
A. Room accommodations	1	2	3	4	5
B. Hotel services	1	2	3	4	5

	Awful		OK		Exceeded expectations
C. Food					
Quality	1	2	3	4	5
Portions	1	2	3	4	5
Variety	1	2	3	4	5
D. Activities					
Games	1	2	3	4	5
Tours	1	2	3	4	5
Lectures	1	2	3	4	5
Dances	1	2	3	4	5
Entertainment	1	2	3	4	5
E. Organization	1	2	3	4	5
F. Variety	1	2	3	4	5
G. Keepsakes/Memorabilia	1	2	3	4	5

12. How old are you?

    0–12 ___   13–19 ___   20–30 ___   31–45 ___   46–64 ___   65+ ___

13. Are you   Male? ____   Female? ____

14. Would you be willing to help organize the next reunion?

    Yes ___   No ___   Maybe ___

    If your answer is "yes" or "maybe," please complete the following:

    Name _____

    Phone _____

    Address _____

    _____

15. Additional comments:

    _____

    _____

    _____

    _____

    Thank you for your time and thoughtful responses.

    Please return this to: _____

COMMITTEE EVALUATION

1. Were working relationships supportive?

2. Did we start planning early enough? Were effective timelines set for completion of each important task?

3. Was the event well publicized? Were new members found and recognized?

4. How did registration go? Who attended? From where? Who did not attend? Why not? Compare with previous reunions. Are there trends?

5. Was the site effective? Did we adequately inform the hotel of all our requirements?

6. Were room layouts for events adequate?

7. Were we satisfied with audiovisual aids, seating, lighting, etc.?

8. Was there good support from the facility's departments: food and beverage, sales, reservations, front desk, bell service, etc.?

9. Were day-to-day operations satisfactory?

10. Did we have a sufficient number of people to cover everything?

Sandy Brass Jenkins, who reviewed the Jenkins Family Reunion, says that after all the hard work it is important to receive kudos along with constructive suggestions. Here are some reponses to a survey taken at the Jenkins Family Reunion.

Question: What was the funniest thing you experienced at the reunion?

Answers: The talent show. Singing "Happy Birthday" to Uncle James at the airport. Little Cousin Jamie "winning" the last musical chair from big Uncle Scott.

Question: What was your most exciting experience?

Answers: Uncle James and Aunt Jennie's family coming all the way from North Carolina to Phoenix. The anticipation of it all. Paper airplane and water balloon fight.

Question: What was the most important thing you learned at the reunion?

Answers: The power we have when we work together as an extended family. That family is *still* more important than anything else. We can all be different and still love each other.

Question: What was the best part of the reunion?

Answers: The blessing of being together. Loving. Going to church together and meeting afterward for family pictures.

Question: What could we do to bring our extended family closer together?

Answers: Start a kids' family letter—on cassette or videotape for those who don't write yet. Exchange children during the summer. Have more reunions.

The survey asked five questions, but a sixth response was recorded: "Meeting Jill, who was just a baby when we last saw her and now she's—a person!" Isn't that what family reunions are all about?

Glossary

R eunion organizers are usually volunteers dealing with professionals in the hospitality industry. It helps, then, to know the language of the industry. This glossary, adapted from *Reunions magazine*, was prepared by Joe Quade of Montville, New Jersey, to provide reunion organizers with the language they'll need to negotiate for accommodations and other services.

ACCOMMODATIONS

Amenities: complimentary items provided by a hotel for use by guests (bathrobes, toilet articles, writing paper, in-room coffee machines, irons, hair dryers, and occasionally, fruit baskets or chocolates).

Confirmation: notice sent by hotel to registrant confirming dates, type of room, and rate.

Corporate rate: the cost agreed to by prior arrangement between the hotel and an organization for a room.

Double: a room for two persons, with a queen or king-size bed.

Double-double: a room for two persons or a family, with two double beds.

Group rate: the cost for a room when a block of rooms has been contracted; always lower than rack rate and often lower than the corporate rate.

Occupancy rate: the total number of rooms occupied compared with the total number of rooms available; expressed as a percent. The higher the occupancy rate, the higher the room rate (high season). The lower the occupancy rate, the better the opportunity to negotiate favorable room rates (low or shoulder season).

Rack rate: the cost quoted to the general public for a room.

Room block: the number of rooms reserved for future use.

Suite: two or more connecting rooms, typically a bedroom and living room.

Twin: a room for two people, with two separate single beds.

EQUIPMENT

AV: audiovisual equipment, including slide and overhead projectors, VCRs, television, and other electronic equipment.

Lectern: A reading desk used by speakers to hold their speech or notes. May be floor or table model; usually equipped with reading light and microphone.

Podium: platform on which a speaker stands.

FINANCIAL

Cancellation clause: contract provisions that specify penalties for failure to meet terms of the contract.

Comp room rates: contract provision stating the ratio of complimentary rooms to the number of rooms contracted for and used. Industry standards vary from 1 to 25 to 1 to 50. It is desirable to calculate this on a cumulative rather than on a per-night basis.

Inclusive rate: the rate quoted, which includes taxes and gratuities.

Master account: the accounting form that lists and explains all authorized charges made by the reunion chairperson (or authorized persons) for services rendered or goods provided by the hotel.

Plus-plus: taxes and gratuities not included but added to the quoted price; usually shown as a percent.

FOOD AND REFRESHMENT SERVICE

À la carte: individual selections made from the menu.

American plan: per-day room rate that includes some meals.

Cash bar: when drinks are paid for in cash or by tickets by individuals as served.

European plan: per day room rate that does not include meals.

Full American plan (FAP): per-day room rate that includes three meals.

Hotel bar: public bar service at the hotel bar.

Modified American plan (MAP): per-day room rate that includes two meals, usually breakfast and dinner.

Open bar: when drinks are paid for by the host, sponsor, or organization; drink charges are made to the master account either per person, number of drinks served, or bottles opened.

Surcharge: an additional charge for special food provided or service rendered.

Table d'hôte: preset menu with limited choice per course.

Note: Open and cash bars are usually special setups in or near function or hospitality rooms. They are staffed by hotel bartending personnel and, if needed, a cashier.

MISCELLANEOUS

Americans with Disabilities Act (ADA): requires public buildings, including hotels and restaurants, to meet minimum standards in making their facilities accessible to physically challenged individuals.

Familiarization tour (FAM): an organized visit hosted by a convention bureau or hotel, usually with several members from a number of reunion organizations, to acquaint them with the area and available facilities; host provides lodging and meals and sometimes airfare.

Site inspection: a personal visit to a prospective reunion site to assess the property and its facilities as they relate to your reunion's needs. May be done by invitation or unannounced.

OPERATIONS

Cutoff dates: dates, designated in the contract, when the hotel will release rooms that have not been booked. Contract provisions can dictate that some of these rooms may be charged to the master account if they are not released by the reunion organization before the cutoff date.

Function sheet: a checklist detailing all your reunion's needs, including rooms to be used, registration, signage, security, food and beverage plans, room setups, audiovisual and other equipment needed. Review this document closely with the convention service manager.

Pre-con meeting: meeting of reunion committee and hotel personnel to go over final details of reunion activities for which the hotel is responsible; held just prior to arrival of reunion members.

Registration packet: collection of materials assembled for reunion members (program, agenda, schedule of events, maps, tickets for meals and tours, etc.).

Turnaround: time needed to rearrange a room from one physical setup to another.

PERSONNEL

Catering manager: hotel staff person responsible for all food and beverage functions contracted for your reunion.

Concierge: hotel staff person responsible for providing special guest services such as obtaining theater tickets and making tour or restaurant arrangements.

Convention service manager: hotel staff person assigned to your reunion as liaison to all involved hotel departments; the hotel's chief assistant to reunion organizers.

Sales director: head of hotel sales department; the person to whom sales managers report. Often involved in final contractual arrangements.

Sales manager: hotel staff person with whom initial contact is made and contractual arrangements developed.

Resources

Reunions magazine
P.O. Box 11727
Milwaukee WI 53211-0727
Phone: (414) 263-4567
E-mail: reunions@execpc.com
www.reunionsmag.com

STARTING A FAMILY ASSOCIATION

To learn more, call the IRS at 1-800-829-1040 to request Publication 557, *Tax-Exempt Status for Your Organization*; Form 1024, *Application for Recognition of Exemption*; and Form SS-4, *Application for Employer Identification Number*. Also read *Family Associations, Organization and Management: A Handbook* by Christine Rose, C.G., F.A.S.G.

Here are some public places to find information.

Colleges/universities

Federal law allows library or alumni association personnel to release information about current and former students, including address, phone number, major, date and place of birth, and dates of attendance.

Computer and Internet

Directories available on CD-ROMs generally provide telephone number; city, state, house, and apartment numbers; zip code; and name. The national telephone directories www.switchboard.com, www.four11.com, and www.look upusa.com supply names, addresses, and phone numbers of people who are "listed." The site www.lookupusa.com includes a map to the address.

County courthouses

Many records are available to the public. Check for birth, marriage, and death records; deeds; professional licenses; tax information; trial records; and voter registration.

Libraries

Public and specialized (genealogy, history) libraries have countless directories and searching sources. If you don't own a computer, most libraries can link you to Web sites or offer CD-ROM programs to help you search.

Post office

If you know a former address, it's possible to obtain a new one if a change-of-address was filed within the last eighteen months. Complete the post office's Freedom of Information request form. There may be a fee. At the Web site www.usps.gov, you can key in a city and get the zip code or key in a zip code and find out what city it matches.

Veterans administration

Any VA office will forward a letter to a veteran at his or her last known address. Include name, year and place of birth, military and other history you know, and names of parents. If the person is deceased, you will be notified. Next of kin can obtain complete military and medical records, including name; service number; birthdate; dates entered, discharged, or retired from service; promotions; assignments (units or ships); courts-martial, awards, and decorations; education level; pay; photograph, if available; and names of spouse and children.

WORKSHOPS AND CONFERENCES

Check *Reunions magazine* for regular updates of workshops and conferences. Often genealogy societies include family reunion planning in their conference programs. The following organizations have regularly sponsored conferences and classes:

Ione Vargus, Ph.D.
African American Family Reunion Conference
Family Reunion Institute
School of Social Administration
Temple University
Ritter Hall Annex
Philadelphia, PA 19122

Myra Quick
The University of Memphis
127 Fogelman Executive Center
Memphis, TN 39152

Patricia Liddell Researchers
P.O. Box 438652
Chicago, IL 60643

FUND-RAISING—MEMENTOS, SOUVENIRS, BUTTONS, T-SHIRTS

AAA Manufacturing
4500 N. Palafox St.
Pensacola, FL 32505
Phone: 1-888-200-4875
Web: www.aaamfg.com

Make your own souvenirs. Quality button machines, parts, and accessories.

AADCO Advertising
4250 Pacific Hwy., #108
San Diego, CA 92110-3218
Phone: (619) 222-2221

Quality military emblematic items such as patches, decals, pins, caps, T-shirts, cups, steins, pens, and plaques.

Aardvark Design & Screenprint
P.O. Box 613265
Dallas, TX 75261
Phone: 1-888-398-1600
Web: www.ardvarktee.com

Top-quality logos and silkscreening for T-shirts.

Atlanta Image Line
5315 Dividend Dr.
Decatur, GA 30035-3006
Phone: 1-800-320-5508

All printed apparel customized: T-shirts, caps, jackets. Art services available.

Badge-a-Minit
Box 800
LaSalle, IL 61301
Phone: 1-800-223-4103
E-mail: questions@badgeaminit.com
Web: www.badgeaminit.com

Make professional quality 2¼" buttons for your reunion. Free catalog and shipping.

Buttons by Bobby
P.O. Box 588
Bloomfield, NJ 07003-0588
Phone: 1-800-339-5107
E-mail: bobbedee@aol.com
Web: www.reunionbuttons.com

Reunion favors: No-to-low minimum quantities. Reunion buttons, T-shirts, caps, certificates. Family trees.

Civitella's Print Source Inc.
52 Center St.
Shelton, CT 06484
Phone: 1-800-441-6423
E-mail: Tnbig@aol.com

T-shirts.

Customized Creations
2297 Benning Dr.
Powell, OH 43065
Phone: (614) 889-5222
E-mail: rob@ccreations.com
Web: www.ccreations.com

Buttons and magnets. Design and manufacture.

Design Factory Tees
2173 Greenspring Dr.
Timonium, MD 21093
Phone: (410) 560-9800
E-mail: Rwaxman@aol.com

Dynamic Advertising Specialties
5031 56th Ave.
Hyattsville, MD 20781
Phone: 1-888-699-1232

Thousands of promotional products: mugs, key chains, buttons, pens.

Emblem & Badge Inc.
859 N. Main St.
Providence, RI 02904
Phone: (401) 331-5444
E-mail: sales@recognition.com
Web: www.recognition.com

Awards and recognition products. Free catalog.

Galapagos Studios Inc.
4172 Center Park Dr.
Colorado Springs, CO 80916
Phone: 1-800-932-5713
Web: www.galapagos-studios.com/reunion

Top-quality custom T-shirts.

Glass Mountain Co.
313 Cowell Ave.
Oil City, PA 16301
Phone: (814) 677-5147
E-mail: glassmt@mail.usachoice.net
Web: www.usachoice.net/glassmt

H. Ford Enterprises
8009 E. 117th Terr.
Kansas City, MO 64134
Phone: (816) 765-7122

T-shirts, hats, cups, mugs, jackets, pens, pencils, personalized items, golf shirts, sweatshirts. Embroidered and silk screen.

Marnex Products Co.
P.O. Box 08058
Cleveland, OH 44108
Phone: (216) 283-8883

Personalized items: T-shirts, caps, pencils, cups, mugs.

Marty McCormick & Associates Inc.
3775 40th Ln. South, #B
St. Petersburg, FL 33711
Phone: (813) 864-1406

Embroidered and screen-printed apparel.

Memphis Net & Twine
2481 Matthews Ave.
Memphis, TN 38108
Phone: 1-800-238-6380

Personalized T-shirts and caps. Free price list.

Passport International
1007 Johnnie Dodds Blvd.
Mount Pleasant, SC 29464-1225
Phone: 1-800-233-1225
Web: www.passprt.com

Screen-printed and embroidered T-shirts, sweatshirts, polos, caps, and tote bags personalized with any family name. Quantity discounts. Call for info.

Reunion Puzzles
P.O. Box 11727 PZ
Milwaukee, WI 53211-0727
Phone: (414) 263-4567

Custom-made porcelain puzzle; individual pieces are pins to be worn on lapel, tie, or dress. Minimum three-month advance orders essential. SASE for info.

Reunion Research
3145 Geary Blvd., #14
San Francisco, CA 94118
Phone: (209) 855-2101

Reunion stickers and custom-made crossword puzzles.

Temtec/Tempbadge Plus
100 Rt. 59
Suffern, NY 10901-4901
Phone: 1-800-628-0022
E-mail: Meetingprod@tempbadge.com

Buttons and name tags.

The Dak Company Inc.
1052 N.W. 3rd St.
Hallandale, FL 33009
Phone: 1-800-817-4491
E-mail: daki@hotmail.com

Custom-designed, imprinted mugs/glassware. Full-scale art department.

What's Nu? Inc.
1601 E. Oklahoma Ave.
Milwaukee, WI 53207
Phone: 1-800-736-9519

FUND-RAISING—PUBLISHING PROJECTS, MEMORY BOOKS, CALENDARS, COOKBOOKS

Anton & Company
3301 Veterans Dr., Ste. 203
Traverse City, MI 49684
Phone: (616) 935-0111
Web: www.northportbay.com

"The Castle"
126 Ocean Blvd.
Isles of Palms, SC 29451
Phone: 1-800-440-6023

Cookbook Publishers Inc.
P.O. Box 115920
10800 Lakeview Ave.
Lenexa, KS 66285-5920
Phone: 1-800-227-7282, (913) 492-5900
E-mail: info@cookbookpublishers.com
Web: www.cookbookpublishers.com

Free step-by-step kit.

Daily Memories
R.D. #2 Box 69
Bear Lake, PA 16402-9628
Phone: (814) 489-3123

Custom calendars for your family: 12 pictures, 365 special dates, low prices, free quotes, samples.

Family History Publishers
845 S. Main St.
Bountiful, UT 84010
Phone: (801) 295-7490

Fundcraft
P.O. Box 340
Collierville, TN 38017
Phone: 1-800-853-1363, 1-800-325-1994

Personalized cookbooks. Free family cookbook kit.

G&R Publishing
507 Industrial St.
Waverly, IA 50677
Phone: 1-800-383-1679
E-mail: gandr@gandrpublishing.com
Web: www.cookbookprinting.com

Custom cookbooks for reunions; preserve favorite recipes. Free cookbook guide.

Heritage Publications
P.O. Box 335
Church St.
Arkville, NY 12406
Phone: (914) 586-3810

Promoworks
P.O. Box 372
Yarmouth, ME 04096
Phone: (207) 781-0942

Family Favorites: a step-by-step guide to creating your family cookbook.

Ruth Press Inc.
P.O. Box 12293
Silver Spring, MD 20908
Phone: (301) 929-1535

Memoirs; preserve family history.

Walters Cookbooks
215 5th Ave. SE
Waseca, MN 56093
Phone: 1-800-447-3274

Quick and easy program to publish your own family cookbook.

REUNION PLANNERS

Carnevale & Associates
P.O. Box 1230
Sonoita, AZ 85637
Phone: (520) 455-5844
E-mail: carne@dakotacom.net

The Reunion Brat
4005 S. Ione St.
Kennewick, WA 99337
Phone: (509) 582-9304
E-mail: BratEmail@aol.com

GAMES

Conestoga Book Service
Box 7
West Willow, PA 17583
Phone: (717) 464-0963

Games: Questions and Ancestors and Table Talk.

Familytime Products Inc.
4071 Championship Ct.
Annandale, VA 22003
Phone: 1-888-547-8899
Website: www.generationsgame.com

Generations: The Game of Family Knowledge, a board game.

Talicor
8845 Steven Chase Ct.
Las Vegas, NV 89129
Phone: 1-800-433-GAME

Games: LifeStories, The UnGame, IceBreakers.

GENEALOGY DISPLAYS

Erie Landmark Company
4449 Brookfield Corporate Dr.
Chantilly, VA 22021
Phone: 1-800-874-7848

Time capsule, documents, and mementos; preserve your family history. Bronze and aluminum plaques for dedications and presentations.

Jane Brenner Family Trees
334 Pala Ave.
Piedmont, CA 94611
Phone: (510) 652-3035

Progeny Wall Charts
232 Main St.
Wolfville, Nova Scotia
Canada BOP 1XD
Phone: (902) 542-5147
E-mail: info@progenysoftware.com
Web: www.progenysoftware.com

Window In Time
4321 Laurelwood Way
Sacramento, CA 95864-0821
Phone: (916) 481-4234

An 8½" x 11" computer printout. Factual information for any year and date from 1900 to 1990.

Ye Olde Charts
P.O. Box 3188, Dept. R
Evergreen, CO 80437-3188
Phone: (303) 595-8003

Five- and ten-generation Family Fan Charts.

PRESERVING REUNIONS

Group Photo Systems
4815 E. Main St., Ste. 3
Mesa, AZ 85205
Phone: 1-800-556-7222
E-mail: info@gps8x10.com

Imagination Studio
2812 Tanglewood Dr.
Sarasota, FL 34239
Phone: (941) 922-9553

Ancestor photo reprints. Photos and documents restored.

Just Black & White
54 York St.
P.O. Box 4628
Portland, ME 04112
Phone: 1-800-827-5881

Copying, enhancement, and restoration of old family photographs. Request catalog and info.

Pearl Copy and Restoration
P.O. Box 7058
San Mateo, CA 94403
Phone: 1-800-874-7327

Point Marketing
P.O. Box 1242
Redlands, CA 92373
Phone: (909) 275-8165

Camcording Reunions for Profit, book and video. How to videotape, edit, produce, market, and sell reunion videos.

Vanlienden's Masterpiece Photography
1322 N. Tamiami Trail
Sarasota, FL 34236
Phone: (941) 951-6614
E-mail: vanlienden@aol.com

PRESERVING ON VIDEO

Gift of Heritage Video
P.O. Box 17233
Minneapolis, MN 55417
Phone: (612) 726-9432
E-mail: giftofheritage@worldnet.att.net
Web: www.giftofheritage.com

Demonstrates the process of creating your own family documentary.

Roots & Wings Life Stories
28402 Plantation Dr., N.E.
Atlanta, GA 30324-2966
Phone: (404) 816-6331
E-mail: audrey@rootswings.com
Web: www.RootsWings.com

Commissioned family histories on video and audio and in print. Video sampler available.

Trail Visions Video
5800 N. Ames
Glendale, WI 53209
Phone: (414) 228-1328

Reflective, entertaining videos to show at reunions. Combine with videotape of your reunion for a complete memorable souvenir. Ask for demo tape.

VIDEOCONFERENCING

Pellien Research
P.O. Box 17213
Alexandria, VA 22302
Phone: (703) 998-5250
E-mail: jpellien@bellatlantic.net
Web: http://members.bellatlantic.net/~jpellien/rr-leasing.htm.

CEMETERY MARKERS FOR VETERANS

Most veterans discharged under honorable conditions are eligible for a free marker. You'll need proof of military service as well as the soldier's name on a muster roll, a pension record, or extracts from state files. Federal or Confederate military service and pension records are in the national or state archives where the soldier enlisted. Confederate pension records are found in the state archives where a veteran applied for pension.

With proof of military service, you can ask Uncle Sam for one of the following: (1) a monument for a soldier's grave, (2) a memorial for a soldier whose remains aren't recoverable, (3) a plaque for a soldier's crypt. To order a plaque or an upright or flat monument, complete VA Form 40-1330: Application for Standard Government Monument, from Monument Services (42), Dept. of Veterans Affairs, 810 Vermont Ave., N.W., Washington, D.C. 20420.

Markers weigh about 230 pounds and are shipped free of charge but do not include installation costs. All markers remain federal property. Anyone with knowledge of a deceased veteran may apply for a monument, though only next of kin may apply for a memorial. Applicants must certify there's no privately placed marker already in place.

"LABOR DAY" REUNIONS

Boeing Aircraft, Seattle, Washington; (206) 655-2121.

Celestial Seasonings Tea Company, Boulder, Colorado; (303) 530-5300.

Crayolas, Binney and Smith, Two Rivers Landing, Pennsylvania;
   (610) 253-3758 (advance registration required).

Harley-Davidson Motorcycles, Milwaukee, Wisconsin; (414) 535-3666.

Levi Strauss Factory, San Francisco, California; (415) 565-9100.

The Lionel Train Visitors Center, Chesterfield, Michigan; (810) 949-4100.

Tabasco, Avery Island, Louisiana; 1-800-634-9599.

COMMEMORATIONS TO CELEBRATE YOUR ANCESTORS

The White House salutes reunions. Make your requests months in advance to assure that you will have greetings before you need them rather than after, which can be very disappointing. For greetings to your family, send request to Carmen Fowler, Room 91, The White House, Washington, D.C. 20500. Include reunion name, reunion purpose, date, and place, along with the name of a contact person. If your reunion will be celebrating a special birthday (over eighty) or wedding anniversary (over fifty years), provide details about the honorees and your reunion and send to Greetings Office, White House, 1600 Pennsylvania Ave., Washington, D.C. 20400.

How about a flag?
Flags flown over the Capitol building in Washington, D.C., are available to mark extra-special events for a small fee. Contact your representative or senator for instructions.

Family reunions cited in Wisconsin
One certificate for each fifth reunion of a Wisconsin family. Provide name of family; and number of reunion, reunion date and place; and name and address where certificate should be mailed. Send to Clifford Sweet, Wisconsin State Genealogical Society, Rt. 2, Box 210, N3854 Savage Rd., Brandon, WI 53919-9447.

Wisconsin Pioneer or Century Ancestors

The Wisconsin State Genealogical Society's Pioneer/Century Family Certificate Program recognizes families with Wisconsin roots. You must prove direct descent of settlers in Wisconsin prior to 1851 or, in the case of Century Ancestors, for 100 years preceding the date of application. Certificates cost $4 each. Send SASE to WSGS, P.O. Box 5106, Madison, WI 53705-0106.

Arizona Pioneers

Honors ancestors in Arizona before its statehood date, February 14, 1912. For the Children of Arizona Pioneers Certificate application, write to Joella Cheek, Pioneer Certification, HC29 Box 359, Prescott, AZ 86301.

Certificate of Chicago Ancestry

Great Migration certificates provided: 1901–1909 Old Settlers; 1910–1920 Great Migration. Contact Certification Program, P.O. Box 438652, Chicago, IL 60643-8652.

Arkansas Ancestry Grants Certificates

For descendants of Arkansas settlers. Territorial ancestors were residents before June 15, 1836; antebellum ancestors before May 6, 1861; nineteenth-century ancestors before December 31, 1900. Send SASE to Desmond Walls Allen, Arkansas Genealogical Society, 99 Lawrence Landing Rd., Conway, AR 72032.

Georgia Pioneers

Honors any direct descendAnt of settlers before 1826. Send SASE to Central Georgia Genealogical Society, P.O. Box 2024, Warner Robins, GA 31099-2024.

Hawaiian ancestry

An ancestry registry to identify and locate Hawaiians worldwide. Must be a direct descendAnt from a person of Hawaiian blood. Contact Kimberly Kau, Operation Ohana, 711 Kapiolani Blvd., Ste. 500, Honolulu, HI 96813; (808) 594-1960.

Idaho Pioneers

Certificates commemorate ancestors who settled in Idaho before July 3, 1890. Send SASE to Idaho Genealogical Society, 4620 Overland Rd., #204, Boise, ID 83705-2867.

Illinois Prairie Pioneer Certificates

These document early Illinois settlements prior to statehood, 1819–1850 and 1851–1880. Send SASE to Prairie Pioneer Chair, Illinois State Genealogical Society, P.O. Box 10195, Springfield, IL 62791-0195.

Forgotten settlers of Kansas

Territorial certificates for direct descendants of people who lived in Kansas prior to January 29, 1861. Pioneer certificates from 1861 to December 31, 1880; Early Settler certificates from January 1, 1881, and December 31, 1900. For surname search, send $2 and a #10 SASE to Kansas Council of Genealogical Societies, P.O. Box 3858, Topeka, KS 66604-6858.

Iowa Genealogical Society's Certificate Program

Honors ancestors who settled in Iowa by 1856 for a Pioneer Certificate, or more than 100 years prior to application for a Century Certificate. Write Certificate Program, Iowa Genealogical Society, P.O. Box 7735, Des Moines, IA 50322-7735.

First Families of the Twin Territories (Pioneer and Indian families of Oklahoma or Indian Territories)

Recognizes residents on or before statehood, November 16, 1907. Send SASE to Liz Codding, Oklahoma Genealogical Society, P.O. Box 12986, Oklahoma City, OK 73157.

First Families of New Mexico

The New Mexico State Genealogical Society honors descendants of pioneers in one of these categories: Native American, The Onate Period (1598–1680), the Reconquest (1692–1821), The Mexican Period (1821–1846), and The Territorial Period (1846–1912). Send request to First Families of New Mexico, P.O. Box 8283, Albuquerque, NM 87198-8283.

First Families of Tennessee

Honors descendants of its first residents. Open to descendants of persons living in Tennessee before June 1, 1796. Write to East Tennessee Historical Society, P.O. Box 1629, Knoxville, TN 37901-1629.

First Families of Texas

Commemoration for descendants of ancestors who lived in Texas on February 19, 1846. Send a legal size SASE with 55¢ postage to Wanda L. Donaldson,

First Families of Texas Certificate, 3219 Meadow Oaks Dr., Temple, TX 76502-1752.

West Texas Pioneer Certificate

The Texas State Genealogical Society (TSGS) issues certificates to direct descendants of settlers in West Texas prior to 1901. Contact Mac Hill, TSGS, 2313 Lakeshore Dr., Cleburne, TX 76031.

Utah Pioneers

Honors forefathers and mothers who crossed the plains and helped develop Utah while it was still part of Mexico, along with territorial pioneers who came to Utah before 1896. For application, write to Utah Genealogical Association, P.O. Box 1144, Salt Lake City, UT 84110.

The American Immigrant Wall of Honor

The Statue of Liberty–Ellis Island Foundation is a memorial and tribute to the "Peopling of America," containing the names of over 500,000 individuals and families honored by their descendants. Contact The Statue of Liberty–Ellis Island Foundation, P.O. Box ELLIS, New York, NY 10163; (212) 883-1986.

Canal Pioneers

Recognizes families whose ancestors played a part in the settlement of the Illinois and Michigan (I&M) Canal National Heritage Corridor, a continental water passageway connecting Lake Michigan to the Mississippi River in 1848. Write to The Canal Corridor Association, 220 S. State St., Ste. 1880, Chicago, IL 60604.

Confederate Descendants Society

Contact them at P.O. Box 233, Athens, AL 35611.

International Society of the Descendants of Charlemagne

Contact them at P.O. Box 5259, Titusville, FL 32783-5259.

Oregon Trail

Descendants of trailblazers between 1811 and 1911. Request information and registration. Send SASE to the Oregon Trail Project, 4620 Overland Rd., #206, Boise, ID 83705.

Oregon-California Trails Association

Contact them at P.O. Box 42, Gerald, MO 63967.

Presidential Families of America

A lineage society whose members share ancestry with a president or descend from a president of the United States of America. Send #10 SASE to Dr. Albert Clinton Walling II, Presidential Families of America, 7011 Spring Briar St., San Antonio, TX 78209.

Sons of Union Veterans of the Civil War

Sons and daughters send name and summary of father's service to Jerome Orton, 231 Dixon Dr., Syracuse, NY 13219-2711; (315) 488-4076.

Southeastern Cherokee Confederacy

Offers membership to persons who are as much as $\frac{1}{16}$ Native American—this includes persons of any Native American heritage. For information, write to Confederacy, National Tribal Office, Rt. 4, Box 120, Albany, GA 31705.

Reunion Budget Worksheet

REUNION INCOME	**In-kind** (goods, services)	**Cash**
Volunteers	$_____	$_____
Contributions/donations	$_____	$_____
Keepsake, memento, and book sales	$_____	$_____
Fees, dues	$_____	$_____
Tickets (meals, tours, activities)	$_____	$_____
Corporate sponsor	$_____	$_____
Door prizes/awards	$_____	$_____
Raffle/auction	$_____	$_____
Total		$_____

REUNION EXPENSES

Organizational costs

Bank account $_____

Checks $_____

Phone calls $_____

Postage $_____

Printing $_____

Supplies $_____

Computer support $_____

                                     Subtotal $_____

Prereunion deposits

Hotel (when reservation made) $_____

Caterer/meals (when order placed) $_____

Keepsakes (when order submitted) $_____

Tours (when booked) $_____

Printing (when job submitted) $_____

                                     Subtotal $_____

Prereunion costs

Registration supplies $_____

Flowers $_____

Awards/certificates/prizes $_____

Paper goods (picnics, refreshments) $_____

Printing (program, directory, memory book, cookbook) $_____

Rentals (A/V equipment, tent, wheelchairs,
    sports equipment, chemical toilets) $_____

Decorations/banners/signs/memorials $_____

Displays $_____

Other (list) $_____

                  Subtotal $_____

Reunion day(s) costs

Meals/food $_____

Beverages $_____

Bartender $_____

Entertainers/musicians $_____

Photo/videographer $_____

Tips/gratuities $_____

Taxes (for your location) $_____

                  Subtotal $_____

Postreunion expenses

Printing $_____

Postage $_____

Pictures, videotapes $_____

Other (list) $_____

                  Subtotal $_____

                  Total $_____

Reunion Sites

The venues and facilities listed here are far from exhaustive—all are eager to host your reunion, but many others are also. Listings are first by category, then by state. New, updated listings appear regularly in "Reunion Resources" in *Reunions magazine* and at www.reunionsmag.com, with direct links to pertinent Web sites.

BED AND BREAKFASTS

Colorado

Foxpine Inn
154 Wheeler Pl.
Copper Mountain, CO 80443
Phone: 1-800-426-7400
E-mail: cralph@hi-country.com
Web: www.hi-country.com

Maine

Ocean Point Inn
Shore Rd.
P.O. Box 409
East Boothbay, ME 04544-0409
Phone: 1-800-552-5554
E-mail: opi@oceanpointinn.com
Web: www.oceanpoint.com

Massachusetts

The Salem Inn
7 Summer St.
Salem, MA 01970
Phone: (978) 741-0682
E-mail: saleminn@earthlink.net
Web: www.salemweb.com/biz/saleminn

Stump Sprouts Guest Lodge
West Hill Rd.
West Hawley, MA 01339
Phone: (413) 339-4265

Montana

Alpinglow Inn on the Big Mountain
3900 Big Mountain Rd.
Whitefish, MT 59937
Phone: 1-800-754-6760
E-mail: info@alpinglow.com
Web: www.alpinglow.com

Vermont

The Oceanfront Inn
Basin Harbor Rd.
Bergennes, VT 05491
Phone: (802) 475-2311
E-mail: info@basinharbor.com
Web: www.basinharbor.com

Wisconsin

Woods Manor Bed and Breakfast
P.O. Box 7
La Pointe, WI 54850
Phone: (715) 747-3102
E-mail: rundra@islandelegance.com
Web: www.islandelegance.com

CAMPING AND CONFERENCE CENTERS

National

American Camping Association
5000 State Rd. 67 North
Martinsville, IN 46151

Bureau of Land Management
1849 C St., NW
Washington, D.C. 20240
Phone: (202) 452-5125
Web: www.rec.gov
Request camping info for land controlled by BLM.

Department of the Army
3909 Halls Ferry
Vicksburg, MS 39180
Phone: (601) 631-6159
Request info about U.S. Army Corps of Engineers campsites near rivers, lakes, and oceans.

Episcopal Camps and Conference Centers
Phone: (315) 994-5417
E-mail: ecccdir@aol.com

International Association of Conference Centers
Phone: (315) 676-4130
E-mail: alfriacca@aol.com

National Association of RV Parks & Campgrounds
8605 Westwood Center Dr.
Vienna, VA 22182
Phone: (703) 847-3900
Web: wwwgocampingamerica.com

U.S.D.A. Forest Service
P.O. Box 96090
Washington, D.C. 20090
Phone: (202) 205-1760
Web: www.fs.fed.us
Request list of national forests.

U.S. Fish and Wildlife Service
4404 N Fairfax Dr., Room 130
Arlington, VA 22203
Phone: (703) 358-1711
Ask about national wildlife refuges that permit camping.

Colorado

Templed Hills Camp & Retreat Center
1364 County Rd. 75
Woodland Park, CO 80863
Phone: (719) 687-9038
E-mail: thercc@kktv.com

YMCA of the Rockies and Snow Mountain Ranch
2515 Tunnel Rd.
Estes Park, CO 80511
Phone: 1-800-777-9622
E-mail: info@ymcarockies.org
Web: www.ymcarockies.org

Florida

Cerveny Conference Center
11057 Camp Weed Pl.
Live Oaks, FL 32060
Phone: (904) 364-5250
E-mail: campweed@hankins.com
Web: www.crcs.net/diocese/cw.htm

Kansas

Tall Oaks Conference Center
12797 189th St.
Linwood, KS 66052-0116
Phone: 1-800-617-1484
E-mail: patti@talloaks.org
Web: www.talloaks.org

Michigan

Camp Henry
5575 Gordon Rd.
Newaygo, MI 49337
Phone: (616) 459-2267
E-mail: camphenry@riverview.net

Myers Lake United Methodist Campground
10575 Silver Lake Rd.
Byron, MI 48418
Phone: 1-800-994-5050
E-mail: cyclawre@shianet.org
Web: www.michcampgrounds.com/myerslake

New Hampshire

Geneva Point Center
HCR 62 Box 469
Center Harbor, NH 03226
Phone: (603) 253-4366
E-mail: geneva@genevapoint.org
Web: www.genevapoint.org

New Mexico

Glorieta Conference Center
P.O. Box 8
Glorieta, NM 87535
Phone: 1-800-797-4222
Web: www.bssb.com/conscalg.htm

North Carolina

Ridgecrest Conference Center
P.O. Box 128
Ridgecrest, NC 28770
Phone: (828) 669-3591
E-mail: rderr@lifeway.com

YMCA Blue Ridge Assembly
84 Blue Ridge Circle
Black Mountain, NC 28711
Phone: (828) 669-8422
E-mail: ymcabra@aol.com

Virginia

Massanetta Springs Conference Center
Rt. 17, Box 138
Harrisonburg, VA 22801-8325
Phone: 1-888-627-7774

CONDOS, VILLAS, AND VACATION HOMES

Arkansas

Vacation Rentals
430 Town Center
Bella Vista, AR 72714
Phone: (501) 855-1111
E-mail: vrlodging@aol.com
Web: www.bellavista-rentals.com

California

Northstar-at-Tahoe
P.O. Box 129
Truckee, CA 96160
Phone: 1-800-466-6784
Web: www.skinorthstar.com

Colorado

Alpine Vacations
P.O. Box 3123
Winter Park, CO 80482
Phone: 1-800-551-9943
E-mail: alpinepeaks@rkymtnhi.com
Web: www.alpinevacations.com

Antlers at Vail
680 W. Lionshead Pl.
Vail, CO 81657
Phone: 1-800-258-8617
E-mail: antlers@csn.net
Web: www.vail.net/antlers

Destinations Resorts-Snowmass
P.O. Box 5629
Snowmass, CO 81615
Phone: 1-800-525-4200
Web: www.destinationsnowmass.com

Simba Run Vail Condominium
1100 N. Frontage Rd.
Vail, CO 81657
Phone: 1-800-746-2278
Web: www.simbarun.com

Vacations Inc.
P.O. Box 3095
Winter Park, CO 80482-3095
Phone: 1-800-228-1025
Web: www.vacationsinc.com

Vail Racquet Club Townhouses & Condos
4690 Vail Racket Club Dr.
Vail, CO 81657
Phone: 1-800-428-4840
Web: www.vailraquetclub.com

Florida

Seabonay Beach Resort
1159 Hillsboro Mile
Hillsboro, FL 33062
Phone: 1-800-777-1961
Web: www.seboney.atsea.com

Michigan

Crystal Mountain Resort
12500 Crystal Mountain Dr.
Thompsonville, MI 49683
Phone: 1-800-968-7686
Web: www.crystalmtn.com

Missouri

Thousand Hills Golf & Conference Resort
245 S. Wildwood
Branson, MO 65616
Phone: 1-800-864-4145
Web: www.thousandhills.com

South Carolina

Hilton Head Discount Rentals
P.O. Box 22436
Hilton Head, SC 29925
Phone: 1-800-445-8664
Web: www.hiltonheaddiscount.com

CONVENTION AND VISITORS AND TOURISM BUREAUS

Alabama

Alabama Bureau of Tourism and Travel
P.O. Box 4927
Montgomery, AL 36103-4927
Phone: (334) 242-4169
Web: www.touralabama.com

Dothan CVB
3311 Ross Clark Circle
Dothan, AL 36303
Phone: (334) 794-6622
E-mail: dothancvb@mail.ala.net
Web: www.dothanalcvb.com

Greater Birmingham CVB
2200 Ninth Ave. North
Birmingham, AL 35203
Phone: 1-800-458-8085
Web: www.birminghamal.org

Mobile CVB
One South Water St.
Mobile, AL 36602
Phone: 1-800-566-2453
E-mail: patriciakieffer@mobile.org
Web: www.mobile.org

Arizona

Arizona Office of Tourism
110 W. Washington St.
Phoenix, AZ 85007
Phone: 1-800-842-8257
Web: www.arizonaguide.com

Arkansas

Ozark Gateway–Ozark Mountains
P.O. Box 4049
Batesville, AR 72503-4049
Phone: 1-800-264-0316
E-mail: ozarks@cei.net
Web: www.ozarkgateway.com

California

Buena Park CVB
6280 Manchester Blvd., Ste. 103
Buena Park, CA 90621
Phone: 1-800-541-3953
E-mail: tourbp@buenapark.com
Web: www.buenapark.com

Catalina Island Chamber of Commerce
P.O. Box 217
Avalon, CA 90704
Phone: (213) 510-1520

Fresno City and County CVB
808 M St.
Fresno, CA 93721
Phone: 1-800-788-0836
E-mail: TourFresno@aol.com

San Diego CVB
401 B St., Ste. 1400
San Diego, CA 92101
Phone: (619) 232-3101
Web: www.sandiego.org

Colorado

Colorado Springs CVB
104 Cascade Ave., Ste. 104
Colorado Springs, CO 80903
Phone: 1-800-368-4748
Web: www.coloradosprings-travel.com/cscvb

Pikes Peak Country Attractions
354 Manitou Ave.
Manitou Springs, CO 80829
Phone: 1-800-525-2250
Web: www.pikespeak.com

Steamboat Springs Chamber Resort Association
P.O. Box 774408
Steamboat Springs, CO 80477
Phone: (303) 879-0882

Vail Valley Tourism & CVB
100 E. Meadow Dr.
Vail, CO 81657
Phone: 1-800-775-8245

Connecticut

Mystic CVB
470 Bank St.
New London, CT 06320
Phone: 1-800-863-6569
Web: www.mysticmore.com

District of Columbia

Washington, D.C. CVB
1212 New York Ave., NW
Washington, D.C. 20005
Phone: (202) 789-7000
Web: www.washington.org

Florida

Central Florida CVB
P.O. Box 61
Cypress Gardens, FL 33884
Phone: 1-800-828-7655
Web: www.cfdc.org/tourism

Daytona Beach Area CVB
126 E. Orange Ave.
Daytona Beach, FL 32114
Phone: 1-800-854-1234
Web: www.daytonabeach-tourism.com

Key West Visitors Bureau
Commerce Department
402 Wall St.
Key West, FL 33040
Phone: (305) 294-2587
Web: www.fla-keywest.com

Key West Welcome Center
3840 N. Roosevelt Blvd.
Key West, FL 33040
Phone: 1-800-284-4482

Lee County CVB
2180 W. First St., Ste. 100
P.O. Box 2445
Fort Myers, FL 33902-2445
Phone: 1-800-533-4753
Web: www.leeislandcoast.com

Palm Beach County CVB
1555 Palm Beach Lakes Blvd., Ste. 204
West Palm Beach, FL 33401
Phone: 1-800-833-5733
Web: www.palmbeachfl.com

Georgia

Columbus CVB
P.O. Box 2825
Columbus, GA 31902
Phone: 1-800-999-1613

DeKalb CVB
750 Commerce Dr., Ste. 200
Decatur, GA 30030
Phone: 1-800-999-6055
Web: www.dcvb.org

Georgia Department of Industry and Trade
P.O. Box 1776, Dept. TIA
Atlanta, GA 30301
Phone: 1-800-847-4842
Web: www.gomm.com

Helen Welcome Center
P.O. Box 730
Helen, GA 30545
Phone: 1-800-858-8027
Web: www.whitecounty.com/helen; www.helenga.org

Jekyll Island CVB
901 Jekyll Causeway
Jekyll Island, GA 31527
Phone: 1-800-841-6586
Web: www.jekyllisland.com

Hawaii

Hawaii Visitors Bureau
75-5719 W. Alii Dr.
Kailua, HI 96740
Phone: (808) 329-7787
Web: www.bigisland.org

Idaho

Boise CVB
P.O. Box 2106
Boise, ID 83701
Phone: 1-800-635-5240
E-mail: admin@boisecvb.org
Web: www.boise.org

Illinois

Aurora Area CVB
44 W. Downer Pl.
Aurora, IL 60506
Phone: 1-800-477-4369

Chicago Southland CVB
2304 173rd St.
Lansing, IL 60438-6006
Phone: 1-888-895-8233
E-mail: Ircscvb@lincolnnet.net
Web: www.Lincolnnet.net/Chicago-Southland-CVB

Galena/Jo Daviess County CVB
101 Bouthillier St.
Galena, IL 61036
Phone: 1-800-747-9377
Web: www.galena.org

Greater Woodfield CVB
1375 E. Woodfield Rd., Ste. 100
Schaumburg, IL 60173
Phone: 1-800-693-1313
Web: www.chicagonorthwest.com

Illinois Bureau of Tourism
100 W. Randolph St., Ste. 3-400
Chicago, IL 60601
Phone: 1-800-223-0121
E-mail: www.ci.chi.il.us/tourism
Web: www.enjoyillinois.com

Indiana

Evansville CVB
623 Walnut St.
Evansville, IN 47708
Phone: 1-800-433-3025
E-mail: tourism@evansvilleCVB.org
Web: www.evansvillecvb.org

Indiana Division of Tourism
1 N. Capital Ave., #700
Indianapolis, IN 46204
Phone: 1-800-289-6646
Web: www.tourism.org

LaPorte County CVB
1503 S. Meer Rd.
Michigan City, IN 46360
Phone: 1-800-634-2650
Web: www.harborcountry-in.org

Iowa

Cedar Rapids CVB
119 First Ave., SE
Cedar Rapids, IA 52406-5339
Phone: 1-800-735-5557
Web: www.cedar-rapids.com/iowa/cvb

Greater Des Moines CVB
Two Ruan Center, Ste. 222
601 Locust St.
Des Moines, IA 50309
Phone: 1-800-346-4289
E-mail: mcvb.1@aol.com
Web: www.desmoinesia.com

Iowa Department of Tourism
200 E. Grand Ave.
Des Moines, IA 50309
Phone: 1-800-345-4692
Web: www.state.ia.us

Kansas

Geary County CVB
425 N. Washington St.
Junction City, KS 66441
Phone: 1-800-528-2489
E-mail: jccvb@flinthills.net
Web: www.junctioncity.org

Newton CVB
500 N. Main
P.O. Box 353
Newton, KS 67114
Phone: (316) 283-7555
E-mail: ncvb1@southwind.net
Web: www.2.southwindnet/~newton /tourism

Kentucky

Kentucky Tourism
Phone: 1-800-225-8747
Web: www.kentuckytourism.com

Lexington CVB
301 E. Vine
Lexington, KY 40507
Phone: 1-800-848-1224
Web: www.visitlex.com

Radcliff/Fort Knox Convention & Tourism Commission
306 N. Wilson
Radcliff, KY 40159-0845
Phone: 1-800-334-7540
E-mail: westour@ekx.infi.net
Web: www.ltadd.org/radcliff

Maryland

Annapolis & Anne Arundel County CVB
26 West St.
Annapolis, MD 21401
Phone: (410) 280-0445
Web: www.visit-annapolis.org

Baltimore Area CVB
100 Light St., 12th Floor
Baltimore, MD 21202-3106
Phone: 1-800-343-3468
Web: www.baltimore.org

CVB of Montgomery County, Maryland
12900 Middlebrook Rd., Ste. 1400
Germantown, MD 20874
Phone: (301) 428-9702

Massachusetts

North Shore Convention Council
Peabody City Hall
24 Lowell St.
Peabody, MA 01960-5400
Phone: (978) 532-3790
E-mail: visitns@shore.net
Web: www.ci.peabody.ma.us

Michigan

Mackinac Island Chamber of Commerce
P.O. Box 451
Mackinac Island, MI 49757
Phone: (906) 847-3783
Web: www.mackinac.com

Michigan Travel Bureau
P.O. Box 3393
Livonia, MI 48151
Phone: 1-800-543-2937
Web: www.michigan.org

Southwestern Michigan Tourist Council
2300 Pipestone Rd.
Benton Harbor, MI 49022
Phone: (616) 925-6301
E-mail: vdunlop@swmichigan.org
Web: www.swmichigan.org

Minnesota

Bloomington Convention Center
1550 E. 79th St., Ste. 450
Bloomington, MN 55425
Phone: (612) 858-8500
E-mail: cvb@bloomington.org
Web: www.bloomingtonmn.org

Bloomington CVB
9801 Dupont Ave. South, #120
Bloomington, MN 55431
Phone: 1-800-346-4289
Web: www.bloomingtonmn.org

Minnesota Office of Tourism
121 7th Pl. East
St. Paul, MN 55101
Phone: 1-800-657-3700
Web: www.exploreminnesota.com

North Metro CVB
6200 Shingle Creek Pkwy., Ste. 248
Brooklyn Center, MN 55430
Phone: 1-800-541-4364
Web: www.northmetrominneapolis.org

Missouri

St. Louis Convention and Visitors Commission
1 Metropolitan Sq., Ste. 1100
St. Louis, MO 63102
Phone: 1-800-888-3861
Web: www.st-louis-cvc.com

Springfield CVB
3315 E. Battlefield Rd.
Springfield, MO 65804-4048
Phone: (417) 881-5300
Web: www.springfieldmo.org

New Hampshire

New Hampshire Meeting Sites
P.O. Box 1175N
Concord, NH 03302-1175
Phone: 1-800-822-2373
Web: www.visitnh.gov

New Mexico

Taos Chamber of Commerce
P.O. Drawer I
Taos, NM 87571
Phone: 1-800-732-8267
Web: www.taoswebb.com/taos

New York

Fingers Lakes Association
309 Lake St.
Penn Yan, NY 14527
Phone: 1-800-548-4386
Web: www.FingerLakes.org

New York CVB
2 Columbus Circle
New York, NY 10019
Phone: 1-800-303-2116
Web: www.nycvisit.com

Saratoga County Chamber of Commerce
494 Broadway
Saratoga Springs, NY 12866
Phone: 1-800-526-8970
E-mail: info@saratoga.org
Web: www.saratoga.org

North Carolina

Asheville Area Chamber of Commerce
151 Haywood St.
Asheville, NC 28801
Phone: 1-800-257-5583
E-mail: asheville@ashevillechamber.org
Web: www.ashevillechamber.org

Cape Fear Coast CVB
24 N. Third St.
Wilmington, NC 28401
Phone: 1-800-222-4757
Web: www.cape-fear.nc.us

Charlotte CVB
330 S. Tryon
Charlotte, NC 28202
Phone: 1-800-231-4636

Greensboro Area CVB
317 S. Green St.
Greensboro, NC 27401-2615
Phone: 1-800-344-2282
E-mail: gso@greensboronc.org
Web: www.greensboronc.org

Greenville-Pitt County CVB
525 S. Evans St.
Greenville, NC 27884-8027
Phone: 1-800-537-5564
E-mail: greenvillenc@globalad.com
Web: www.globalad.com

Ohio

Warren County CVB
1073 Oregonia Rd.
Lebanon, OH 45036
Phone: 1-800-433-1072
Web: www.ohio4fun.org

Pennsylvania

Chester County Tourist Bureau
300 Greenwood Rd.
Kennett Square, PA 19348
Phone: 1-800-228-9933
Web: www.brandyvinevalley.com

Philadelphia CVB
1515 Market St., Ste. 2020
Philadelphia, PA 19102
Phone: 1-800-225-5745
E-mail: tour@libertynet.org
Web: www.libertynet.org/phila-visitor

Pocono Mountains Vacation Bureau
Box K
1004 Main St.
Stroudsburg, PA 18360-1695
Phone: (717) 421-5791
E-mail: pocomts@poconos.org
Web: www.poconos.org

Valley Forge CVB
600 West Germantown Pike
Plymouth Meeting, PA 19462
Phone: 1-800-441-3549
Web: www.valleyforge.org

Rhode Island

Newport County CVB
23 America's Cup
Newport, RI 02840
Phone: 1-800-326-6030
Web: www.gonewport.com

South Carolina

Charleston Convention & Group Services
P.O. Box 1118
Charleston, SC 29402
Phone: 1-800-553-2055
E-mail: ccgs@charlestongrpservices.com
Web: www.charlestongrpservices.com

Texas

Beaumont CVB
P.O. Box 3827
Beaumont, TX 77704
Phone: 1-800-392-4401
E-mail: bmttvb@sat.net
Web: www.beaumontcvb.com

Galveston Island CVB
2106 Sea Wall Blvd.
Galveston, TX 77550
Phone: 1-800-351-4237
Web: www.galvestontourism.com

Texas Tourism, Tourism Division
1700 N. Congress, Ste. 200
Austin, TX 78711-2728
Phone: (512) 462-9191
Web: www.traveltex.com

Utah

Utah Travel Council
Council Hall/Capitol Hill
Salt Lake City, UT 84114
Phone: 1-800-200-1160
Web: www.utah.com

Vermont

Vermont Department of Agriculture
116 State St.
Montpelier, VT 05620
Web: www.cit.state.vt.us/agric

Virginia

Virginia Beach CVB
2101 Parks Ave., Ste. 500
Virginia Beach, VA 23451
Phone: 1-800-700-7702
E-mail: rkuhlman@city.virginia-beach.va.us
Web: www.virginia-beach.va.us

Washington

Seattle-King County CVB
520 Pike St., Ste. 1300
Seattle, WA 98101
Phone: (206) 461-5836
Web: www.seeseattle.org

West Virginia

Charleston WV CVB
200 Civic Center Dr.
Charleston, WV 25301
Phone: (304) 344-5075
Web: www.charleston.wv.com

Wisconsin

Fond du Lac CVB
19 W. Scott St.
Fond du Lac, WI 54935
Phone: 1-800-937-9123
E-mail: visitor@tcccom.net
Web: www.fdl.com

Greater Milwaukee CVB
510 W. Kilbourn Ave.
Milwaukee, WI 53203
Phone: 1-800-231-0903

Oshkosh CVB
2 N. Main St.
Oshkosh, WI 54901-4897
Phone: 1-800-876-5250
Web: www.oshkoshcvb.org

Wisconsin Division of Tourism
123 W. Washington Ave.
Madison, WI 53707
Phone: 1-800-432-TRIP (8747)
Web: www.tourism.state.wi.us/

Jamaica

Negril Chamber of Commerce
P.O. Box 55
Negril, Westmoreland, Jamaica
Phone: (876) 957-4067
E-mail: negrilchamber.cwjamaica.com

CRUISES

Angola Cruise Shop
Peachtree Plaza
1220 N. 200 W., Ste. J
Angola, IN 46703
Phone: 1-800-283-7756
E-mail: cruises@brightnet.com

Celebration River Cruises
2501 River Dr.
Moline, IL 61265
Phone: 1-800-297-0034

Cruise Club Internationale
247 E. Lake St.
Bloomingdale, IL 60108
Phone: 1-800-232-4358

Cruise Consolidators Ltd.
2017 E. Cactus, Ste. G-341
Phoenix, AZ 85022
Phone: (602) 493-8382
E-mail: jackie1@primenet.com
Web: www.crazy4cruisin.com

Cruises Inc.
3523 Fawn Creek Dr.
Kingswood, TX 77339
Phone: (281) 358-9857
E-mail: swej@earthlink.net
Web: www.geocities.com/SouthBeach/Marina/2916

Cruises Only
1011 E. Colonial Dr.
Orlando, FL 32803
Phone: 1-800-683-7447
E-mail: groups@cruisesonly.com
Web: www.cruisesonly.com

Delta Queen Steamboat Co.
Robin Street Wharf
1380 Port of New Orleans Pl.
New Orleans, LA 70130
Phone: 1-800-543-1949
Web: www.deltaqueen.com

Florida Suncoast Tra-Master Cruises
15985 Briarcliff
Fort Myers, FL 33912
Phone: (941) 482-3354

Gotta Go Cruises
11 E. Main St., Ste. 156
Bay Shore, NY 11706
Phone: (516) 969-1785
E-mail: gottaemail@aol.com

JC Cruises Paddlewheeler
2313 Edwards Dr.
Fort Myers, FL 33901
Phone: (941) 334-7474
Web: www.floridatravel.com/attractions/jccruis.htm

LeBoat Inc.
10 S. Franklin Tpk., Ste. 204B
Ramsey, NJ 71446
Phone: 1-800-922-0291

Maine Windjammer Association
251 Jefferson St.
Waldoboro, ME 04572
Phone: 1-800-807-9463
Web: www.midcoast.com

President Riverboat Casino
200 E. 3rd St.
Davenport, IA 52801
Phone: 1-800-331-4145
Web: www.prescasino.com

St. Lawrence Cruise Lines
253 Ontario St.
Kingston, Ontario
Canada K7L 224
Phone: 1-800-267-7868

DORMITORIES

Alabama

Auburn University Hotel & Conference Center
241 S. College St.
Auburn, AL 36830-5400
Phone: (205) 826-8755

Tuskegee Kellogg Conference Center
Tuskegee University
Tuskegee, AL 36088
Phone: (334) 727-3000

Idaho

Idaho State University
P.O. Box 8083
Pocatello, ID 83209
Phone: (208) 236-2120

New York

Hofstra University
200 Hofstra University
Student Center Room 111
Hempstead, NY 11550-1090
Phone: (516) 463-5067

Nova Scotia

Dalhousie University
6136 University Ave., Room 410
Halifax, Nova Scotia
Canada B3H 4J2
Phone: (902) 494-3831

Wisconsin

Lakeland College
P.O. Box 359
Sheboygan, WI 53082-0359
Phone: (414) 565-2111

FORTS

Fort Robinson State Park
P.O. Box 392
Crawford, NE 69339-0392
Phone: (308) 665-2900

Fort Worden State Park Conference Center
200 Battery Way
Port Townsend, WA 98368
Phone: (360) 385-4730
Web: www.olympus.net/ftworden

HOTELS

Arizona

Best Western Grace Inn
10831 S. 51st St.
Phoenix, AZ 85044
Phone: (602) 893-3000

Best Western Phoenix-Glendale
5940 N.W. Grand Ave.
Glendale, AZ 75234
Phone: 1-800-382-2130
E-mail: ksshaw@worldnet.att.com
Web: www.Hotels-HMS.com

Days Inn Scottsdale
4710 N. Scottsdale Rd.
Scottsdale, AZ 85251
Phone: (602) 947-5411

Holiday Inn City Center
181 W. Broadway
Tucson, AZ 85701
Phone: (602) 624-8711

Holiday Inn Select
4300 E. Washington
Phoenix, AZ 85034
Phone: (602) 286-1154

Scottsdale Marriott Suites
7325 E. 3rd Ave.
Scottsdale, AZ 85251
Phone: (602) 951-1550
Web: www.marriott.com/phxst

Arkansas

Best Western Inn of the Ozarks
P.O. Box 431, Hwy. 62 West
Eureka Springs, AR 72632
Phone: 1-800-264-0316
E-mail: ozarks@cei.net
Web: www.ozarkgateway.com

California

Dana Inn and Marina
1710 W. Mission Bay Dr.
San Diego, CA 92109
Phone: 1-800-445-3339

Days Inn-Hotel Circle
543 Hotel Circle South
San Diego, CA 92108
Phone: 1-800-227-4743

Doubletree Club Hotel
11611 Bernardo Plaza Ct.
San Diego, CA 92128
Phone: (619) 485-9250

Doubletree Hotel Ontario
222 N. Vineyard Ave.
Ontario, CA 91764
Phone: (909) 937-0900

Embassy Suites
901 E. Calaveras Blvd.
Milpitas, CA 95035
Phone: (408) 942-0400

Embassy Suites San Francisco Airport/Burlingame
150 Anza Blvd.
Burlingame, CA 94010
Phone: (650) 342-4600

Holiday Inn Northeast-Sacramento
5321 Date Ave.
Sacramento, CA 95841
Phone: 1-800-388-9284

Holiday Inn San Diego Bayside
4875 N. Harbor Dr.
San Diego, CA 92106
Phone: (619) 224-3621

Hotel Queen Mary and Spruce Goose
P.O. Box 8, Pier J
Long Beach, CA 90801
Phone: (213) 435-3511

Humphrey's Half Moon Inn
2303 Shelter Island Dr.
San Diego, CA 92106
Phone: 1-800-542-7400

Quality Hotel, Los Angeles Airport
5249 W. Century Blvd.
Los Angeles, CA 90045
Phone: (310) 645-2200
E-mail: 728dos-losangeles@sunbursthospitality.com
Web: www.sunbursthospitality.com

Radisson Hotel La Jolla
3299 Holiday Ct.
La Jolla, CA 92037
Phone: 1-800-854-2900

San Diego Mission Valley
901 Camino Del Rio South
San Diego, CA 92108
Phone: 1-800-733-2332

Colorado

Association of Historic Hotels West
2080 Pearl St.
Boulder, CO 80302
Phone: (303) 546-9040
E-mail: ahhwest@boulder.earthnet.net
Web: www.historic-hotels.com

Best Western Landmark Hotel
455 S. Colorado Blvd.
Denver, CO 80222
Phone: (303) 388-5561

West Beaver Creek Lodge
P.O. Box 7626
Avon, CO 81620
Phone: 1-888-795-1061
E-mail: wbclodge@vail.net
Web: www.wbclodge.com

Florida

Best Western Harborview
964 S. Harbor City Blvd.
Melbourne, FL 32901
Phone: 1-888-329-8901
Web: www.seawake.com

Best Western Sea Wake Inn
691 S. Gulfview Blvd.
Clearwater Beach, FL 33767
Phone: 1-888-329-8910
Web: www.seawake.com

Embassy Suites Orlando North
225 E. Altamonte Dr.
Altamonte Springs, FL 32701
Phone: (407) 834-2400

Hampton Inn
13000 N. Cleveland Ave.
North Fort Myers, FL 33903
Phone: (813) 656-4000

Holiday Inn Hotel & Suites On The Beach
1401 S. Atlantic Ave.
New Smyrna Beach, FL 32169
Phone: 1-800-232-3414
E-mail: HINSB@aol.com
Web: www.travelpick.com

Holiday Inn Sunspree
600 N. Atlantic Ave.
Daytona Beach, FL 32118
Phone: 1-800-999-1613

Inn at Maingate
3011 Maingate Ln.
Kissimmee, FL 34747
Phone: 1-800-239-6478

Ramada Inn
2011 N. Wheeler St.
Plant City, FL 33566
Phone: (813) 752-3141

Sheraton Inn Lakeside
7769 W. Hwy. 192
Kissimmee, FL 34747
Phone: 1-800-831-1844 x 206

Georgia

Holiday Inn Macon Conference Center
3590 Riverside Dr.
Macon, GA 31210
Phone: 1-888-394-8552
Web: www.holiday-inn/hotels/mcnga

The Lodge on Little St. Simons Island
P.O. Box 21078
St. Simons Island, GA 31522
Phone: 1-888-733-5774
E-mail: iss@mindspring.com
Web: www.pactel.com.au/lssi

Illinois

Radisson Hotel, Alsip
5000 W. 127th St.
Alsip, IL 60803
Phone: (708) 371-7300
E-mail: Radhotelsales@msn.com.

Rosemont Suites Hotel O' Hare
5500 N. River Rd.
Rosemont, IL 60018
Phone: (847) 928-7616

Sheraton Gateway Suites, Chicago O'Hare Airport
6501 N. Mannheim Rd.
Rosemont, IL 60018
Phone: (847) 699-6300

Iowa

Collins Plaza Hotel Cedar Rapids
1200 Collins Rd., NE
Cedar Rapids, IA 52402
Phone: 1-800-541-1067

Wyndham Five Seasons Hotel
350 First Ave. NE
Cedar Rapids, IA 52401
Phone: (319) 363-8161
Web: www.travelweb.com

Louisiana

Dauphine Orleans Hotel
725 Rue Dauphine
New Orleans, LA 70112
Phone: 1-800-521-7111
E-mail: dohfq@aol.com
Web: www.dauphineonleans.com

Doubletree Hotel Lakeside, New Orleans
3838 N. Causeway Blvd.
Metairie, LA 70002
Phone: (504) 836-5254
E-mail: dhlake@aol.com
Web: www.doubletreehotels.com

Maryland

Clarion Hotel
612 Cathedral St.
Baltimore, MD 21201
Phone: (410) 727-7101

Colony South Hotel
7401 Surratts Rd.
Clinton, MD 20735
Phone: (301) 856-4500
Web: www.colonysouth.com

Comfort Suites Laurel Lakes
14402 Laurel Pl.
Laurel, MD 20707
Phone: (301) 206-2600
Web: www.comfortsuiteslaurel.com

Days Hotel
9615 Deerco Rd.
Timonium, MD 21093-6901
Phone: 1-800-235-3297

Holiday Inn Bethesda
8120 Wisconsin Ave.
Bethesda, MD 20814
Phone: (301) 652-2000

Quality Hotel Silver Spring
8727 Colesville Rd.
Silver Spring, MD 20910
Phone: (301) 589-5200

Massachusetts

Doubletree Hotel, Lowell
50 Warren St.
Lowell, MA 018552
Phone: (978) 452-1200

Radisson Hotel Milford
11 Beaver St.
Milford, MA 01757
Phone: (508) 478-7010
E-mail: salesoff@gisnet
Web: www.radissonmilford.com

Sheraton Framingham Hotel
1657 Worcester Rd.
Framingham, MA 01701
Phone: (508) 879-7200

Michigan

Clarion Hotel
2900 Jackson Rd.
Ann Arbor, MI 48103
Phone: (734) 665-4444
E-mail: info@clarionhotelaa.com
Web: www.clarionhotelaa.com

Michigan Lodging Association
222 Washington Sq. North, Ste. 340
Lansing, MI 48933
Phone: (517) 485-8000

Minnesota

Canal Park Inn, Duluth
250 Canal Park Dr.
Duluth, MN 55802
Phone: 1-800-382-2130
E-mail: ksshaw@worldnet.att.com
Web: www.Hotels-HMS.com

Holiday Inn Metrodome
1500 Washington Ave. South
Minneapolis, MN 55454
Phone: (612) 338-1309
E-mail: mborum@metrodome.com
Web: www.metrodome.com

Missouri

Clarion Hotel
3333 S. Glenstone Ave.
Springfield, MO 65804
Phone: (417) 883-6550

Days Inn of Branson
3524 Keeter St.
Branson, MO 65616
Phone: (417) 334-5544

Residence Inn By Marriott
280 Wildwood Dr. South
Branson, MO 65616
Phone: (417) 336-4077
Web: www.residenceinn.com

Montana

Willow Fire Lodge
1866 West Rd.
Eureka, MT 59917
Phone: 1-888-406-3344
Web: www.libby.org/triangle/montana /index.html

Nebraska

Sheraton Four Points Hotel
4888 S. 118th St.
Omaha, NE 68137
Phone: (402) 895-1000
Web: www.sheraton.com

Nevada

Circus Circus
2880 Las Vegas Blvd. South
Las Vegas, NV 89109
Phone: 1-800-765-4449
E-mail: ccsales@ccei.com
Web: www.circuscircus-lasvegas.com

Harveys Resort Hotel/Casino Lake Tahoe
P.O. Box 128
Lake Tahoe, NV 89449
Phone: 1-800-553-1022
E-mail: sales@harveys.com

Imperial Palace Hotel & Casino
3535 Las Vegas Blvd. South
Las Vegas, NV 89109
Phone: (702) 794-3286
E-mail: ip@imperialpalace.com
Web: www.imperialpalace.com

New Jersey

Hanover Marriott
1401 State Rt. 10 East
Whippany, NJ 07981
Phone: (201) 898-6443

Woodcliff Lake Hilton
200 Tice Blvd.
Woodcliff Lake, NJ 07675
Phone: (201) 391-3600

Wyndham Hotel
901 Spring St.
Elizabeth, NJ 07201
Phone: (908) 527-1600

New Mexico

Pueblo Encantado
P.O. Box 31040
Santa Fe, NM 87594
Phone: 1-800-690-8001
E-mail: pueblo@trinl.com
Web: www.puebloencantado.com

North Carolina

Onslow Inn & Phillips Conference Center
201 Marine Blvd.
Jacksonville, NC 28540
Phone: 1-800-763-3151

Pennsylvania

Clarion Suites Convention Center
1010 Race St.
Philadelphia, PA 19107
Phone: 1-800-628-8932

Holiday Inn Philadelphia Stadium
10th & Packer Ave.
Philadelphia, PA 19149
Phone: (215) 755-9500

Mount Airy Lodge
42 Woodland Rd.
Mount Pocono, PA 18344
Phone: 1-800-441-4410 x 7079

Ramada Inn, Lancaster
2250 Lincoln Hwy. East
Lancaster, PA 17602
Phone: (717) 393-5499

South Carolina

Clarion Town House Hotel
1615 Gervais St.
Columbia, SC 29201
Phone: (803) 771-8711

Comfort Inn Capital City
2025 Main St.
Columbia, SC 29201
Phone: (803) 252-6321

Hampton Inn, Charleston/Mount Pleasant
255 Johnnie Dodds Blvd.
Mount Pleasant, SC 29464
Phone: (843) 881-3300

Hampton Inn Riverview
11 Ashley Pointe Dr.
Charleston, SC 29407
Phone: (803) 556-5200 x 105

Sheraton Hotel & Conference Center
2100 Bush River Rd.
Columbia, SC 29210
Phone: (803) 731-0300
E-mail: IMICSHER@aol.com
Web: www.ColumbiaSouthCarolina.com/Sheraton

Tennessee

Comfort Hotel Airport
2411 Winchester Rd.
Memphis, TN 38116
Phone: 1-800-365-2370

Texas

Best Western Dallas North
1333 N. Stemmons Fwy.
Dallas, TX 75234
Phone: 1-800-382-2130
E-mail: ksshaw@worldnet.att.com
Web: www.Hotels-HMS.com

Clarion Hotel, Richardson
1981 N. Central Expwy.
Richardson, TX 75080
Phone: (972) 644-4000

The Dallas Grand Hotel
1914 Commerce St.
Dallas, TX 75201-5205
Phone: 1-800-421-0011
Web: www.dallasgrandhotel.com

Doubletree Hotel at Allen Center
400 Dallas St.
Houston, TX 77002
Phone: 1-800-772-7666

Doubletree Hotel at Post Oak
2001 Post Oak Blvd.
Houston, TX 77056
Phone: (713) 961-9300

Holiday Inn DFW
4441 Hwy. 114
Irving, TX 75063
Phone: (214) 929-8181

Holiday Inn Select, San Antonio Airport
77 N.E. Loop 410
San Antonio, TX 78216-5855
Phone: (210) 349-9900

Radisson Downtown Market Square
502 W. Durango
San Antonio, TX 78207
Phone: (210) 224-7155
E-mail: zip@txdirect.net
Web: www.radisson.com/sanantonio

Virginia

Embassy Suites
1300 Jefferson Davis Hwy.
Arlington, VA 22202
Phone: (703) 979-9799

Embassy Suites Tysons Corner
8517 Leesburg Pike
Vienna, VA 22182
Phone: (703) 883-0707

Holiday Inn Chesapeake
725 Woodlake Dr. at Greenbrier Pkwy.
Chesapeake, VA 23320
Phone: (804) 523-1500

Holiday Inn Fair Oaks
11787 Lee Jackson Memorial Hwy.
Fairfax, VA 22033
Phone: (703) 352-2525
E-mail: hifo@erols.com

Holiday Inn Hampton Hotel & Conference Center
1815 W. Mercury Blvd.
Hampton, VA 23666
Phone: 1-800-631-2662
E-mail: holiday@cvent.net
Web: www.cvent.net/lodging/holiday

Washington

Best Western Executive Inn & Convention Center
5700 Pacific Hwy. East
Tacoma, WA 98424
Phone: (253) 922-0080
E-mail: ccBestWestern@juno.com

Best Western Lakeway Inn
714 Lakeway Dr.
Bellingham, WA 98226
Phone: 1-888-671-1011

Wisconsin

Holiday Inn Aqua Dome
P.O. Box 236
Wisconsin Dells, WI 53965
Phone: 1-800-543-3557
E-mail: holiday.inn@midplains.net
Web: www.dells.com/aquadome.html

Radisson Inn, Madison
517 Grand Canyon Dr.
Madison, WI 53719
Phone: (608) 833-0100
E-mail: Charterone34@earthlink.net
Web: www.Radisson.com/MadisonWi

Ramada Inn West
201 N. Mayfair Rd.
Milwaukee, WI 53226
Phone: 1-800-531-3965

RANCHES

Arizona

Grapevine Canyon Ranch
P.O. Box 302
Pearce, AZ 85625
Phone: 1-800-245-9202
Web: www.gcranch.com

Lazy K Bar Ranch
8401 N. Scenic Dr.
Tucson, AZ 85743
Phone: (520) 744-3050
E-mail: lazyk@theriver.com
Web: www.lazybar.com

California

The Alisal Guest Ranch & Resort
1054 Alisal Rd.
Solvang, CA 93463
Phone: 1-800-425-4725
E-mail: sales@alisal.com
Web: www.alisal.com

Colorado

American Wilderness Experience Inc.
P.O. Box 1486
Boulder, CO 80306
Phone: 1-800-444-3833
Web: www.awetrips.com

Aspen Lodge at Estes Park
6120 Hwy. 7
Estes Park, CO 80517
Phone: 1-800-332-6867

Colorado Dude & Guest Ranch Association
P.O. Box 300
Tabernash, CO 80478
Phone: (970) 887-9248
E-mail: 103104.1071@compuserve.com
Web: www.stout.entertain.com

Emerald Valley Guest Ranch
P.O. Box 38036
Colorado Springs, CO 80937
Phone: (719) 635-2468

Lost Valley Ranch
29555 Goose Creek Rd., Rt. 2
Sedalia, CO 80135-9000
Phone: (303) 647-2311

Idaho

Hidden Creek Ranch
7600 E. Blue Lake Rd.
Harrison, ID 83833
Phone: 1-800-446-3833
E-mail: hiddencreek@hiddencreek.com
Web: www.hiddencreek.com

Montana

Alta Meadow Ranch
9975 W. Fork Rd.
Darby, MT 59829
Phone: 1-800-808-2464
Web: www.altameadow.com

B Bar Guest Ranch
818 Tommner Creek Rd.
Emigrant, MT 59027
Phone: (406) 848-7523
E-mail: guestranch@bbar.com
Web: www.bbar.com

White Tail Ranch
82 White Tail Ranch Rd.
Ovando, MT 59854
Phone: 1-888-987-2624
Web: www.whitetailranch.com

New York

Rocking Horse Ranch-Resort
600 Rt. 44-65
Highland, NY 12528
Phone: 1-800-647-2624
Web: www.rhranch.com

Texas

Guadalupe River Ranch
605 FM 474
Boerne, TX 78006
Phone: 1-800-460-2005
E-mail: grranch@gvtc.com
Web: www.guadalupe-river-ranch.com

Utah

Rockin' R Ranch
10274 S. Eastdell Dr.
Sandy, UT 84092
Phone: (801) 733-9538

RESORTS

Arizona

Prescott Resort Conference Center & Casino
1500 Hwy. 69
Prescott, AZ 86301
Phone: (520) 776-1666
E-mail: ranniker@northlink.com
Web: www.prescottresort.com

Arkansas

Clarion Resort
4813 Central Ave.
Hot Springs, AR 71913
Phone: (501) 525-1391
Web: gwww.clarionresort.com/

Scott Valley Resort & Guest Ranch
223 Scott Valley Trail
Mountain Home, AR 72653
Phone: (870) 425-5136
Web: www.scottvalley.com

Colorado

Beaver Run Resort
620 Village Rd.
Breckenridge, CO 80424
Phone: 1-800-288-1282 x 8719
E-mail: brbyrnnes@colorado.net
Web: www.beaverrunresort@colorado.net

Beaver Village Resort
P.O. Box 21
Winter Park, CO 80482
Phone: 1-800-666-0281

Vail/Beaver Creek Resort Properties
P.O. Box 36
Avon, CO 81620

Phone: (970) 845-5851
E-mail: lees@vailresorts.com
Web: www.vail.net/vbcrp

Connecticut

Sunrise Resort
P.O. Box 415
Moodus, CT 06469
Phone: (860) 873-8681
Web: www.sunriseresort.com

Florida

Best Western Sea Stone Resorts & Suites
445 Hamden Dr.
Clearwater Beach, FL 33767
Phone: 1-888-329-8910
Web: www.seawake.com

Clarion Suites Resort & Conference Center
20 Via De Luna
Pensacola, FL 32561
Phone: 1-800-874-5303

Krista's Kastle Oceanside Resort
1208 N. Ocean Blvd.
Pompano Beach, FL 33062
Phone: 1-800-327-1132

Naples Beach Hotel and Golf Club
851 Gulf Shore Blvd. North
Naples, FL 34102
Phone: (941) 261-2222
Web: www.naplesbeachhotel.com

The Pensacola Grand Resort
200 E. Gregory St.
Pensacola, FL 32501
Phone: 1-800-348-3336
Web: www.pensacolagrandhotel.com

Saddlebrook Resort, Tampa
5700 Saddlebrook Way
Wesley Chapel, FL 33543-4499
Phone: 1-800-729-8383 x 4477

Secret Lake Resort
8550 W. Irlo Bronson Memorial Hwy.
Kissimmee, FL 34747
Phone: 1-800-400-9304

South Seas Resorts
12800 University Dr., Ste. 350
Fort Myers, FL 33907
Phone: (941) 481-5600 x 512
E-mail: ellis.staten@ssrc.com
Web: www.southseas.com

Steinhatchee Landing Resort
P.O. Box 789
Steinhatchee, FL 32359
Phone: 1-800-584-1709
Web: www.SLI@dixie.4ez.com

Vistana Resort
8800 Vistana Center Dr.
Lake Buena Vista, FL 32830-2197
Phone: 1-800-877-8787

The Wyndham Resort & Spa
250 Racquet Club Rd.
Fort Lauderdale, FL 33326
Phone: 1-800-225-5331
Web: www.wyndham.com

Georgia

Clarion Resort Buccaneer
85 S. Beachview Dr.
Jekyll Island, GA 31520
Phone: 1-800-253-5955

Forest Hills Mountain Hideaway
Rt. 3, Box 510
Dahlonega, GA 30533
Phone: 1-800-654-6313
Web: www.foresths.com

Jekyll Island Club Hotel
371 Riverview Dr.
Jekyll Island, GA 31527
Phone: 1-800-535-9547
E-mail: jiclub@technonet.com
Web: www.jekyllclub.com

Illinois

Eagle Ridge Inn & Resort
P.O. Box 777
Galena, IL 61036
Phone: (815) 777-2444
E-mail: eri@galenalink.com
Web: www.eagleridge.com

Missouri

Clarion at Falls Creek Resort
1 Falls Creek Dr.
Branson, MO 65616

Lakeview Resort
HCR 69, Box 505
Sunrise Beach, MO 65079
Phone: 1-800-936-5655

New Jersey

Golden Inn Resort
7849 Dune Dr.
Avalon, NJ 08202
Phone: (609) 368-5155
E-mail: sloan@goldeninn.com
Web: www.goldeninn.com

Marriott's Seaview Resort
401 S. New York Rd.
Absecon, NJ 08201
Phone: (609) 652-1800

New Mexico

Angel First Resort & Conference Center
P.O. Drawer B
Angel Fire, NM 87710
Phone: 1-888-472-0124
E-mail: groupsales@angelfireresort.com
Web: www.angelfireresort.com

New York

Jeronimo's Resort & Conference Center
P.O. Box 155
Walker Valley, NY 12588
Phone: (914) 733-5652
E-mail: jeronimo@warwick.net
Web: www.jeronimo.com

North Carolina

Nantahala Village
9400 Hwy. 19 West
Bryson, NC 28713
Phone: 1-800-438-1507
E-mail: nvinfo@nvnc.com
Web: www.nvnc.com

Rainbow Lake Resort
Rt. Box 233
Brevard, NC 28712
Phone: (828) 862-5354
E-mail: Innkeeper@Rainbowlake.com
Web: www.Rainbowlake.com

Pennsylvania

Woodloch Pines Resort
R.R.1, Box 290
Hawley, PA 18428
Phone: 1-800-453-8263
E-mail: woodmark@woodloch.com
Web: www.woodloch.com

Texas

Columbia Lakes Resort
188 Freeman Blvd.
West Columbia, TX 77480
Phone: 1-800-231-1030

Vermont

Smuggler's Notch Resort
4323 Rt. 108 South
Smuggler's Notch, VT 05464
Phone: 1-800-521-0536
E-mail: gvacations@smuggs.com
Web: www.smuggs.com

Virginia

Holiday Inn-1776
725 Bypass Rd.
Williamsburg, VA 23185
Phone: 1-800-446-2848 x 312

Quality Inn Lake Wright Resort and Convention Center
6280 Northampton Blvd.
Norfolk, VA 23502
Phone: 1-800-228-5157 x 511

Wisconsin

Wagon Trail Resort & Conference Center
1041 Hwy. ZZ
Ellison Bay, WI 54210
Phone: (920) 854-2385
Web: www.wagontrail.com

Wyoming

Grand Targhee Ski & Summer Resort
Ski Hill Rd., Box SKI
Alta, WY 83422
Phone: 1-800-827-4433 x 1315

Jamaica

Ponciana Beach Resort
P.O. Box 44
Negril, Jamaica
Phone: 1-800-468-6728

REUNITING WITH HISTORY

Mystic Seaport
Mystic, CT
Phone: (860) 572-5331
Web: www.mysticseaport.org

Living History Farms
2600 N.W. 111th St.
Urbandale, IA 50322
Phone: (515) 278-5286
Web: www.lhf.org

Old Bardstown Village
310 E. Broadway
Bardstown, KY 40004
Phone: (502) 349-0291
Web: www.win.ent/bardstown/civilwar.html

Shaker Village of Pleasant Hill
3501 Lexington Rd.
Harrodsburg, KY 40330
Phone: (606) 734-5411
Web: www.shakervillageky.org

Hancock Shaker Village
P.O. Box 927
Pittsfield, MA 01202
Phone: (413) 443-0188
Web: www.hancockshakervillage.org

Historic St. Mary's City
Rosecroft Rd., Rt. 5
St. Mary's City, MD 20686
Phone: 1-800-762-1634
Web: www.webgraphic.com/hsmc

The Statue of Liberty–Ellis Island Foundation
52 Vanderbilt Ave.
New York, NY 10017-3808

Colonial Williamsburg
P.O. Box 1776
Williamsburg, VA 23187-1776
Phone: 1-800-822-9127 x 7461
Web: www.history.org

Old World Wisconsin
S.103 W. 37890 Hwy. 67
Eagle, WI 53119
Phone: (414) 594-6300

THEME PARKS

Dollywood Entertainment Park & The Music Mansion
1020 Dollywood Ln.
Pigeon Forge, TN 37863-4101
Phone: 1-800-618-9283

Silver Dollar City Entertainment Park & The Showboat Branson Belle
2800 W. Hwy. 76
Branson, MO 65616
Phone: 1-800-618-9283

TRAVEL AGENTS

Crested Butte Accommodations & Travel Agency Ltd.
P.O. Box 5004
Mount Crested Butte, CO 81225-5004
Phone: 1-800-821-3718
Web: www.crestedbutte-lodging.com

Rosenbluth Vacations
18 Campus Blvd., Ste. 210
Newton Square, PA 19073-3286
Phone: 1-800-257-8279
Web: www.savtraveler.com

Taylor-Made Reservations
39 Touro St.
Newport, RI 02840
Phone: 1-800-847-6820
Web: www.4Taylor-Made.com

Travel Service Corporation
188 W. Randolph St., Ste. 1700
Chicago, IL 60601-3079
Phone: 1-800-634-2153
E-mail: traserco@megsinet.net

Travel Services Worldwide
1150 Lake Heran Dr., NE
Atlanta, GA 30342-1506
Phone: 1-800-717-3231
E-mail: condo#4less@iname.com
Web: www.thetravelagency.com

Uniglobe Elite Travel Inc.
824 E. Aurora Rd.
Macedonia, OH 44056
Phone: (330) 468-2294
E-mail: me.elite@uniglobe.com
Web: www.uniglobe.com/me.elite

TOURS

AlaskaPass Inc.
P.O. Box 351
Vashon, WA 98070-0351
Phone: 1-800-248-7598
Web: www.alaskapass.com

American Bus Association
1100 New York Ave., NW, Ste. 1050
Washington, DC 20005-3934
Phone: 1-800-283-2877
Web: www.buses.org

Fountain Head Tours
P.O. Box 2266
Branson, MO 65615-2266
Phone: 1-800-334-2723
E-mail: GOBRANSON@aol.com
Web: www.gobranson.com

Santa Catalina Island Company
P.O. Box 737
Avalon, CA 90704
Phone: 1-800-428-2566

CHAPTER 2

Culligan, Joseph J. *You, Too, Can Find Anybody*. Miami: Hallmark Press, 1994.

———. *Find Anyone FAST*. Spartanburg, S.C.: MIE Publishing, 1995. [P.O. Box 17118, Spartanburg, S.C. 29301]

Johnson, Richard. *How to Locate Anyone Who Is Or Has Been in the Military*. Spartanburg, S.C.: MIE Publishing, 1997. [P.O. Box 17118, Spartanburg, S.C. 29301]

Mitchell, Jann. Home Sweeter Home: *Creating a Haven of Simplicity and Spirit*. Hillsboro, Ore.: Beyond Words Publishing, Inco, 1996.

Rose, Christine, C.G., F.A.S.G. *Family Associations, Organization and Management: A Handbook*. San Jose, Calif.: Rose Family Association, 1991. [1474 Montelegre Dr., San Jose, CA 95120]

CHAPTER 3

Anthenat, Kathy Smith. *Fantastic Family Gathers, Tried and True Ideas for Large and Small Family Reunions*. Bowie, Md.: Heritage Books, 1995. [1540-E Pointer Ridge Place, Ste. 300, Bowie, MD 20716]

Bagley, Nancy Funke. *Reunions for Fun-Loving Families*. St. Paul, Minn.: Brighton Publications, 1994. [P.O. Box 120706, St. Paul, MN 55112]

Beasley, Donna. *The Family Reunion Planner*. New York: Macmillan, 1997.

Brown, Barbara, and Tom Ninkovich. *Family Reunion Handbook*. San Francisco: Reunion Research, 1992. [3145 Geary Blvd., #14, San Francisco, CA 94118]

Brown, Vandella. *Celebrating the Family: Steps to Planning a Family Reunion*. Orem, Utah: Ancestry, 1990. [P.O. Box 990, Orem, UT 84058]

Cox, Meg. *The Heart of a Family: Searching America for New Traditions That Fulfill Us.* New York: Random House, 1998.

Crichton, Jennifer. *Family Reunion.* New York: Workman Publishing, 1998.

Duncan, Ed E. *The Complete Guide to Planning Your Family Reunion.* Cleveland, Ohio: Cleve-Coast Enterprises, 1993. [P.O. Box 93792, Cleveland, OH 44101]

Fournoy, Valerie, illustrated by Jerry Pinkney. *Tanya's Reunion.* New York: Dial Books for Young Readers, 1995.

Johnson, Audrey Weldon. *The Road Back Home: Family Reunions,* 2d ed. St. Paul, Minn.: Audrey Weldon Johnson, 1996. [171 Downs Ave., St. Paul, MN 55117-1912]

Keitt, Frances M. *So You're Going to Plan a Family Reunion.* Philadelphia: FMK Publishing, 1997. [P.O. Box 25254, Philadelphia, PA 19119]

Mitchell, Jann. *Home Sweeter Home: Creating a Haven of Simplicity and Spirit.* Hillsboro, Ore.: Beyond Words Publishing, 1997. [4443 NE Airport Rd., Hillsboro, OR 97124]

Reunions Workbook and Catalog. Reunions magazine annual ed. [P.O. Box 11727, Milwaukee, WI 53211-0727]

Singer, Marilyn, illustrated by R.W. Alley. *Family Reunion.* New York: Macmillan, 1995.

Smith, Gloria J., illustrated by Beth Simon. *A Family Reunion Planning Guide.* Greensburg, Pa.: G&L Publications, 1994. [P.O. Box 866, Dept. RR, Greensburg, PA 15601-0866]

———. *Once Upon a Family Reunion.* Greensburg, Pa.: G&L Publications, 1994. [P.O. Box 866, Dept. RR, Greensburg, PA 15601-0866]

Westheimer, Dr. Ruth, and Ben Yagoda. *The Value of Family: A Blueprint for the 21st Century.* New York: Warner Books, 1996.

CHAPTER 5

Barile, Mary. *Food from the Heart.* Arkville, N.Y.: Heritage Publications, 1991. [Church St., Arkville, NY 12406]

Hackleman, Phyllis A. *Reunion Planner.* Baltimore: Clearfield Co., 1993. [200 E. Eager St., Baltimore, MD 21202]

Hoffman, Linda Johnson, and Neal Barnett. The Complete Reunion Planner Version 3.0. Los Angeles: Goodman Lauren Publishing, 1998. [11661 San Vicente Blvd., Ste. 505, Los Angeles, CA 90049]

———. *The Reunion Planner: The Step-by-Step Guide Designed to Make Your Reunion a Social and Financial Success!* 2d ed. Los Angeles: Goodman Lauren Publishing, 1998. [11661 San Vicente Blvd., Ste. 505, Los Angeles, CA 90049]

Holloman, Elsie G. *How to Have a Successful Family Reunion.* Bend, Ore.: Maverick Publications, 1992. [P.O. Box 5007, Bend, OR 97708]

———. *Family Reunion Organizer.* Nashville: Post Oak Publications, 1992. [P.O. Box 70455, Nashville, TN 37207-0455]

Wisdom, Emma. *A Practical Guide to Planning a Family Reunion.* Nashville: Post Oak Publications, 1988. [P.O. Box 70455, Nashville, TN 37207-0455]

CHAPTER 6

Campus Lodging Guide. Fullerton, Calif.: B&J Publications, 1999. [P.O. Box 5486, Fullerton, CA 92635-0486]

Condominium Travel Associates. *Renting Vacation Condominiums: A Suite Experience.* Prospect, Conn.: Condominium Travel Associates, 1998. [33 Union City Rd., Ste. 2B, Prospect, CT 06712]

Dude Ranchers Association. *Dude Ranch Directory.* La Porte, Colo.: Dude Ranchers Association, 1997. [P.O. Box 471, La Porte, CO 80535]

Independent Innkeepers Association. *The Innkeepers Register: A Guide to 315 Distinctive Destinations.* Marshall, Mich.: Independent Innkeepers Association, 1997. [Box 150, Marshall, MI 49068]

CHAPTER 7

Brown, Barbara, and Tom Ninkovich. *The Family Reunion Handbook.* San Francisco: Reunion Research, 1992. [3145 Geary Blvd., #14, San Francisco, CA 94118]

CHAPTER 8

Akan, Obasi Haki, and Lynn Harvey-Akan. *Family Ties: Fun Activities for Collecting Family Historical & Heritage Information*. Cleveland, Ohio: 24th Century Solutions, 1998. [16033 Brewster Rd., East Cleveland, OH 44112]

Akeret, Robert U., with Daniel Klein. *Family Tales, Family Wisdom. How to Gather the Stories of the Lifetime and Share Them with Your Family*. New York: William Morrow, 1991.

Anderson, Adrienne E. *Fun & Games for Family Gatherings*. San Francisco: Reunion Research, 1996. [3145 Geary Blvd., #14, San Francisco, CA 94118]

Carlson, Fran. *Growing Your Family Medical Tree*. Lafayette Hill, Penn.: Keep It Simple Solutions, 1997. [Lafayette Hills, PA 19444-0136]

Carmack, Sharon DeBartolo. *The Geneology Sourcebook*. Los Angeles, Calif.: Lowell House, 1997.

Feldscher, Sharla, and Susan Lieberman. *The KIDFUN Activity Book*. New York: HarperCollins, 1995.

Flock, Shari L. *Family Reunions and Clan Gatherings*. Yreka, Calif.: Coyote Publishing, 1991.

Keeshan, Robert. *Family Fun Activity Book*. Minneapolis, Minn.: Deaconess Press, 1994. [2450 Riverside Ave. South, Minneapolis, MN 55454]

Sachs, Patty. *Pick a Party*. Minnetonka, Minn.: Meadowbrook Press, 1997. [5451 Smetana Dr., Minnetonka, MN 55343]

Turner, Geneva, Ph.D., R.N., C.F.L.E. *How to Plan a Spectacular Family Reunion*. Columbus, Ga.: Turner and Associates, 1993. [2901 Cody Rd., Ste. 12, Mission Square, P.O. Box 6427, Columbus, GA 31907]

Vargus, Ione. *Reviving the Legacy: African American Family Reunions*. Forthcoming.

Wolfman, Ira. *Do People Grow on Family Trees? Genealogy for Kids & Other Beginners*. New York: Workman Publishing, 1991.

CHAPTER 9

Fry, Patricia. *The Mainland Luau: How to Capture the Flavor of Hawaii in Your Own Backyard.* Ojai, Calif.: Matilija Press, 1996. [323 E. Matilija St., Ste. 110-123, Ojai, CA 92023]

Index